Party Pursuits and the Presidential–House Election Connection, 1900–2008

This study proposes and assesses an alternative explanation of the changes in the relationship between presidential and House of Representatives election results during the last century. Jeffrey M. Stonecash argues that the separation of presidential and House election results that occurred from the 1960s to 1980 was a party-driven process, with both parties seeking to change their electoral base. Republicans sought a more conservative electoral base to counter what they saw as disturbing liberal trends in the nation. Democrats sought to reduce their reliance on the South and its conservativism. Presidential and House election results changed at different rates, creating an appearance that they were unconnected, but they eventually came together. Although many saw these changes in election results as evidence of parties' decline, this study reaffirms the position of the parties as central actors in bringing about change.

Jeffrey M. Stonecash is Maxwell Professor of Political Science at Syracuse University. He is the author of *Understanding American Political Parties* (forthcoming); *Reassessing the Incumbency Effect* (Cambridge University Press 2009); *Political Parties Matter: Realignment and the Return of Partisan Voting* (2005); *Political Polling: Strategic Information in Campaigns* (2005), and *The Emergence of State Government: Parties and New Jersey Politics, 1950–2000* (2002). He coauthored *Counter Realignment: Political Change in the Northeast* (with Howard L. Reiter, Cambridge University Press 2011); *Dynamics of American Political Parties* (with Mark D. Brewer, Cambridge University Press 2009); *Split: Class and Cultural Divides in American Politics* (with Mark D. Brewer, 2007); and *Diverging Parties: Realignment, Social Change, and Political Polarization* (with Mark D. Brewer and Mark Mariani, 2002). He is the editor of *New Directions in American Political Parties* (2010).

Party Pursuits and the Presidential–House Election Connection, 1900–2008

JEFFREY M. STONECASH

Maxwell School, Syracuse University

CAMBRIDGE UNIVERSITY PRESS

CAMBRIDGE UNIVERSITY PRESS
Cambridge, New York, Melbourne, Madrid, Cape Town,
Singapore, São Paulo, Delhi, Mexico City

Cambridge University Press
32 Avenue of the Americas, New York, NY 10013-2473, USA

www.cambridge.org
Information on this title: www.cambridge.org/9781107616752

First published 2013

Printed in the United States of America

A catalog record for this publication is available from the British Library.

Library of Congress Cataloging in Publication Data

Stonecash, Jeffrey M.
Party pursuits and the presidential-house election connection, 1900–2008 / Jeffrey M. Stonecash.
  p.   cm.
Includes bibliographical references and index.
ISBN 978-1-107-02948-4 (hardback : alk. paper) – ISBN 978-1-107-61675-2 (pbk. : alk. paper)
1. Elections – United States – History.   2. Presidents – United States – Election.   3. United
States. Congress – Elections.   4. Political parties – United States.   I. Title.
JK1957.S76   2012
324.973'09–dc23   2012027322

ISBN 978-1-107-02948-4 Hardback
ISBN 978-1-107-61675-2 Paperback

Contents

Preface

The present is confusing because we do not really understand the past.[1]

Our understandings of politics evolve. At one time – much of the first half of the 1900s – it was widely understood that presidential and House election results were closely tied together. The partisan votes for presidential and House candidates in House districts were very similar, and we presumed that voting was primarily for a party and not individuals. Then in the 1960s the relationship between presidential and House results declined. By the 1970s a new interpretation emerged about what was dominating elections and how the presidential–House connection was being altered. The conclusion was that House elections were becoming dominated by incumbency, elections were candidate-centered, and parties were of less relevance in voting choices. House incumbents were becoming more immune to shifts in partisan presidential electoral support in the nation. The conventional wisdom quickly became that we were witnessing a diminished capability for elections to simultaneously register voter sentiment in the institutions of the presidency and the House.

[The House elections of the 1960s represent] a set of electoral arrangements that is . . . quite unresponsive to shifts in the preferences of voters. (1973)[2]

Incumbents have become quite effectively insulated from the electoral effects, for example, of adverse presidential landslides. As a result, a once-notable phenomenon, the so-called coattails effect, has virtually been eliminated. (1975)[3]

[1] Gregory Koger, *Filibustering: A Political History of Obstruction in the House and Senate* (Chicago: University of Chicago Press, 2010), 3.

[2] Edward T. Tufte, "The Relationship between Seats and Votes in Two-Party Systems," *American Political Science Review*, Vol. 67, No. 2 (June 1973).

[3] Walter D. Burnham, "Insulation and Responsiveness in Congressional Elections," *Political Science Quarterly*, Vol. 90, No. 3 (Fall 1975a), 411–413.

The incumbency advantage in House races has increased to such a level during the last decade that the electoral outcomes for president and Congress have become virtually independent. (1983)[4]

Voting in congressional elections has become detached from broad national currents reflecting reactions to the president and national issues and problems. (1985)[5]

No matter which party wins the White House each four years, presidential elections seem to have little impact on the partisan balance in Congress. The discrepancy between presidential and congressional election results is frequently attributed . . . to a decline in presidential coattails. (1995)[6]

Then evidence began to emerge that created doubts about the consensus. In the elections of 1996 and after, presidential and House election results were once more highly associated. The 2008 presidential and House election results appeared to be dominated by reactions to parties, not candidates. This renewed relationship is puzzling if we rely on an interpretation of the past – the 1950s–1980s – that presumes House incumbents have become independent of presidential voting. That interpretation does not explain how these two election results might once again be *consistently* closely associated. Was it just chance? Or was something much more systematic occurring? If the latter, had we perhaps misinterpreted the past, missed some intended and coherent source of change, and developed an understanding that was erroneous? Do we need to reinterpret the past to provide an explanation of the present?

This analysis argues that the answer to these last questions is yes. The argument presented here is that the separation of presidential and House results that occurred in the 1960s–1980s was not because candidates had suddenly figured out how to create personal constituencies. Rather, a lengthy and sometimes uncoordinated secular realignment was under way. Parties were not peripheral to the process but central. The process was party-driven. Parties were developing differing interpretations of what were the most important problems in American society. They were seeking constituencies compatible with these changing views. In the pursuit of change the wings of each party sometimes acted independently and sometimes together. As the process unfolded over decades, presidential and House results came apart and then gradually came back together. Incumbents lost or retired. Party control and partisan voting percentages in districts changed. By the mid-1990s most of the changes for both wings of each party had worked themselves out and results across districts were once again very similar.

---

4 Randall L. Calvert and John A. Ferejohn, "Coattail Voting in Recent Presidential Elections," *American Political Science Review*, Vol. 77, No. 2 (June 1983), 408.

5 John A. Ferejohn and Morris P. Fiorina, "Incumbency and Realignment in Congressional Elections," in John E. Chubb and Paul E. Peterson, Editors, *New Directions in American Politics* (Washington, DC: Brookings Institution, 1985), 94.

6 Gregory N. Fleming, "Presidential Coattails in Open-Seat Elections," *Legislative Studies Quarterly*, Vol. 20, No. 2 (May 1995), 197–211.

At issue here is our understanding of the past. Reinterpreting the past as party-driven and not candidate-centered explains the present. The current situation of highly associated presidential–House results is not a puzzle but the logical conclusion to a lengthy party-engineered process in response to social, economic, and ultimately political concerns.

PART I

ELECTION PATTERNS AND INTERPRETIVE FRAMEWORKS

I

Disconnecting and Reconnecting Presidential–House Election Results

In the early 1900s presidential and House election results were highly correlated. When a Republican presidential candidate did well within a district, the Republican House candidate also did well. When a presidential candidate did poorly, the House candidate of the same party also did poorly. There was a consistency of partisan electoral expressions across House districts. The result was that a president generally came into office with his party holding a majority in the House.[1] The presumption was that the electorate was reacting primarily to parties.[2] Divided partisan control of institutions was not the norm.[3] If the electorate shifted significantly toward one party, it carried that party to power in the presidency and the House.

That connection persisted even when the critical realignment of 1932 occurred. That election is viewed as one that fundamentally changed electoral alignments;[4] however, the major change involved relatively uniform movements to the Democrats in districts where the party had been weak. A shift toward Democrat Franklin Roosevelt for president was accompanied by a shift toward the Democratic House candidate, regardless if it was an incumbent or a

---

[1] The Senate, with only one-third of seats up for election every two years, was less sensitive to shifts in voter sentiment because most of its membership was not up for election in any given year.

[2] There is also the argument that the way the voting and districting processes were structured played a significant role in creating these outcomes. See Erik J. Engstrom and Samuel Kernell, "Manufactured Responsiveness: The Impact of State Electoral Laws on Unified Party Control of the Presidency and House of Representatives, 1840–1940," *Journal of Politics*, Vol. 49, No. 3 (July 2005), 531–549.

[3] Morris P. Fiorina, *Divided Government*, Second Edition (Boston: Allyn and Bacon, 1996).

[4] James L. Sundquist, *Dynamics of the Party System: Alignment and Realignment of Political Parties in the United States, Revised Edition* (Washington, DC: Brookings Institution, 1983), 198–239.

candidate for an open seat. The shift in voter sentiment in the presidential race also occurred in House elections, and the association between the two sets of results remained high. For the first half of the century the correlation between presidential and House election results was consistently .8 or higher.[5] The percentage of House districts with split-outcomes (different parties winning the presidential and House vote within a district) rarely reached 20 percent.

Then this political relationship began to disconnect. The change was at first gradual and then dramatic. In the 1948 presidential campaign there were three major presidential candidates, and the association between presidential and House results declined. The 1952, 1956, and 1960 elections lowered the relationship somewhat more. Divided control of government was more prevalent. Then the association declined even more between 1964 and 1976. The relationship between presidential and House results appeared to unravel, to become disconnected. The correlation between presidential and House results dropped to .10 and .25 in some of those years. Split-outcomes were becoming much more common. By 1984, 46 percent of all House districts had split-outcomes.

Concerns about Political Responsiveness

These changes prompted considerable concern about the ability of American elections to register the sentiments of voters in political institutions. Presidential campaigns are times when candidates make arguments for the policies and direction the country should take. If the public supports a party candidate and the policy proposals presented, we hold some hope that a shift in voter reaction to a party moves both presidential and House election results so that the president has a House majority with the same electoral base and policy concerns. That commonality may provide a basis for overcoming the separation of powers built into American politics and make it possible for electoral sentiments to result in policy changes.[6]

For electoral sentiments to be registered in both institutions, presidential and House results must move somewhat together. Such shifts must change partisan control of many House seats. The concern was that an array of evidence was emerging suggesting that the conditions necessary for elections to register changing sentiments were declining, resulting in a disconnection of presidential and House election results. The primary changes appeared to involve House incumbents and their ability to control their own destiny, separate from presidential results. Incumbents were increasingly successful in winning reelection, warding off partisan swings in the vote. As Figure 1.1 indicates, among incumbents choosing to run for reelection, their success rate has been steadily increasing since the late 1800s. It is now common for 95 percent of incumbents

---

[5] The exception was 1912 when Teddy Roosevelt ran as a third-party candidate for president.

[6] For discussions of this issue, see David R. Mayhew, *Divided We Govern: Party Control, Lawmaking, and Investigations* (New Haven, CT: Yale University Press, 2005).

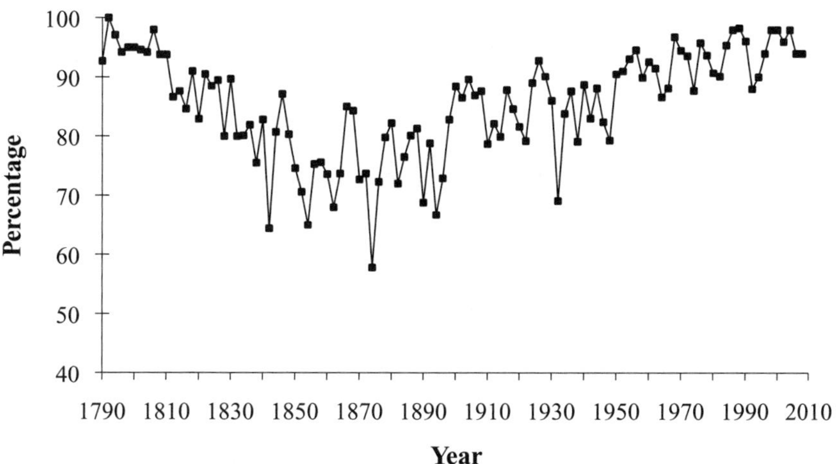

FIGURE 1.1. Reelection Rates for House of Representatives, 1790–2008

to win. Even in 2006, 2008, and 2010, when more incumbents than usual lost, at least 88 percent won. If incumbents were less and less susceptible to losing, the concern was that they might be less responsive to shifting public opinion. Members presumably have set opinions and are unlikely to change them, particularly if the members are safe.[7] If voters wish different policies, the solution is to replace the members with ones with different opinions.

Shifts in voter sentiment are more likely to change party control of House seats if there are many close elections. The evidence indicated that the percentage of close elections was declining.[8] In the post–World War II era, incumbents

---

[7] The idea that members of Congress do not change was presented in Aage R. Clausen, *How Congressmen Decide: A Policy Focus* (New York: St. Martin's Press, 1973), 70–84. The idea that members of Congress have ideal points was later represented in scores measuring positions for members: Keith T. Poole and Howard Rosenthal, "The Polarization of American Politics," *Journal of Politics*, Vol. 46, No. 4 (November 1984), 1061–1079; Keith T. Poole and Howard Rosenthal, "A Spatial Model for Legislative Roll Call Analysis," *American Journal of Political Science*, Vol. 29, No. 2 (May 1985), 357–384; and Keith Krehbiel, "Where's the Party?" *British Journal of Political Science*, Vol. 23, No. 2 (April 1993), 235–266. For a more recent review of this issue, see Thomas Stratmann, "Congressional Voting over Legislative Careers: Shifting Positions and Changing Constraints," *American Political Science Review*, Vol. 94, No. 3 (September 2000), 665–676. For challenges to the idea that members have set views that do not change, see Kenny J. Whitby and Frank D. Gilliam, Jr., "A Longitudinal Analysis of Competing Explanations for the Transformation of Southern Congressional Politics," *Journal of Politics*, Vol. 53, No. 2 (May 1991), 504–518; and Gary C. Jacobson, "Explaining the Ideological Polarization of the Congressional Parties since the 1970s," in David W. Brady and Mathew D. McCubbins, Editors, *Party, Process, and Political Change in Congress*, Volume 2 (Palo Alto, CA: Stanford University Press, 2007), 91–101.

[8] David R. Mayhew, "Congressional Elections: The Case of the Vanishing Marginals," *Polity*, Vol. 6, No. 3 (Spring 1974a), 295–317; David R. Mayhew, *The Electoral Connection* (New Haven, CT: Yale University Press, 1974b). There is some disagreement about the impact of

FIGURE 1.2. Vote Percentages for Contested House Incumbents, 1946–1988

appeared to be winning with higher percentages of the vote. Studies found that in the years between 1946 and 1950 incumbents averaged about 60 percent of the two-party vote. By the late 1980s, as shown in Figure 1.2, studies indicated incumbents were averaging 68 percent. Incumbents were more likely to want to stay in office and run for reelection.[9] They had more resources in the form of staff, government-funded trips to the district, and access to mailings to constituents.[10] House members were seen as more successful in creating a "personal vote" base of support that was separate from some base partisan vote in districts.[11]

marginality on voting. See Morris P. Fiorina, "Electoral Margins, Constituency Influence, and Policy Moderation: A Critical Assessment," *American Politics Quarterly*, Vol. 1, No. 4 (October 1973), 479–498; and John D. Griffin, "Electoral Competition and Democratic Responsiveness: A Defense of the Marginality Hypothesis," *The Journal of Politics*, Vol. 68, No. 4 (November 2006), 911–921.

[9] Nelson W. Polsby, "The Institutionalization of the U.S. House of Representatives," *American Political Science Review*, Vol. 62, No. 1 (March 1968), 144–168. As noted by some, the trend toward wanting to stay in office had started increasing in the 1800s. See Samuel Samuel Kernell, "Toward Understanding 19th Century Congressional Careers: Ambition, Competition, and Rotation," *American Journal of Political Science*, Vol. 21, No. 4 (November 1977), 669–693; and Robert Struble, Jr., "House Turnover and the Principle of Rotation," *Political Science Quarterly*, Vol. 94, No. 4 (Winter 1979–1980), 649–667.

[10] Gary C. Jacobson, *The Politics of Congressional Elections*, Seventh Edition (New York: Pearson-Longman, 2009), 31–32.

[11] Bruce E. Cain, John A. Ferejohn, and Morris P. Fiorina, "The Constituency Basis of the Personal Vote for U.S. Representatives and British Members of Parliament," *American Political Science Review*, Vol. 78, No. 1 (March 1984), 110–125; and Bruce E. Cain, John A. Ferejohn,

The result of higher vote percentages for incumbents was fewer close elections and declining susceptibility of incumbents to the periodic shifts in public opinion that occur.[12] From the 1870s through the first half of the twentieth century, the percentage of competitive House elections was relatively high, and there was considerable turnover in who held House seats.[13] Shifts in partisan sentiment affected a substantial number of House outcomes. A relatively high percentage of seats changed party from one election to another.[14] The swing ratio, or the change in party control of House seats in response to a shift in presidential voting, was higher in the past.[15] As Figure 1.3 indicates, the percentage of seats in which party control changed following elections was declining. The percentage of incumbents losing was also steadily declining.[16] There was less and less turnover.[17] Fewer House members were feeling the threat of a competitive race.[18] Fewer lived with the anxiety of possible defeat, and presumably these members were less likely to worry about knowing and representing their constituents.

The concern was that incumbents were acquiring the ability to systematically increase their average vote above the normal partisan vote, thus creating a

and Morris P. Fiorina, *The Personal Vote: Constituency Service and Electoral Independence* (Cambridge, MA: Harvard University Press, 1990). There was also the argument that this personal vote could make members more vulnerable because it could create a less predictable vote. See Thomas E. Mann, *Unsafe at Any Margin* (Washington, DC: American Enterprise Institute, 1978).

[12] Albert D. Cover and David R. Mayhew, "Congressional Dynamics and the Decline of Competitive Congressional Elections," in Lawrence C. Dodd and Bruce I. Oppenheimer, Editors, *Congress Reconsidered* (Washington, DC: CQ Press, 1977), 62–82; Albert D. Cover, "One Good Term Deserves Another: The Advantage of Incumbency in Congressional Elections," *American Journal of Political Science*, Vol. 21, No. 3 (August 1977), 523–541; James A. Stimson, Michael B. MacKuen, and Robert S. Erikson, "Dynamic Representation," *American Political Science Review*, Vol. 89, No. 3 (September 1995), 543–565.

[13] Kernell, "Toward Understanding 19th Century Congressional Careers"; Erik Engstrom, "The Partisan Impact of Malapportionment on the 19th Century and Early 20th Century House of Representatives." Presented at the 2005 Midwestern Political Science Association Meetings, Chicago, Illinois, April; and, Erik Engstrom, "Stacking the States, Stacking the House: The Partisan Consequences of Congressional Redistricting in the 19th Century," *American Political Science Review*, Vol. 100, No. 3 (August 2006), 419–427.

[14] Charles O. Jones, "Inter-Party Competition in Congressional Seats," *Western Political Quarterly*, Vol. 17, No. 3 (September 1964), 465.

[15] For a review of that literature, see Jeffrey M. Stonecash, "The Declining Swing Ratio: Incumbent Insulation or Realignment?" Paper presented at the 2010 American Political Science Association Meetings, Washington, DC, September.

[16] The percentages are calculated only for pairs of years for which the districts were the same: 1902 is compared to 1904, 1904 with 1906, 1906 with 1908, 1908 with 1910, 1912 with 1914, and so forth.

[17] Morris P. Fiorina, David W. Rhode, and Peter Wissell, "Historical Change in House Turnover," in Norman J. Ornstein, Editor, *Congress in Change* (New York: Praeger, 1975), 24–46.

[18] Jamie L. Carson and Carrie P. Eaves, "Congressional Elections: Why Some Incumbent Candidates Lose," in Stephen K. Medvic, Editor, *New Directions in Campaigns and Elections* (New York: Routledge, 2011), 184–185.

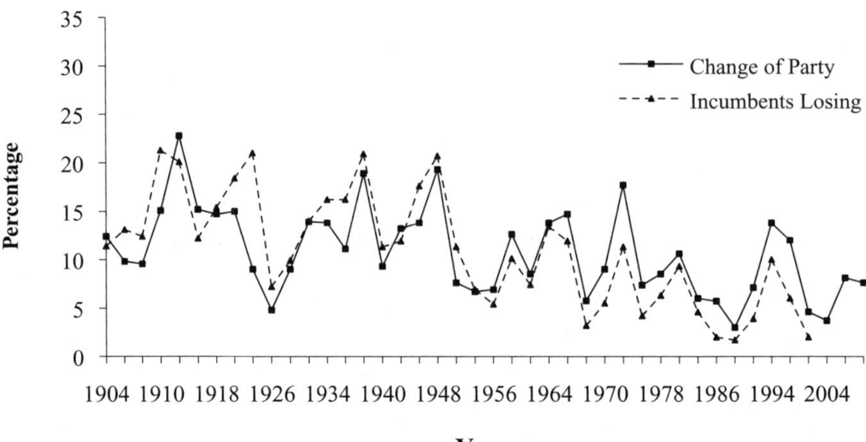

FIGURE 1.3. Percentage of House Seats Changing Party Control and Incumbents Losing, 1900–2008

greater deviation from the presidential vote. They could disconnect themselves from presidential voting. The effect presumed to be occurring is illustrated in Figure 1.4. Assume that there is some "normal vote"[19] for a set of districts, or a consistent level of partisan support.[20] In this case assume that the district is politically divided and has a consistent or normal vote of 50 percent Democratic. For this set of districts, Democratic incumbents might be able to gradually raise their vote above the normal vote and create positive deviations from that base partisan sentiment in the district. Republican incumbents would

[19] Philip E. Converse, "The Concept of a Normal Vote," in Angus Campbell, Philip E. Converse, Warren E. Miller, and Donald E. Stokes, *Elections and the Political Order* (New York: John Wiley, 1966), 6–39.

[20] This normal vote need not be a fixed percentage. Some define it as largely stable: Matthew S. Levendusky, Jeremy C. Pope, and Simon Jackman, "Measuring District-Level Partisanship with Implications for the Analysis of U.S. Elections," *Journal of Politics*, Vol. 70, No. 3 (July 2008), 736–753.

  Some see it as changeable as conditions change: Arthur H. Miller, "Normal Vote Analysis: Sensitivity to Change over Time," *American Journal of Political Science*, Vol. 23, No. 2 (May 1979), 406–425. Others treat it more as a moving average of results over a number of elections: Peter F. Nardulli, "A Normal Vote Approach to the Study of Electoral Change: Presidential Elections, 1828–1984," *Political Behavior*, Vol. 16, No. 4 (December 1994), 467–503; and Peter F. Nardulli, *Popular Efficacy in the Democratic Era: A Reexamination of Electoral Accountability in the United States, 1828–2000* (Princeton, NJ: Princeton University Press, 2007). It is important to note that in using presidential vote percentages in House districts, the focus is on the vote percentage as a reflection of the party's support within that district. Some use this vote as an indicator of the ideological position of the median voter. For difficulties with the latter use, see Georgia Kernell, "Giving Order to Districts: Estimating Voter Distributions with National Election Returns," *Political Analysis*, Vol. 17, No. 3 (Summer 2009), 215–235.

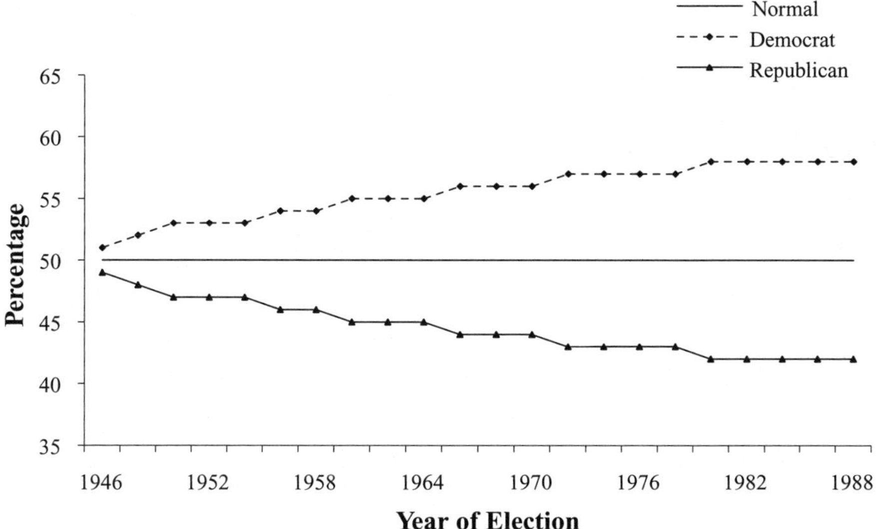

FIGURE 1.4. Incumbent Vote Deviations from the Normal Democratic Vote

achieve greater safety by creating partisan votes for Democratic challengers less than the normal 50 percent Democratic vote.

In fact, the differences of House vote from the presidential vote within districts were steadily increasing. Figure 1.5 indicates the average difference of House votes from the presidential vote from 1900 to 1988. The figure uses the average absolute difference (with the sign of whether the difference is

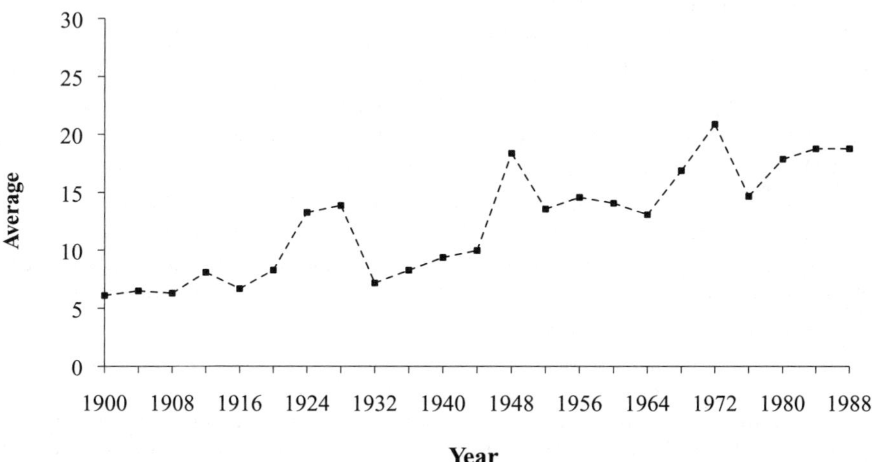

FIGURE 1.5. Average Absolute Difference of House Vote from Presidential Vote, 1900–1984

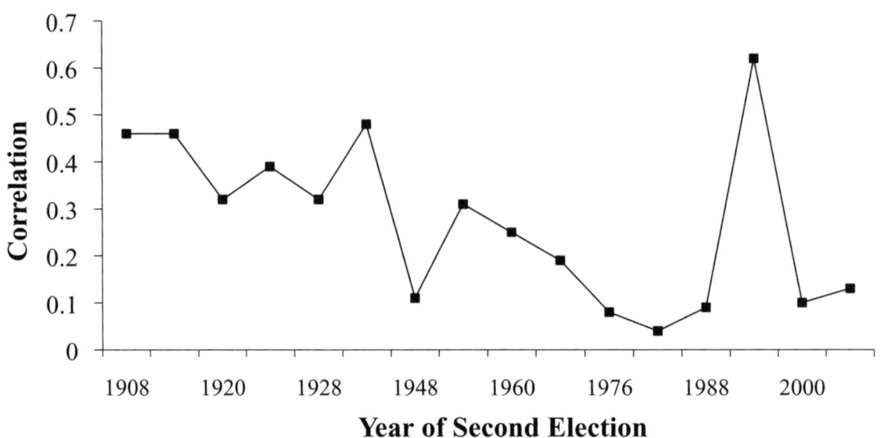

FIGURE 1.6. Correlation of Changes in Presidential–House Percentages from Prior Presidential Election, 1900–2008

positive or negative removed). If a simple average was used, it would measure the average net difference (positives offset by negatives), which would conceal the extent of deviations. Over time the average absolute difference of House results from presidential results gradually increased, moving from about 5 points in 1900 to almost 20 in 1988. There was also concern that differences in House percentages from one election to the next were changing less uniformly, reflecting the ability of members to create unique changes. That is, the national partisan vote might shift five percentage points but the changes for individual members might vary remarkably.[21]

The result would be a decline in the association between changes in presidential and House results from one presidential election to another. From the election in 1904 to the one in 1908, both presidential and House results within each district change, and the issue is how much those changes are correlated. These changes can be calculated only for election pairs in which the same set of districts existed, so the results shown in Figure 1.6 are for the pairs of elections ending in the years 1908, 1912, 1916, 1920, 1924, 1928, 1936, 1940, 1948, 1956, 1960, 1968, 1976, 1980, 1988, 1996, 2000, and 2008. Except for the year 1996, the trend is toward a declining association of changes from one presidential election to the next.[22]

---

[21] Gary C. Jacobson, "The Marginals Never Vanished: Incumbency and Competition in Elections to the U.S. House of Representatives, 1952–1982," *American Journal of Political Science*, Vol. 31, No. 1 (February 1987), 126–141.

[22] This is for all districts and not just those with an incumbent present because the general concern is the overall relationship between presidential and House results.

The Consequences for Democratic Responsiveness

The accumulated evidence seemed to establish that House members were reducing their tie to presidential results. House members were creating a personally based vote that diverged from the normal vote within the district. This was reducing the closeness of elections, and shifts in voter sentiment from prior elections were less likely to register across House districts.[23] The relationship between presidential and House elections was declining because House members were pushing House district election results away from being competitive. The concern was that the ability of presidential elections to serve as a means to register shifting political opinions was declining. Members were becoming more insulated from the threat of defeat and less responsive to shifting political views.[24]

The changes developing in House elections were particularly evident by the 1960s.[25] The electorate might shift its support from one party to another in the presidential election, but swings in presidential elections were having less effect on the net shift in partisan success in House elections. As Tufte expressed it, by the 1960s we had "a set of electoral arrangements that is . . . quite unresponsive to shifts in the preferences of voters."[26] Shifts in the national partisan vote were producing less change in partisan seat distributions.[27] Responsiveness to changing voter sentiments was declining.[28] The sense was that "we are witnesses to the blunting of a blunt instrument,"[29] and "Congress has become increasingly isolated from electoral tides."[30] By the 1980s and 1990s, divided control of government was more common than unified party control, and scholars offered theories that voters were voting for divided government to

---

[23] Burnham, "Insulation and Responsiveness in Congressional Elections."

[24] For relevant studies, see Kathryn Harmon and Marsha L. Brauen, "Joint Electoral Outcomes as Cues for Congressional Support of U.S. Presidents," *Legislative Studies Quarterly*, Vol. 4, No. 2 (May 1979), 281–299; Ferejohn and Fiorina, "Incumbency and Realignment in Congressional Elections"; Suzanna De Boef and James A. Stimson, "The Dynamic Structure of Congressional Election," *Journal of Politics*, Vol. 57, No. 3 (August 1995), 630–648.

[25] Tufte, "The Relationship between Seats and Votes in Two-Party Systems," 548.

[26] Tufte, "The Relationship between Seats and Votes in Two-Party Systems," 550.

[27] Edward R. Tufte, "Determinants of the Outcomes of Midterm Congressional Elections," *American Political Science Review*, Vol. 69, No. 3 (September 1975), 812–826; David W. Brady and Bernard Grofman, "Sectional Differences in Partisan Bias and Electoral Responsiveness in US House Elections, 1850–1980," *British Journal of Political Science*, Vol. 21, No. 2 (April 1991), 247–256.

[28] Gary King and Andrew Gelman, "Systematic Consequences of Incumbency in U.S. House Elections," *American Journal of Political Science*, Vol. 35, No. 1 (February 1991), 126–127.

[29] Mayhew, "Congressional Elections: The Case of the Vanishing Marginals," 314.

[30] Gary C. Jacobson, "Presidential Coattails in 1972," *Public Opinion Quarterly*, Vol. 40, No. 2 (Summer 1976), 194–200.

balance the diverging ideologies each party represented.[31] A Democratic majority persisted in the House for decades because Republican incumbents thought they would never be in the majority and retired more often than Democrats.[32] Presidential candidates were experiencing shrinking coattails, or the ability to move the vote to bring in members of Congress sympathetic to their policies.[33] All in all, there was considerable concern that elections were less and less useful as vehicles to register shifts in political support. Incumbents were becoming harder to defeat. Those in office tended to stick with their views, meaning that when the electorate shifted its opinions, there was less of a shift in what views were represented.

These changes and their interpretation fit with the larger understanding of what was occurring in American politics. From the 1960s through the 1990s, the dominant interpretation was that parties meant less to voters and that partisan dealignment was occurring.[34] Voters were less and less attached to parties, and the percentage choosing independent was increasing. Those identifying with a party were defecting and voting for candidates of the other party.[35] Congressional elections were localized and detached from national voting.[36] Split-ticket voting, or voting for candidates of differing parties for different offices, was increasing.[37] Party conflict in Congress was declining, presumably because members were operating independently of

---

[31] Gary C. Jacobson, *The Electoral Origins of Divided Government: Competition in U.S. House Elections, 1946–1988* (Boulder, CO: Westview Press, 1990); Fiorina, *Divided Government*. For a detailed critique of these arguments, see Richard Born, "Split-Ticket Voters, Divided Government, and Fiorina's Policy-Balancing Model," *Legislative Studies Quarterly*, Vol. 19, No. 1 (February 1994), 95–115.

[32] Stephen Ansolabehere and Alan Gerber, "Incumbency Advantage and the Persistence of Legislative Majorities," *Legislative Studies Quarterly*, Vol. 22, No. 2 (May 1997), 161–178.

[33] Calvert and Ferejohn, "Coattail Voting in Recent Presidential Elections"; John A. Ferejohn and Randall L. Calvert, "Presidential Coattails in Historical Perspective," *American Political Science Review*, Vol. 28, No. 1 (February 1984), 127–146; and, Stephen Ansolabehere, David Brady, and Morris Fiorina, "The Vanishing Marginals and Electoral Responsiveness," *British Journal of Political Science*, Vol. 22, No. 1 (January 1992), 21–38.

[34] Martin P. Wattenberg, "The Decline of Political Partisanship in the United States: Negativity or Neutrality?," *American Political Science Review*, Vol. 75, No. 4 (December 1981), 941–950; Martin P. Wattenberg, *The Decline of American Political Parties 1952–1988* (Cambridge, MA: Harvard University Press, 1990); and Martin P. Wattenberg, *The Rise of Candidate-Centered Politics: Presidential Elections of the 1980s* (Cambridge, MA: Harvard University Press, 1991).

[35] Richard W. Boyd, "Presidential Elections: An Explanation of Voting Defection," *American Political Science Review*, Vol. 63, No. 2 (June 1969), 498–514.

[36] Laura L. Vertz, John P. Frendreis, and James L. Gibson, "Nationalization of the Electorate in the United States," *American Political Science Review*, Vol. 81, No. 3 (September 1987), 961–966.

[37] Barry Burden and David C. Kimball, *Why Americans Split Their Tickets: Campaigns, Competition, and Divided Government* (Ann Arbor: University of Michigan Press, 2004); and Jeffrey M. Stonecash, *Parties Matter: Realignment and the Return of Partisanship* (Boulder, CO: Lynne Rienner, 2006), 9.

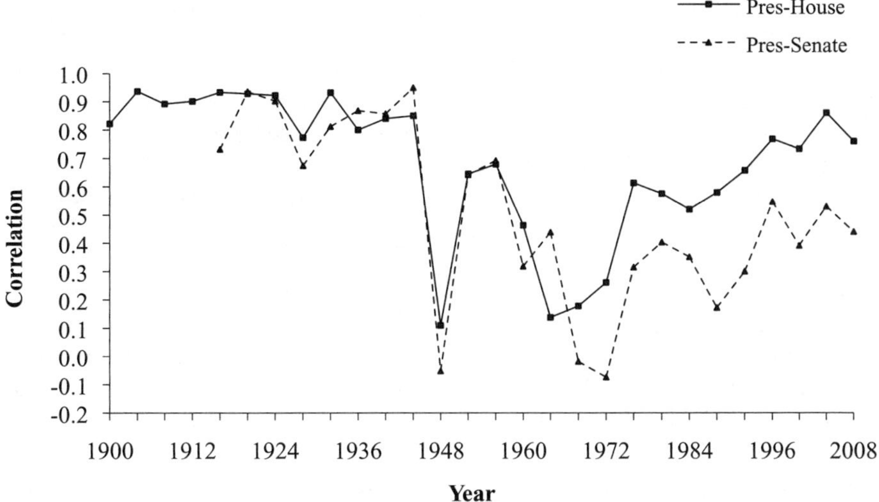

FIGURE 1.7. Correlation of Democratic Presidential Results with Senate (by State) and House Results (by District), 1900–2008

party.[38] Within that context, it seemed logical to analyze how much voters were consciously seeking split partisan choices in presidential and House contests and wanted divided control of government.[39]

A Reversal of Trends and the Concern of the Analysis

Then just as this decline-of-party interpretation seemed firmly established, the relevant trends began to reverse. The correlation between presidential and House results began to increase,[40] and by 1996 the relationship was close to the level of the first half of the 1900s (Figure 1.7).[41] The vote percentages for House candidates were becoming closer to that of presidential candidates.

[38] Melissa P. Collie, "Electoral Patterns and Voting Alignments in the U.S. House, 1886–1986," *Legislative Studies Quarterly*, Vol. 14, No. 1 (February 1989), 107–127.

[39] Richard W. Born, "Congressional Incumbency and the Rise of Split-Ticket Voting," *Legislative Studies Quarterly*, Vol. 25, No. 3 (August 2000), 365–387; Jacobson, *The Electoral Origins of Divided Government*; Fiorina, *Divided Government*; and Michael S. Lewis-Beck and Richard Nadeau, "Split-Ticket Voting: The Effects of Cognitive Madisonianism," *Journal of Politics*, Vol. 66, No. 1 (February 2004), 97–112.

[40] Sean M. Theriault, *Party Polarization in Congress* (New York: Cambridge University Press, 2008), 95–101; Gary C. Jacobson, *The Politics of Congressional Elections*, 163.

[41] The correlation presented is for Republican percentages. The correlation for Democrats follows a roughly similar pattern, but the correlation begins its decline in 1948. The creation of this correlation back to 1900 is not without some problems. It requires estimating for 1900–1948 the presidential vote for urban counties with multiple House districts. For an explanation of this process, see Appendix I. There is also an issue of whether uncontested races (with percentages of 100) and their variation over time may affect the correlation: They do not. For an indication of

The percentage of House districts with split-outcomes was declining. Unified party control prevailed from 2000 to 2006 and then in 2009–2010. Partisanship in the electorate was increasing.[42] This phenomenon of separation and then reconnection of election results has also occurred for presidential–Senate election results.[43] The trend of the relationship between presidential and congressional election results was general and not confined to one house.[44] These changes became part of the growing documentation and concern about partisan polarization.[45] The focus here will be only on the presidential–House relationship, but that pattern is reflective of a more general pattern in congressional elections.

The intriguing matter, and the focus of this analysis, is what accounts for the disconnection of presidential and House results and then their reconnection. Did incumbents gain and then lose their ability to influence vote percentages? Or was something fundamentally different affecting the relationship between presidential and House voting patterns? Is another interpretation of these trends possible? The conclusions developed about dealignment and an increasing incumbency effect emerged largely without consideration of alternative explanations. The pattern was to embrace the two notions of declining parties and the rise of candidate-centered politics as the dominant narrative for explaining American politics as a given, and then search for supporting evidence.

---

the Democratic correlation and how both Republican and Democratic correlations are affected by the inclusion or exclusion of uncontested races, see Appendix II.

[42] Larry M. Bartels, "Partisanship and Voting Behavior, 1952–1996," *American Journal of Political Science*, Vol. 44, No. 1 (January 2000), 35–49; Marc J. Hetherington, "Resurgent Mass Partisanship: The Role of Elite Polarization?," *American Political Science Review*, Vol. 95 (September 2001), 619–632; and Stonecash, *Parties Matter*.

[43] The pattern for the Senate is particularly impressive because in any given year only one-third of Senate seats are up for election. That means that the presidential–Senate correlation involves only about 33 cases compared to 435 for the House. This considerably fewer cases over a varying set of states could easily yield a more erratic correlation, but it still roughly tracks the pattern for House elections. The Senate has also polarized as much as the House. See Kathryn Pearson, "Party Loyalty and Discipline in the Individualistic Senate," in Nathan W. Monroe, Jason M. Roberts, and David W. Rohde, Editors, *Why Not Parties? Party Effects in the United States Senate* (Chicago: University of Chicago Press, 2008), 100–120.

[44] For an overview of the changes, see Hahrie Han and David W. Brady, "A Delayed Return to Historical Norms: Congressional Party Polarization after the Second World War," *British Journal of Political Science*, Vol. 37, No. 3 (July 2007), 505–531.

[45] Jon R. Bond and Richard Fleisher, *Polarized Politics* (Washington, DC, CQ Press, 2000); Gary C. Jacobson, "Party Polarization in Presidential Support: The Electoral Connection," *Congress and the Presidency*, Vol. 30, No. 1 (Spring 2003), 1–36; Jeffrey M. Stonecash, Mark D. Brewer, and Mack D. Mariani, *Diverging Parties: Social Change, Realignment, and Party Polarization* (Boulder, CO: Westview, 2003); Nelson W. Polsby, *How Congress Evolves: Social Bases of Institutional Change* (New York: Oxford University Press, 2004); Ronald Brownstein, *The Second Civil War: How Extreme Partisanship Has Paralyzed Washington and Polarized America* (New York: Penguin Press, 2007); and Sean M. Theriault, "Congressional Parties and the Policy Process," in Mark D. Brewer and L. Sandy Maisel, Editors, *The Parties Respond*, Fifth Edition (Boulder, CO: Westview Press, forthcoming).

In retrospect the evidence for an increased incumbency effect does not hold up, and there is a need for an alternative explanation.[46]

The argument to be made here is that there is a much more plausible interpretation of the changes that have occurred. That argument is about more than just this relationship. At issue is how we interpret much of the last 60-plus years of electoral patterns in American politics. Although the focus has been largely on the fortunes of incumbents as a means of explaining the decline in the presidential–House connection, that focus has taken us away from examining the pursuits of parties and the corresponding impact of secular realignment on the presidential–House election relationship. As realignment gradually unfolded over the decades it created a separation between results for the two offices. Then, as the process continued, election results came together again. This alternative interpretation is not built from a view that parties are playing less of a role, but from an argument that party actions and their interactions with voters have been central to explaining change.

Parties sought and created electoral change, and their efforts yielded the patterns of the last 60-plus years. The long-term process of disconnection and reconnection has been driven largely not by House incumbents but by the lengthy pursuits of political parties. Political parties represent voters' concerns and seek voters' support. Over time social and political change occurred, voters reacted, parties responded and staked out positions, elections occurred, parties struggled to interpret results, and a gradual process of change evolved. In an effort to create majority coalitions, parties were seeking to bring together people who reacted to society in the same way.

The process of change developed differently for the presidential and congressional wings. Presidential candidates seeking to change their party's electoral base played a major role. First, presidential candidates must plot a strategy that they believe will give them a majority in the Electoral College.[47] In working with the nature of the Electoral College, candidates must assess the past base of the party and how often their party has won with that base, and decide if they need to expand that base, and, if so, where.[48] Second, they must decide if the ideological and policy focus of the existing base is compatible with where they see the party and themselves going in the future. Candidates must work with a multitude of groups to secure the nomination and mobilize resources.[49]

---

[46] Jeffrey M. Stonecash, "Reconsidering the Trend in Incumbent Vote Percentages in House Elections," *American Review of Politics* (Fall 2003), 225–239; Jeffrey M. Stonecash, *Reassessing the Incumbency Effect* (New York: Cambridge University Press, 2008).

[47] Scott C. James, *Presidents, Parties, and the State: A Party System Perspective on Democratic Regulatory Choice* (New York: Cambridge University Press, 2000).

[48] Jeffrey M. Stonecash, "The Electoral College and Democratic Responsiveness," in Gary Baugh, Editor, *Electoral College Reform: Challenges and Possibilities* (Burlington, VT: Ashgate, 2010), 65–76.

[49] Marty Cohen, David Karol, Hans Noel, and John Zaller, *The Party Decides: Presidential Nominations before and after Reform* (Chicago: University of Chicago Press, 2008); David Karol,

They must decide if they wish to replicate support among the past base and groups or if they wish to try to pursue a new base and groups.

Parties are not defined just by presidential candidates, and parties should not be seen as unitary actors. House candidates and their party organizations engage in an ongoing process of assessing partisan conditions in local districts and seeking House seats across the nation. These assessments and pursuits are more diverse in nature and they receive considerably less attention. The cumulative outcomes of these pursuits can shift the geographical and ideological composition of the party and the issues that dominate the agenda of a congressional party.[50] That in turn can help the party attract seats in new districts.

Change can result from the calculations of presidential or congressional candidates. Changes in electoral bases are sometimes abrupt and sometimes gradual. Partisan shifts can first emerge in presidential elections with shifts for congressional and state election results lagging for some time.[51] Other times House candidates may make initial inroads into a region. Voters often take some time to recognize the changes occurring and to reconsider their partisan loyalties, creating further lags.[52]

This process of change can create changes in electoral patterns very different from that shown in Figure 1.3. That presentation assumes that House candidates can pull away from some normal vote within the district. If presidential candidates lead change, it is more likely that any divergence in results is a product of presidential results diverging from House results. Figure 1.8 provides an illustration of such a sequence. Assume that at some initial time period presidential and House election results in a set of districts are similar. Then Republican presidential election results in this set of districts start to increase while House results remain at the same level for a number of years. As presidential candidates increase their vote percentage, there is a greater divergence in results, creating a diminished correlation and more split-outcomes. Eventually the House results begin to catch up with the presidential results and the correlation returns.

Party Position Change in American Politics: Coalition Management (New York: Cambridge University Press, 2009).

[50] Nicole Mellow, *The State of Disunion: Regional Sources of Modern American Partisanship* (Baltimore, MD: Johns Hopkins University Press, 2008).

[51] Merle Black and Earl Black, *Politics and Society in the South* (Cambridge, MA: Harvard University Press, 1987); Thomas L. Brunell and Bernard Grofman, "Explaining Divided U.S. Senate Delegations, 1788–1996: A Realignment Approach," *American Political Science Review*, Vol. 92, No. 2 (June 1998), 391–399; Merle Black and Earl Black, *The Rise of Southern Republicans* (Cambridge, MA: Harvard University Press, 2002); Howard L. Reiter and Jeffrey M. Stonecash, *Counter Realignment: Political Change in the Northeast* (New York: Cambridge University Press, 2010).

[52] Morris Fiorina, *Retrospective Voting in American National Elections* (New Haven, CT: Yale University Press, 1981).

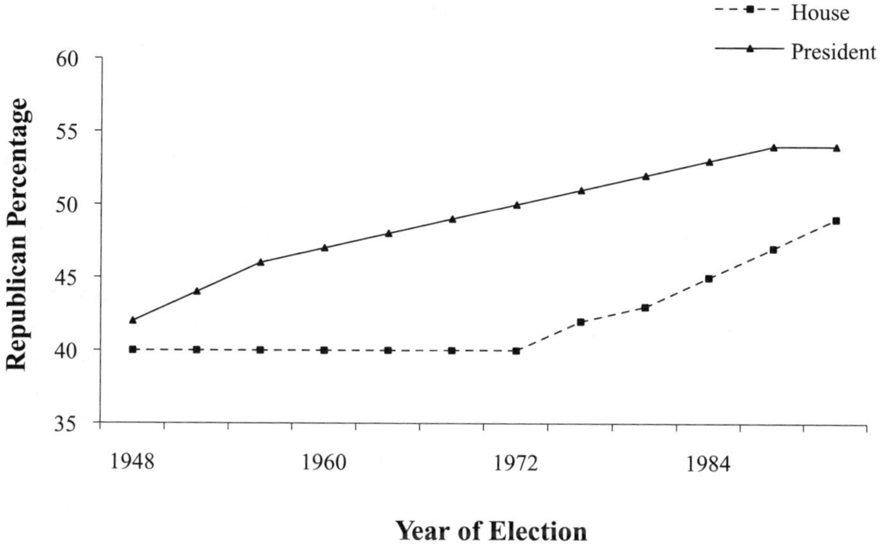

Year of Election

FIGURE 1.8. Presidential Vote Divergences from House Election Results

In other cases, House candidates of a party may steadily gain votes ahead of their presidential candidates in a previously unreceptive region and expand the party's base. If enough are successful, then their success may persuade presidential candidates of the virtues of appealing to voters in that region. Their success may also change the party composition sufficiently to change the agenda and appeal of the party nationally.

The essential difference in interpretations of change is that the candidate-centered framework presumes House incumbents pull away from presidential voting by enhancing their visibility and popularity. The alternative presumes that the pursuit of constituencies by the different wings of a party can separate the results until something brings them back together. The presumption of declining partisanship and a growing incumbency effect may well be inaccurate interpretations of what has been occurring in recent decades. Although this framework seemed to make sense of American politics for some time, it is difficult to use this framework and explain the recent trends toward greater partisanship and an increasing correlation between presidential and House results.

The Nature of Explanations: Change, Time, and Political Response

Although this book is about the patterns of American elections over the last century, it is also about the equally important matter of how we analyze elections. Over the last 40 years, we have drifted into studying House elections and incumbents in isolation and largely via cross-sectional analyses. The relevance of presidential campaigns, what they mean for long-term efforts to reposition parties and respond to change, and how to incorporate and analyze change have received considerably less attention.[53] There once were numerous studies about the presidential–House connection, but those have declined, probably because the conclusion developed that there was less and less of a connection between the two. The focus was largely on House elections and incumbents in isolation from other elections.

That shift was accompanied by a tendency to focus on cross-sectional analyses. Sometimes the prior election of a House candidate was included to assess changes from that "base," but the tendency was to focus on current conditions such as the quality of challengers and the amount of money the incumbent and challenger spent, with the presidential vote sometimes included as a control variable. The result of this analytical approach was that somehow party strategies, time, and change largely disappeared. The argument of this analysis is that history and change matter, and we need to bring them in as we think about studying elections. To quote Pierson: "The ambition . . . is to flesh out the often-invoked but rarely examined declaration that history matters."[54] He also quotes Douglass North as follows: "Without a deep understanding of time, you will be lousy political scientists, because time is the dimension in which ideas and institutions and beliefs evolve."[55] The argument to be made here is that the study of the relationship of House and presidential elections proceeded with little acknowledgment of gradual realignment over time. There is only occasional recognition of a fundamental shift in the geographical bases of parties and efforts to grapple with the consequences of that shift. The challenge of this analysis is to incorporate historical change and its effects and assess why neglecting it matters.[56]

The Issue of Political Responsiveness

The connection between presidential and House elections is important as an indication of how elections work to reflect or not reflect voter sentiments. The central issue is political responsiveness. The candidate-centered literature of recent decades suggests that elections are less useful as a vehicle for registering concerns at the same time for the presidency and the House. The framework for thinking about responsiveness being proposed here involves a more long-term notion of responsiveness. Voters have concerns about the direction of the nation. Their expressions of those concerns may not always be articulate, but

---

53 Karol, *Party Position Change in American Politics.*
54 Paul Pierson, *Politics in Time: History, Institutions, and Social Analysis* (Princeton, NJ: Princeton University Press, 2004), 2.
55 Pierson, *Politics in Time,* 1.
56 Richard Johnston and Byron Shafer, "Structural Foundations of Divided Government, 1952–2008: A Reconsideration." Presented at the 2010 Annual American Political Science Association Meetings, Washington, DC, September 2010.

they are there. Parties represent ideas and interests. They can play a role as vehicles to try to respond to social change and make voter concerns part of the political dialogue. The process generally does not happen quickly, and it is filled with uncertainty as parties seek to discern the meaning of elections.[57]

If presidential and House candidates pursue constituencies different from their historical base, it can create electoral change and lead to the representation of ideas and interests their party had previously not represented and to electoral realignments. If presidents lead in a region and create a disjuncture in results for a number of years, and even decades, that disconnection of results may not indicate unresponsiveness within the political system, but just the slow and differential pace of change for different offices. If House candidates can win in selected areas where the party had previously not done well, it may take time for presidential candidates to exploit the same electoral base as House candidates attract. The separation between presidential and House results witnessed in recent decades may indicate, quite the contrary to existing suggestions, slow and gradual responsiveness to shifting voter concerns as parties seek to respond and pursue a new electoral base. What looks like disconnection when the focus is short term may be seen as steady and purposeful change and responsiveness if the focus is long term.

The change that has occurred in recent decades is the product of a long shift in geographical partisan voting. As Kevin Phillips (and others) noted long ago, the conditions in the 1950s and 1960s were ripe for realignment.[58] There were more conservatives in the South, and many within the Republican Party wanted to attract more conservatives.[59] The Sunbelt was growing and Republicans emphasized individualism and antigovernment views in an effort to capitalize on the increasing prosperity of the region.[60] Republican presidential candidates were acutely aware that they needed a broader base to win and to create a party ideologically compatible with their goals. They pursued changes that brought us to where we are now. We might presume that large-scale changes have worked themselves out and a new stability is now in place.

Although the concern here is the last 100 or so years, it is not just the past that is at issue. Change is a phenomenon that will occur in the future in American society. About the time we think that change is slowing down, there are often signs it may be occurring again. At one time it seemed clear that Republicans could rely on whites within the growing Sunbelt to build a strong base. That presumption may now be in doubt and prompt a new round

---

[57] Mark D. Brewer and Jeffrey M. Stonecash, *Dynamics of American Political Parties* (New York: Cambridge University Press, 2009); and Jeffrey M. Stonecash, *Understanding American Political Parties: Democratic Ideals, Political Uncertainty, and Strategic Positioning* (New York: Routledge, forthcoming).

[58] Kevin Phillips, *The Emerging Republican Majority* (New York: Anchor, 1969).

[59] Rick Perlstein, *Before the Storm* (New York: Hill and Wang, 2001).

[60] Merle Black and Earl Black, *Politics and Society in the South* (Cambridge, MA: Harvard University Press, 1987).

of change. Immigration into the Sunbelt has increased significantly, shifting the importance of whites. A recent report indicates that a majority of public school children in the South are now nonwhite.[61] Many of the states that were once thought to be solidly Republican now are experiencing large increases in the presence of nonwhites.[62] If these trends continue, it may set off another round of change in the geography of party bases as parties search for a majority. Whether that will occur we will have to wait and see. The point is that change in where the parties obtain their votes is likely to persist, so understanding how change affects the relationship between presidential and House election results is both a past and a future concern.

The Plan of the Book

The first step is to briefly review the development of the study of presidential and House elections and the results that have emerged. That will be followed by a critique of the findings developed. That critique will lead to the questions that are not answered by existing approaches and that need to be answered. Then an alternative framework, focusing on party pursuits, realignment, and the implications for elections, will be presented. Successive chapters will present analyses based on the expectations of the framework, focusing on how the relationship between presidential and House elections has changed over time as realignment proceeded. What follows is not the presentation of a theory followed by tests, but a narrative and interpretation of what has created change, followed by supporting evidence.

---

[61] Shaila Dewan, "Southern Schools Mark Two Majorities," *The New York Times*, January 7, 2010: A20.

[62] Chris Cillizza, "The Republicans' Hispanic Problem," *Washington Post*, March 28, 2011, http://www.washingtonpost.com/politics/the-republicans-hispanic-problem/2011/03/27/ AFiMXokB_story.html.; and Karen R. Humes, Nicholas A. Jones, and Roberto R. Ramirez, *Overview of Race and Hispanic Origin: 2010*, U.S. Census Bureau, March 2011, http://www.census.gov/prod/cen2010/briefs/c2010br-02.pdf.

2

The Study of Presidential–House Elections

The study of presidential *and* House elections developed slowly. The progression of analyses, in conjunction with the timing of major changes in American politics, combined to significantly affect what has become the focus of studies. The ability to examine presidential *and* House elections was limited for much of the first half of the 1900s because data were hard to acquire from individual states.[1] Presidential results were being collected but only for states and counties.[2] Lacking results by House districts, the early quantitative studies focused on aggregate-level results, either at the national or regional level.[3] Apparently the first publication that gathered presidential *and* House results by House districts was that of Malcolm Moos, *Politics, Presidents and Coattails*, in 1952.[4] He presented results for both offices by district for the years 1938–1950. That data set was incomplete because he could not get results for all states. For some states there were also no presidential results by House district in counties containing multiple districts.

[1] Charles E. Merriam, "Research Problems in the Field of Parties, Elections, and Leadership," *American Political Science Review*, Vol. 24, No. 1 (February 1930), 33–38; and Idella G. Swisher, "Election Statistics in the United States," *American Political Science Review*, Vol. 27, No. 3 (June 1933), 422–432.

[2] Edgar E. Robinson, *They Voted for Roosevelt* (Palo Alto, CA: Stanford University Press, 1934); Edgar E. Robinson, *The Presidential Vote, 1896–1932* (Palo Alto, CA: Stanford University Press, 1947); Walter D. Burnham, "The Changing Shape of the American Political Universe," *American Political Science Review*, Vol. 59, No. 1 (March 1965), 7–28.

[3] Louis H. Bean, "Tides and Patterns in American Politics," *American Political Science Review*, Vol. 36, No. 4 (August 1942), 637–655; Cortez A. Ewing, *Congressional Elections 1896–1944: The Sectional Basis of Political Democracy in the House of Representatives* (Norman: University of Oklahoma Press, 1947).

[4] Malcolm Moos, *Politics, Presidents, and Coattails* (Baltimore, MD: Johns Hopkins University Press, 1952).

By the mid-1950s data for all House districts were becoming more available, and subsequent studies focused on House elections over time.[5] In 1957 Congressional Quarterly published an *Almanac* containing the first data on presidential and House elections by House district, covering the years 1952 and 1956.[6] The availability of these data[7] resulted in efforts to assess the relationship between presidential and House results, and soon there were numerous efforts to assess the extent of presidential coattails.[8] The general conclusion was that the connection was declining.[9]

Despite the importance of understanding this relationship, the study of coattails did not develop as much as might be expected. It was soon displaced as a focus because of a growing interest in what was happening with House election results. Analyses indicated that competition in House elections was declining. It appeared that incumbent members of Congress were increasing their vote percentages.[10] More and more incumbents were in safe seats, or those in which the winner received 60 percent or more of the vote.[11]

[5] Edward F. Cox, "Congressional District Party Strength and the 1960 Election," *The Journal of Politics*, Vol. 24, No. 2 (May 1962), 277–302; Lewis A. Froman, "Inter-Party Constituency Differences and Congressional Voting Behavior," *American Political Science Review*, Vol. 57, No. 1 (March 1963), 57–61; Lewis A. Froman, *Congressmen and Their Constituencies* (Chicago: McNally, 1963); Jones, "Inter-Party Competition in Congressional Seats."

[6] Congressional Quarterly, *Congressional Quarterly Almanac* (Washington, DC: CQ Press, 1957).

[7] The book by Milton C. Cummings, Jr., *Congressmen and the Electorate: Elections for the U.S. House and the President, 1920–1964* (New York: Free Press, 1966) contains data back to 1920. He reports that presidential data were available for "four-fifths of the districts for 1920–1944 and for virtually all districts from 1948–1964" (viii). Those data came from Ruth Silva and were lost once she retired from Penn State.

[8] Charles Press, "Voting Statistics and Presidential Coattails," *American Political Science Review*, Vol. 52, No. 4 (December 1958), 1041–1050; Cummings, *Congressmen and the Electorate*; and Stan Kapolwitz, "Using Aggregate Voting Data to Measure Presidential Coattail Effects," *Public Opinion Quarterly*, Vol. 35, No. 3 (Autumn 1971), 415–419.

[9] Jacobson, "Presidential Coattails in 1972"; Richard Born, "House Incumbents and Inter-Election Vote Change," *Journal of Politics*, Vol. 39, No. 4 (November 1977), 1008–1034; George T. Edwards, "The Impact of Presidential Coattails on Outcomes of Congressional Elections," *American Politics Quarterly*, Vol. 7, No. 1 (January 1979), 94–108; Calvert and Ferejohn, "Coattail Voting in Recent Presidential Elections"; Ferejohn and Calvert, "Presidential Coattails in Historical Perspective." For a dissenting view, see Richard W. Born, "Reassessing the Decline of Presidential Coattails: U.S. House Elections from 1952–1980," *The Journal of Politics*, Vol. 46, No. 1 (February 1984), 60–79.

[10] Robert S. Erikson, "The Advantage of Incumbency in Congressional Elections," *Polity*, Vol. 3, No. 3 (Spring 1971), 395–405; Robert S. Erikson, "Malapportionment, Gerrymandering and Party Fortunes in Congressional Elections," *American Political Science Review*, Vol. 66, No. 4 (March 1972), 1234–1245: 1240.

[11] Mayhew, "Congressional Elections: The Case of the Vanishing Marginals"; and, Mayhew, *The Electoral Connection*; Burnham, "Insulation and Responsiveness in Congressional Elections," 423.

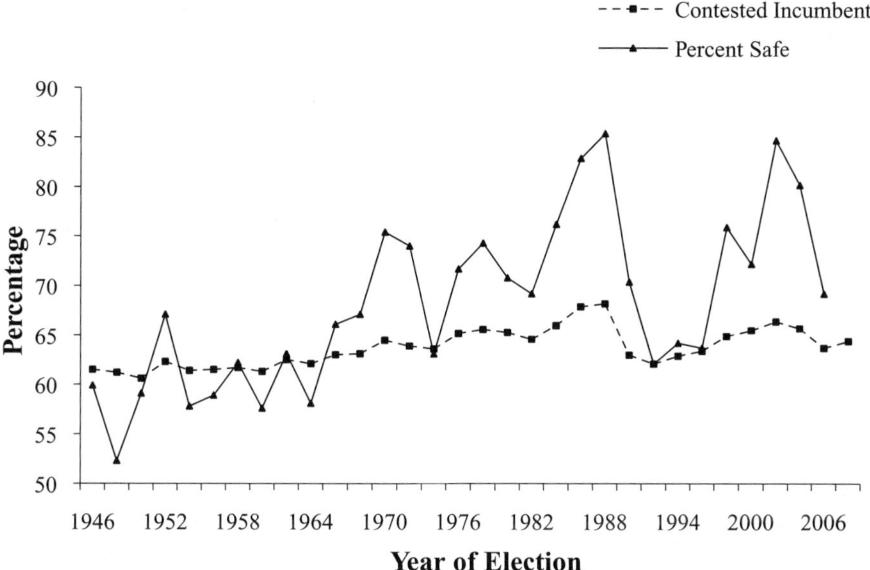

FIGURE 2.1. Incumbent Vote Percentages and the Percent Safe, 1946–2008

Incumbency was steadily displacing party as a source of the vote percentages of candidates.[12]

The conclusions from subsequent studies provided further support for the argument that incumbents were safer. Figure 2.1 presents the essential evidence that House incumbents were safer. It indicates the average percentage of the vote received by incumbents contested by a major party candidate and the percentage of incumbents who were safe (60 percent or above). The average vote percentage was gradually, if erratically, increasing, and the percentage of safe seats had clearly increased beginning in 1966. The increase in vote percentages for incumbents fit with the evidence that the percentage of seats changing party control within a decade had declined since the early 1900s.[13]

Mayhew, in commenting on the ability of elections to create accountability, concluded "we are witnesses to the blunting of a blunt instrument."[14] This conclusion was quickly embraced by others.

[12] Warren L. Kostrowski, "Party and Incumbency in Postwar Senate Elections: Trends, Patterns, and Models," *American Political Science Review*, Vol. 67, No. 4 (December 1973), 1213–1234: 1229–1233; Cain, Ferejohn, and Fiorina, "The Constituency Basis of the Personal Vote for U.S. Representatives and British Members of Parliament."

[13] Jones, "Inter-Party Competition in Congressional Seats;" David W. Brady, "A Research Note on the Impact of Interparty Competition on Congressional Voting in a Competitive Era," *American Political Science Review*, Vol. 67, No. 1 (March 1973), 153.

[14] Mayhew, "Congressional Elections: The Case of the Vanishing Marginals," 314.

Incumbents have become quite effectively insulated from the electoral effects, for example, of adverse presidential landslides. As a result, a once notable phenomenon, the so-called coattails effect, has virtually been eliminated.[15]

[O]ur data lend support to the notion of a robust two-tiered system in which the influences of presidential electoral competition have become increasingly remote from the level of congressional district electoral politics.[16]

The incumbency advantage in House races has increased to such a level during the last decade that the electoral outcomes for president and Congress have become virtually independent.[17]

Voting in congressional elections has become detached from broad national currents reflecting reactions to the president and national issues and problems.[18]

The growing variance in congressional elections over the past 20 years indicates an insulation of congressional votes from the national political scene.[19]

Given this conclusion there appeared to be less reason to study the relationship between presidential and House results. There might be reasons to study the effects of presidential voting on House results in open seats,[20] but the question that became intriguing to academics was what was happening to the situation of House incumbents.[21] A steady stream of studies began to emerge seeking to establish the reasons for a rising incumbency effect.[22] The presumption

---

[15] Burnham, "Insulation and Responsiveness in Congressional Elections," 411–413.

[16] Charles M. Tidmarch and Douglas Carpenter, "Congressmen and the Electorate, 1968 and 1972," *Journal of Politics*, Vol. 40, No. 2 (May 1978), 479–487.

[17] Calvert and Ferejohn, "Coattail Voting in Recent Presidential Elections."

[18] Ferejohn and Fiorina, "Incumbency and Realignment in Congressional Elections," 94.

[19] Sadafumi Kawat, "Nationalization and Partisan Realignment in Congressional Elections," *American Political Science Review*, Vol. 81, No. 4 (December 1987), 1235–1250.

[20] Jeffrey Mondak, "Presidential Coattails and Open Seats," *American Politics Research*, Vol. 21, No. 3 (July 1993), 307–319; Fleming, "Presidential Coattails in Open-Seat Elections;" Ronald Keith Gaddie and Charles S. Bullock, *Elections to Open Seats in the U.S. House: Where the Action Is* (Lanham, MD: Rowman & Littlefield, 2000); and Franco Mattei and Joshua Glasgow, "Presidential Coattails, Incumbency Advantage, and Open Seats: A District-Level Analysis of the 1976–2000 Elections," *Electoral Studies*, Vol. 24, No. 1 (March 2005), 619–641.

[21] John R. Alford and David W. Brady, "Personal and Partisan Advantage in U.S. Congressional Elections, 1846–1986," In Lawrence C. Dodd and Bruce I. Oppenheimer, Editors, *Congress Reconsidered*, Fourth Edition (Washington, DC: Congressional Quarterly, 1989), 153–169.

[22] The focus soon became almost exclusively on the effect of incumbency. There were prior studies that had included the role of constituency characteristics, but those variables soon fell away as the focus became just incumbency. Constituency traits were included in works by Julius Turner, *Party and Constituency: Pressures on Congress* (Baltimore, MD: The Johns Hopkins Press, 1951); W. Wayne Shannon, *Party, Constituency and Congressional Voting* (Baton Rouge: Louisiana University Press, 1968); Julius Turner and Edward V. Schneier, *Party and Constituency: Pressures on Congress*, Revised Edition (Baltimore, MD: Johns Hopkins Press, 1970); and Barbara Sinclair Deckard, "Political Upheaval and Congressional Voting: The Effect of the 1960s on Voting Patterns in the House of Representatives," *Journal of Politics*, Vol. 38, No. 2 (May 1976), 326–345.

was that House incumbents were creating more of a personal vote and were able to stay in office despite shifts in partisan presidential voting. Shifts in partisan support for presidential candidates mattered less for House elections. Incumbents survived as presidential voting fluctuated, resulting in an increase in divided governments.[23]

This apparent increase in a personal vote, achieved by the efforts of incumbents, made considerable sense given the conclusions of other studies. More and more legislators were seeking to stay in office and were successful in their efforts.[24] They were operating in a context in which partisan politics seemed to matter less. There was concern among academics that the two major political parties did not differ much[25] and that most voters lacked coherent beliefs about politics.[26] Studies were emerging indicating that American political parties were "decomposing."[27] The accumulating evidence indicated that voter identification with the two major parties was declining.[28] There was a decline in the percentage of party identifiers voting for candidates of their party. The percentage of voters voting for a candidate of one party for one office and the candidate of another party for another office, or split-ticket voting, was increasing.[29] A growing percentage of voters, and particularly independents, were choosing incumbents over challengers.[30] It appeared that attachments to parties and voting on that basis were declining. There were dissents to the view

[23] Herbert M. Kritzer and Robert Eubank, "Presidential Coattails Revisited: Partisanship and Incumbency Effects," *American Journal of Political Science*, Vol. 23, No. 3 (August 1979), 615–626; and Gary C. Jacobson, *The Electoral Origins of Divided Government*; and, Fiorina, *Divided Government*.

[24] Polsby, "The Institutionalization of the U.S. House of Representatives"; Charles S. Bullock, "House Careerists: Changing Patterns of Longevity and Attrition," *American Political Science Review*, Vol. 66, No. 4 (December 1972), 1295–1300: 1296; David Ray, "Membership Stability in Three State Legislatures: 1869–1969," *American Political Science Review*, Vol. 68, No. 1 (March 1974), 106–112.

[25] American Political Science Association, Committee on Parties, "Toward a More Responsible Two-Party System," *American Political Science Review*, Vol. 44, No. 3, Part 2, Supplement (September 1950), v–96.

[26] Angus Campbell, Philip E. Converse, Warren E. Miller, and Donald E. Stokes, *The American Voter* (New York: John Wiley & Sons, 1960).

[27] Walter D. Burnham, "The Changing Shape of the American Political Universe," *American Political Science Review*, Vol. 59, No. 1 (March 1965): 7–28.

[28] Philip E. Converse, *The Dynamics of Party Support* (Beverly Hills, CA: Sage, 1976), 32; Paul R. Abramson, "Generational Change and the Decline of Party Identification in America: 1952–1974," *American Political Science Review*, Vol. 70, No. 2 (June 1976), 469–478.

[29] Norman Nie, Sidney Verba, and John Petrocik, *The Changing American Voter* (Cambridge, MA: Harvard University Press, 1976). For a criticism of some of these conclusions, see Robert B. Eubank, "Incumbent Effects on Individual-Level Voting Behavior in Congressional Elections: A Decade of Exaggeration," *Journal of Politics*, Vol. 47, No. 3 (August 1985), 958–967.

[30] Keith Krehbiel and John R. Wright, "The Incumbency Effect in Congressional Elections: A Test of Two Explanations," *American Journal of Political Science*, Vol. 27, No. 1 (February 1983), 140–157.

that parties did not differ,[31] that candidate positioning did not matter,[32] or that voters could not discern differences,[33] but the dominant view was that parties were on the decline and voters were less attached to political parties. Campaigns were seen as candidate-centered, not party-centered.

There was also evidence that incumbent election results were separating from presidential results. There was a marked increase in the percentage of House districts with split outcomes, or outcomes within House districts in which the party winning the House and presidential contests differed.[34] The correlation between presidential and House elections had steadily declined since the late 1800s.[35] Presidential elections were having less of a uniform effect on the vote percentages for House incumbents. If House election percentages move in accord with presidential changes, there would be high uniformity in changes in House vote percentages from one election to another. If the national vote moved five points more Democratic then all House vote percentages would move five points more Democratic. In comparing the early 1900s with the 1960s–1980s, the diversity of changes in House percentages from one election to the next was steadily increasing.[36] Uniformity of change was declining. Incumbents were safer and steadily buffering themselves from changes in sentiment registered in presidential elections. The sense was that House elections were becoming disconnected from presidential elections.

Given the accumulated evidence, the relationship between presidential and House results declined as a focus of analyses. It became a given that incumbents were able to separate themselves from presidential results and reduce the impact on local House races of a swing in presidential results from one party to another. Incumbents wanted to survive,[37] and survival meant being less tied to national swings.[38] Members were able to separate themselves from the actions of Congress, leading to a declining connection with the public and a decline

---

[31] Julius Turner, "Responsible Parties: A Dissent from the Floor," *American Political Science Review*, Vol. 45, No. 1 (March 1951), 143–152; Turner, *Party and Constituency*; Froman, "Inter-Party Constituency Differences and Congressional Voting Behavior"; Evron M. Kirkpatrick, "Toward a More Responsible Two-Party System: Political Science, Policy Science, or Pseudo-Science," *American Political Science Review*, Vol. 65, No. 4 (December 1971), 965–990.

[32] Gerald C. Wright and Michael B. Berkman, "Candidates and Policy in United States Senate Elections," *American Political Science Review*, Vol. 80, No. 2 (June 1986), 567–588.

[33] Gerald M. Pomper, "From Confusion to Clarity: Issues and American Voters, 1956–1968," *American Political Science Review*, Vol. 66, No. 2 (June 1972), 415–428.

[34] Walter D. Burnham, "Insulation and Responsiveness in Congressional Elections," *Political Science Quarterly*, Vol. 90, No. 3 (Fall 1975), 411–435; Tidmarch and Carpenter, "Congressmen and the Electorate, 1968 and 1972," 481–483.

[35] Burnham, "Insulation and Responsiveness in Congressional Elections," 428.

[36] Jacobson, "The Marginals Never Vanished."

[37] Mayhew, "Congressional Elections."

[38] John R. Petrocik and Scott W. Desposato, "Incumbency and Short-Term Influences on Voters," *Political Research Quarterly*, Vol. 57, No. 3 (September 2004), 363–373.

in collective responsibility.[39] The primary explanation for any disconnection between presidential and House results, and for a declining swing ratio, became the growing incumbency effect.[40]

Research efforts soon shifted to attempts to estimate the magnitude of the incumbency effect. The presumption was that "Incumbency is without question the most important single factor in congressional elections,"[41] and the challenge was to find out how incumbents achieved this effect. There were studies of the sophomore surge, the increase in the vote percentage in the first reelection bid.[42] Was the generation of incumbents entering after 1966 enjoying greater electoral success?[43] There were studies focusing on increases in vote percentages over a career,[44] the average percentage of the vote won by incumbents from year to year,[45] and the retirement slump, or the drop in the partisan vote after an incumbent left office.[46] An alternative was to simply estimate the growing overall incumbency effect.[47]

[39] Morris P. Fiorina, "The Decline of Collective Responsibility in American Politics," *Daedalus*, Vol. 109, No. 3 (Summer 1980), 25–45. This theme that members of Congress are increasingly disconnected from the public is continued in Morris P. Fiorina, *Cultural War: The Myth of a Polarized America*, Third Edition (New York: Pearson Longman, 2010), and Morris P. Fiorina, with Samuel J. Abrams, *Disconnect: The Breakdown of Representation in American Politics* (Norman: University of Oklahoma Press, 2009). For an analysis that argues that any separation of the fate of a member from the public's view of congressional performance was a product of the state of parties in the 1970s and now a member's fate is tied to collective performance see David R. Jones, "Partisan Polarization and Congressional Accountability in House Elections," *American Journal of Political Science*, Vol. 54, No. 2 (April 2010), 323–337.

[40] There were some efforts to assess how redistricting affected the swing ratio. See Alan I. Abramowitz, "Partisan Redistricting and the 1982 Congressional Elections," *Journal of Politics*, Vol. 45, No. 3 (August 1983), 767–770; and Gary Cox and Jonathan Katz, "The Reapportionment Revolution and Bias in U.S. Congressional Elections," *American Journal of Political Science*, Vol. 43, No. 3 (July 1999), 812–841.

[41] Gary C. Jacobson, "Incumbents' Advantages in the 1978 U.S. Congressional Elections," *Legislative Studies Quarterly*, Vol. 6, No. 2 (May 1981), 183–200.

[42] John R. Alford and John R. Hibbing, "Increased Incumbency Advantage in the House," *Journal of Politics*, Vol. 43, No. 4 (November 1981), 1042–1061.

[43] Richard W. Born, "Generational Replacement and the Growth of Incumbent Reelection Margins in the U.S. House," *American Political Science Review*, Vol. 73, No. 3 (September 1979), 811–817.

[44] John R. Hibbing, "Contours of the Modern Congressional Career," *American Political Science Review*, Vol. 85, No. 2 (June 1991), 405–428; and John R. Hibbing, *Congressional Careers: Contours of Life in the U.S. House of Representatives* (Chapel Hill: University of North Carolina Press, 1991).

[45] Gary C. Jacobson, *The Politics of Congressional Elections* (Boston: Little, Brown, 1983).

[46] James L. Payne, "The Personal Electoral Advantage of House Incumbents," *American Politics Quarterly*, Vol. 8, No. 4 (October 1980), 375–398.

[47] Andrew Gelman and Gary King, "Estimating Incumbency Effect without Bias," *American Journal of Political Science*, Vol. 34, No. 4 (November 1990), 1142–1164; Michael Krashinsky and William J. Milne, "The Effects of Incumbency in U.S. Congressional Elections, 1950–1988," *Legislative Studies Quarterly*, Vol. 18, No. 3 (August 1993), 321–344.

Assuming that incumbents were doing better, a primary concern became trying to determine the causes of this rising incumbency effect. Was it advantages in campaign spending,[48] the use of office resources,[49] mailings to constituents,[50] the ability to do casework for constituents and curry their favor,[51] or the overall attention devoted to the district?[52] Was it the amount of "pork" brought to the district?[53] Were incumbents able to create more contact with constituents?[54] Were all these activities creating greater visibility and name recognition within

[48] Alan I. Abramowitz, "Campaign Spending in U.S. Senate Elections," *Legislative Studies Quarterly*, Vol. 14, No. 4 (November 1989), 487–507; Gary C. Jacobson, "The Effects of Campaign Spending in House Elections: New Evidence for an Old Argument," *American Journal of Political Science*, Vol. 34, No. 2 (May 1990), 334–362; and Alan I. Abramowitz, "Incumbency, Campaign Spending, and the Decline of Competition in U.S. House Elections," *Journal of Politics*, Vol. 53, No. 1 (February 1991), 34–56.

[49] Mayhew, "Congressional Elections"; Mayhew, *The Electoral Connection*.

[50] Albert D. Cover, "Baby Books and Ballots: The Impact of Congressional Mail on Constituent Opinion," *American Political Science Review*, Vol. 76, No. 2 (June 1982), 347–359.

[51] Morris Fiorina, "The Case of the Vanishing Marginals: The Bureaucracy Did It," *American Political Science Review*, Vol. 71, No. 1 (March 1977), 177–181; Glenn R. Parker and Roger H. Davidson, "Why Do Americans Love Their Congressmen So Much More Than Their Congress?" *Legislative Studies Quarterly*, Vol. 4, No. 1 (February 1979), 53–61; Diana E. Yiannakis, "The Grateful Electorate: Casework and Congressional Elections," *American Journal of Political Science*, Vol. 25, No. 3 (August 1981), 568–580; John R. Johannes and John C. McAdams, "The Congressional Incumbency Effect: Is It Casework, Policy Compatibility, or Something Else?" *American Journal of Political Science*, Vol. 25, No. 3 (August 1981), 512–542; Morris P. Fiorina, "Some Problems in Studying the Effects of Resource Allocation in Congressional Elections," *American Journal of Political Science*, Vol. 25, No. 3 (August 1981), 543–567; Fiorina, *Retrospective Voting in American National Elections*; John C. McAdams and John R. Johannes, "Does Casework Matter? A Reply to Professor Fiorina," *American Journal of Political Science*, Vol. 25, No. 3 (August 1981), 581–604; John C. McAdams and John R. Johannes, "Constituency Attentiveness in the House: 1977–1982," *Journal of Politics*, Vol. 47, No. 4 (November 1985), 1108–1139; George Serra and Albert D. Cover, "The Electoral Consequences of Perquisite Use: The Casework Case," *Legislative Studies Quarterly*, Vol. 17, No. 2 (May 1992), 233–246; Gary King, "Constituency Service and Incumbency Advantage," *British Journal of Political Science*, Vol. 21, No. 1 (June 1991), 119–128; George Serra, "What's in It for Me: The Impact of Congressional Casework on Incumbent Evaluation," *American Politics Quarterly*, Vol. 22, No. 4 (October 1994), 403–420. For a review of many of these studies and an argument that there was no evidence that activities such as casework had any impact on voting for incumbents, see John C. McAdams and John R. Johannes, "Congressmen, Perquisites, and Elections," *Journal of Politics*, Vol. 50, No. 2 (May 1988), 412–439.

[52] Jon R. Bond, "Dimensions of District Attention over Time," *American Journal of Political Science*, Vol. 29, No. 2 (May 1985), 330–347; and Glenn R. Parker, "Is There a Political Life Cycle in the House of Representatives?," *Legislative Studies Quarterly*, Vol. 11, No. 3 (August 1986), 375–392.

[53] Morris Fiorina, *Congress: Keystone to the Washington Establishment* (New Haven, CT: Yale University Press, 1977).

[54] Thomas E. Mann and Raymond E. Wolfinger, "Candidates and Parties in Congressional Elections," *American Political Science Review*, Vol. 74, No. 3 (September 1980), 627; Barbara Hinckley, "The American Voter in Congressional Elections," *American Political Science Review*, Vol. 74, No. 3 (September 1967), 644.

districts[55] and discouraging challengers?[56] Was it the quality of challengers?[57] Were incumbents increasingly successful in warding off primary opponents?[58] Was incumbent "success" largely a function of the strategic entry of challengers and exit of incumbents as political conditions changed?[59] Was there a new generation, a new type of legislator?[60] Were members putting "very little emphasis on articulating issues" and focusing on "cultivating personal relationships" as a means to create "candidate-centered bases for tendering electoral support"?[61] How much did redistricting matter?[62] Others took a

[55] Alan I. Abramowitz, "Name Familiarity, Reputation and the Incumbency Effect in a Congressional Election," *Western Political Quarterly*, Vol. 28, No. 4 (December 1975), 668–684; Alan I. Abramowitz, "A Comparison of Voting for U.S. Senator and Representative in 1978," *American Political Science Review*, Vol. 74, No. 3 (September 1980), 633–640; Glenn R. Parker, "The Advantage of Incumbency in House Elections," *American Politics Quarterly*, Vol. 8, No. 4 (October 1980), 375–398; John A. Ferejohn, "On the Decline of Competition in Congressional Elections," *American Political Science Review*, Vol. 71, No. 1 (March 1977), 166–176; Candice J. Nelson, "The Effect of Incumbency on Voting in Congressional Elections," *Political Science Quarterly*, Vol. 93, No. 4 (Winter 1978–1979), 665–678; and James E. Campbell, "The Return of the Incumbents: The Nature of the Incumbency Advantage," *Western Political Quarterly*, Vol. 36, No. 3 (September 1983), 434–444.

[56] Thomas A. Kazee, "The Deterrent Effect of Incumbency on Recruiting Challengers in U.S. House Elections," *Legislative Studies Quarterly*, Vol. 8, No. 3 (August 1983), 469–480.

[57] Jon R. Bond, Cary Covington, and Richard Fleisher, "Explaining Challenger Quality in Congressional Elections," *Journal of Politics*, Vol. 47, No. 2 (June 1985), 510–529; Jonathon S. Krasno and Donald P. Green, "Preempting Quality Challengers in House Elections," *Journal of Politics*, Vol. 50, No 4 (November 1988), 920–936; and Jamie L. Carson, Erik J. Engstrom, and Jason M. Roberts, "Candidate Quality, the Personal Vote, and the Incumbency Advantage in Congress," *American Political Science Review*, Vol. 101, No. 2 (May 2007), 289–302.

[58] Stephen Ansolabehere, John Mark Hansen, Shigeo Hirano, and James M. Snyder, Jr., "The Incumbency Advantage in U.S. Primary Elections," *Electoral Studies*, Vol. 26, No. 3 (September 2007), 660–668; and Stephen Ansolabehere, Shigeo Hirano, and James M. Snyder, Jr., "What Did the Direct Primary Do to Party Loyalty in Congress?," in David W. Brady and Mathews D. McCubbins, Editors, *Party, Process, and Political Change in Congress*, Volume 2 (Palo Alto, CA: Stanford University Press, 2007), 1–36.

[59] Gary C. Jacobson, and Samuel Kernell, *Strategy and Choice in Congressional Elections* (New Haven, CT: Yale University Press, 1981); Gary C. Jacobson, "Strategic Politicians and the Dynamics of U.S. House Elections, 1946–86," *American Political Science Review*, Vol. 83, No. 3 (September 1989), 773–793.

[60] Fiorina, *Congress: Keystone to the Washington Establishment*, 1977; Born, "Generational Replacement and the Growth of Incumbent Reelection Margins in the U.S. House"; Glenn R. Parker and Suzanne L. Parker, "Correlates and Effects of Attention to District by U.S. House Members," *Legislative Studies Quarterly*, Vol. 10, No. 2 (May 1985), 223–242; Richard Herrera and Michael Yawn, "The Emergence of the Personal Vote," *Journal of Politics*, Vol. 61, No. 1 (February 1999), 136–150.

[61] Richard F. Fenno, "U.S. House Members in Their Constituencies: An Exploration," *American Political Science Review*," Vol. 71, No. 3 (September 1977), 902 and 915; and Richard F. Fenno, *Home Style: House Members in Their Districts* (New York: HarperCollins, 1978).

[62] Tufte, "The Relationship between Seats and Votes in Two-Party Systems;" Charles S. Bullock, "Redistricting and Congressional Stability, 1962–72," *Journal of Politics*, Vol. 37, No. 2 (May 1975), 569–575; Richard G. Niemi and John Deegan, Jr., "A Theory of Political Districting,"

more eclectic approach, trying to sort out the relative importance of different factors.[63]

Although it proved to be difficult to produce clear evidence linking any of the above factors to higher incumbent percentages,[64] it soon became a widely stated fact in American government texts that incumbents were safer.[65] It is now not unusual to encounter statements that America has "arguably the most radically candidate-centered system in the world," even while partisan voting has increased.[66] The search continues for an explanation of why incumbents

The American Political Science Review, Vol. 72, No. 4 (December 1978), 1304–1323; Born, "Reassessing the Decline of Presidential Coattails"; Richard W. Born, "Partisan Intentions and Election Day Realities in the Congressional Redistricting Process," *American Political Science Review*, Vol. 79, No. 2 (June 1985), 305–319.

Amihai Glazer, Bernard Grofman, and Marc Robbins, "Partisan and Incumbency Effects of 1970s Congressional Districting," *American Journal of Political Science*, Vol. 31, No. 3 (August 1987), 680–707; Michael Lyons and Peter F. Galderisi, "Incumbency, Reapportionment, and U.S. House Redistricting," *Legislative Studies Quarterly*, Vol. 48, No. 4 (December 1995), 857–871; Stephen Ansolabehere, James M. Snyder, Jr., and Charles Stewart, III, "Old Voters, New Voters, and the Personal Vote: Using Redistricting to Measure the Incumbency Advantage," *American Journal of Political Science*, Vol. 44, No. 1 (January 2000), 17–34; Gary W. Cox and Jonathan N. Katz, *Elbridge Gerry's Salamander: The Electoral Consequences of the Reapportionment Revolution* (New York: Cambridge University Press, 2002), 127–139; Scott W. Desposato and John R. Petrocik, "The Variable Incumbency Advantage: New Voters, Redistricting, and the Personal Vote," *American Journal of Political Science*, Vol. 47, No. 1 (January 2003), 18–32.

[63] Robert D. Brown and James A. Woods, "Toward a Model of Congressional Elections," *Journal of Politics*, Vol. 53, No. 2 (May 1991), 454–473; Gary Cox and Jonathan Katz, "Why Did the Incumbency Advantage Grow?," *American Journal of Political Science*, Vol. 40, No. 2 (May 1996), 478–497; Steven D. Levitt and Catherine D. Wolfram, "Decomposing the Sources of Incumbency Advantage," *Legislative Studies Quarterly*, Vol. 22, No. 1 (February 1997), 45–60.

[64] It is not uncommon to come across statements such as the following. "Despite the face validity of the personal vote argument, scholars have had difficulty finding empirical evidence supporting the hypothesis that using these resources [the perks of office] influences election outcomes," Herrera and Yawn, "The Emergence of the Personal Vote," 138. In a 2000 conference paper, Alford and Arceneaux comment: "The sources of the incumbency advantage in congressional elections, and its increase in the mid-1960s – despite all that has been written about it – remain largely enigmatic" (1); or, "Although there is little doubt that incumbents have a substantial advantage over non-incumbents in congressional elections, there is considerably less agreement over the sources of the incumbency advantage and the causes of its growth over time," Carson and Eaves, "Congressional Elections: Why Some Incumbent Candidates Lose." The practice has been to assume there is a growing incumbency effect and presume that some source can be found.

[65] Stonecash, *Reassessing the Incumbency Effect*, 5–6.

[66] Eric McGhee, "National Tides and Local Results in US House Elections," *British Journal of Political Science*, Vol. 38, No. 4 (October 2008), 722. The view that elections are candidate-centered is expressed in many works, such as Paul Herrnson, *Congressional Elections: Campaigning at Home and Washington*, Fifth Edition (Washington, DC: CQ Press, 2008), 6–70.

are presumably safer. The important consequence was that studies of the relationship between presidential and House elections largely disappeared. It was accepted that the relationship had declined, so there was less need to explore different explanations of how or why it was changing. The focus shifted almost exclusively to the activities of individual candidates and particularly incumbents. Parties became secondary in analyses.

3

Reconsidering Conclusions

A Critique

In recent decades analyses of the relationship between presidential and House election results were largely set aside to examine the factors affecting House elections and why incumbents were increasingly safe. There are, however, fundamental problems with the premises underlying the focus on House elections in isolation and with the resulting neglect of the presidential–House election connection. One involves the relevant evidence about incumbents, and the other involves doubts about the candidate-centered framework that has dominated analyses.

First, with regard to the evidence, two matters are important. The empirical evidence about an increased incumbency effect does not indicate what is generally presumed. There is also accumulating evidence that the relationship between presidential–House results is gradually returning to its prior levels. It appears that something sustained and systematic is increasing this relationship in recent decades.

Second, there are reasons to wonder if adherence to the framework dominating analyses – the candidate-centered interpretation – has largely precluded considering an alternative explanation of change. The pattern has been to accept a view of political change apparently built on the twin pillars of the "Michigan model" and critical realignment. Together those two provided the basis for the conclusion that candidate-centered politics had emerged and that presidential and House elections were unconnected. This led to a neglect of the possible role of presidential and party plans in creating gradual change in the presidential–House relationship. An alternative explanation of change will be developed in the next chapter. Before doing that it is necessary to review the existing evidence about elections and the nature and limits of the dominant framework.

Questionable Evidence about Incumbents

The focus on incumbents began with evidence that something was changing in House election results. The essential evidence was that incumbents were increasing their percentage of the vote, and a higher percentage of incumbents were safe, or had a vote percentage of 60 percent or more. This evidence became the basis of the presumption that incumbents were pulling away from the presidential vote. The difficulty is that the evidence of changing incumbent situations does not hold up to reexamination.[1]

The first fact – that the average vote of incumbents was increasing – was derived by examining only those races contested by a major party. For whatever reasons, scholars chose to exclude uncontested races along with some others. This had significant implications because there were more uncontested races in the 1940s and 1950s than in later years.[2] As more districts became contested, they were added to the pool of those forming the average. Those incumbents previously uncontested and now contested had relatively high average vote percentages in the first election they were contested. The result was that as uncontested seats declined over time this resulted in adding in relatively high vote percentages to the existing average for previously contested seats. That raised the overall average from the 1960s through the 1990s.[3] The "fact" of an increasing incumbency vote percentage was essentially a result of more House elections being contested. Figure 3.1 indicates the trend in average vote percentages for all incumbents and for only those contested. From 1946 to 2008, there is no upward trend in the vote percentage of all incumbents.[4]

---

[1] There were earlier works covering a shorter time period that questioned whether incumbents were doing better. See Melissa P. Collie, "Incumbency, Electoral Safety, and Turnover in the House of Representatives, 1972–1976," *American Political Science Review*, Vol. 75, No. 1 (March 1981), 119–131.

[2] Peverill Squire, "Competition and Uncontested Seats in U.S. House Elections," *Legislative Studies Quarterly*, Vol. 14, No. 2 (May 1989), 281–295; J. Mark Wrighton and Peverill Squire, "Uncontested Seats and Electoral Competition for the U.S. House of Representatives over Time," *Journal of Politics*, Vol. 59, No. 2 (May 1997), 452–468.

[3] This is analyzed in some detail in Stonecash, *Reassessing the Incumbency Effect*, 18–29.

[4] Garand, Wink, and Vincent made an effort to point out the consequences of considering only contested races versus all races. They also separated trends by party (31). See James C. Garand, Kenneth Wink, and Bryan Vincent, "Changing Meanings of Electoral Marginality in U.S. House Elections, 1824–1978," *Political Research Quarterly*. Vol. 46, No. 1 (March 1993), 27–48. Jacobson regarded the inclusion of uncontested races as "a fundamental mistake" because it "distorts measurement" (49). He noted that "The extensive literature on postwar changes in the incumbency advantage would certainly have taken a different direction had researchers employed Garand, Wink, and Vincent's index" (50). The difference in the trends by party was also apparently of no interest (50–52). See Gary C. Jacobson, "Getting the Details Right: A Comment on 'Changing Meanings of Electoral Marginality in U.S. House Elections, 1824–1978,'" *Political Research Quarterly*, Vol. 46, No. 1 (March 1993), 49–65. For a further defense of excluding uncontested races, see Gary C. Jacobson, "Reconsidering 'Reconsidering the Trend

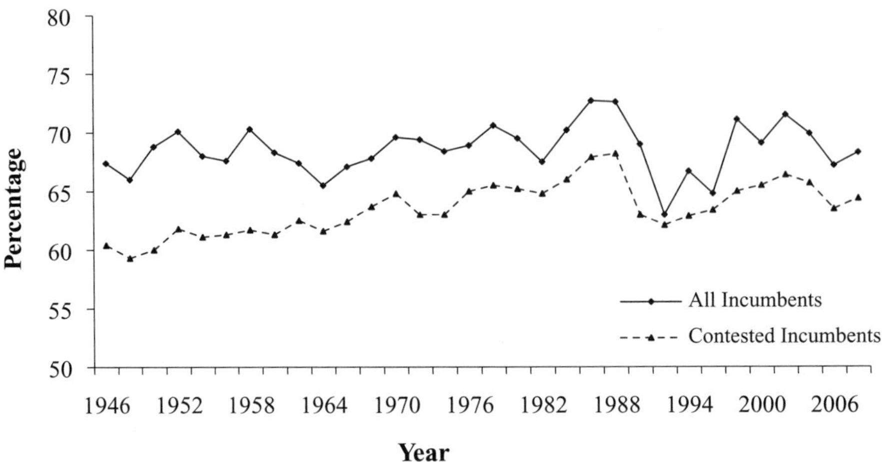

FIGURE 3.1. Vote Percentages for All and Contested Incumbents, 1946–2008

Not only were the data for post-WWII trends not quite what they seemed, but there were reasons to wonder whether the repeated focus on increases after 1946 was missing a more-relevant time period. Incumbent vote percentages were relatively low in the late 1800s and gradually increased from then until 1930. They dipped somewhat in the early 1930s and then rose gradually and only slightly until 1988.[5]

The change from the late 1800s to 1930 occurred before there were all the resources that are presumed to be the source of an increased incumbency effect. Given that, the puzzle becomes what happened before the 1930s that explains the rise in incumbent vote percentages. The very modest increase in incumbent vote percentages from 1936 through the 1980s also casts doubt on any explanation that begins with the presumption that something abrupt occurred in the 1960s.

A second important "fact" was that more incumbents were safe. Mayhew found a significant increase in the percentage of safe seats in the 1966 elections, and that finding became the basis for research on why this general increase occurred.[6] The difficulty with this conclusion was that this change did *not*

<hr>

in Incumbent Vote Percentages in House Elections': A Comment," *American Review of Politics*, Vol. 24 (2003), 241–244.

[5] Donald A. Gross and James C. Garand, "The Vanishing Marginals, 1824–1980," *Journal of Politics*, Vol. 46, No. 1 (February 1984), 224–237; James C. Garand and Donald A. Gross, "Changes in the Vote Margins for Congressional Candidates: A Specification of Historical Trends," *American Political Science Review*, Vol. 78, No. 1 (March 1984), 17–30; Garand, Wink and Vincent, "Changing Meanings of Electoral Marginality in U.S. House Elections, 1824–1978."

[6] Mayhew, "Congressional Elections"; Mayhew, *The Electoral Connection*.

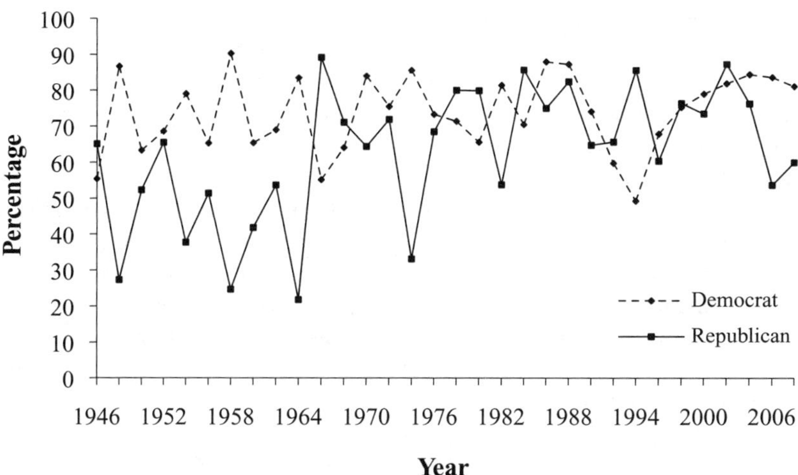

FIGURE 3.2. Percentage of House Incumbents with 60 Percent or More of Vote, by Party, 1946–2008

occur for both parties.[7] *Only* Republicans experienced an increase in safe seats. Figure 3.2 indicates the percentage of incumbents with "safe" seats (more than 60 percent of the total vote) over time for Democrats and Republicans.

From 1946 through 1964 Democratic incumbents had a higher percentage of safe seats than Republican incumbents did. Then in 1966 the situation of Republican incumbents abruptly improved and has largely persisted. The overall change in safeness that many scholars found and focused on was actually experienced by only one party and did not apply to all incumbents. The much-discussed rise in safe seats in 1966 was partisan in nature and not a general change.[8] The evidence that incumbents in general had improved their fortunes does not hold up well under reexamination.

Nonetheless, efforts to precisely estimate the changing incumbency effect proceeded with the presumption that it had occurred.[9] If it had occurred, then a coefficient for the presence of an incumbent in an estimation technique must be picking up changes in the effect. Gelman and King proposed an estimate of the incumbency effect[10] that seemed to make sense, but because of multicollinearity

---

[7] Cox and Katz, *Elbridge Gerry's Salamander*, 127; Stonecash, *Reassessing the Incumbency Effect*, 88–98.

[8] For an analysis of what happened in 1966, see Jeffrey M. Stonecash, "The 1966 Incumbency Effect Increase and the Study of Elections." Presented at the 2011 Southern Political Science Association Meetings, New Orleans, Louisiana, January.

[9] There was also the argument that incumbents were not really doing better, but they were getting better at anticipating the likelihood that they might lose and exiting via retirement instead. This left those who were in a better situation, which made it look as if incumbents were safer. Cox and Katz, *Elbridge Gerry's Salamander*, 167.

[10] Gelman and King, "Estimating Incumbency Effect without Bias."

problems really ends up tracking partisan shifts in open seat races.[11] It does not track greater deviations of incumbents from some base level of support, but the deviations from the expected that occur when an open-seat occurs. Because an increased incumbency effect was presumed, the coefficient's value was accepted as valid.

The other major indicator of incumbents becoming safer, the retirement slump, also has its problems. The retirement slump is the drop in partisan support from the incumbent's last election before retirement to the vote for the same party in the next election. The increased drop-off in partisan votes following retirement in the 1960s and after was presumed to reflect the extent to which the incumbent had raised the party vote. The problem with this indicator is that much of the drop in the partisan percentages was not a reflection of the return to the base partisanship of the district but reflected a shift away from the prior partisanship of the district.[12] Districts were shifting in their partisan inclinations and when incumbents left – many with no increase in their vote percentage over the course of their career – the drop in the partisan vote between the last vote of the incumbent and the next vote for the same party was mistakenly seen as the effect of incumbents.[13]

In short, the evidence does not indicate that incumbent vote percentages increased abruptly in the 1960s. The major increase in this percentage took place before 1946, and any post-1946 increase reflects which districts are included in the analysis. The major change has been in the percentage of Republican incumbents with safe seats, suggesting the need to understand partisan changes more than incumbent percentages. The evidence for an increased incumbency effect is very questionable. If incumbents have not changed their situation, then the presumption that House races are now disconnected from presidential results might well also be questionable.

Accumulating Evidence: The Return of a Relationship

Not only is the evidence about an increased incumbency effect suspect, but other data trends indicate something is wrong with our understanding of the relationship of presidential and House results. If the power of incumbency

[11] For a detailed explanation of this, see Stonecash, *Reassessing the Incumbency Effect*, 130–150.

[12] Stonecash, *Reassessing the Incumbency Effect*, 119–129.

[13] It should also be noted that the presumption is questionable that incumbents generally increase their vote percentage over a career. In reality most members exit the House with a lower percentage than their initial percentage. From 1900 to 2008, more than 4,000 members have been elected and have departed the House: For those members elected since 1900 through 2008 there have been approximately 4000 members elected and departing the House. Over that time 61.2 percent of exiting members – whether through retirement of a loss – have experienced a net loss in vote percentages from their first to last election. For those exiting between 1902 and 1949, 65.0 percent of members had a net loss. Among those exiting 1950–2008, 54.7 percent had a net loss. Even for those members elected in recent decades the situation is not very different. Among those elected since 1975, 46.5 percent experienced a net loss in vote percentage from their first to last election.

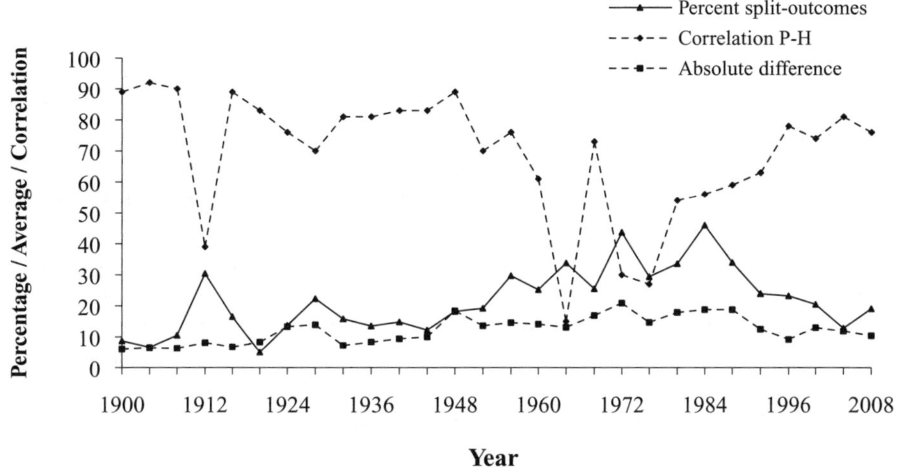

FIGURE 3.3. Republican Presidential–House Election Relationships, 1900–2008, all Districts

and candidate-centered politics is increasing, then House members should be able to steadily separate themselves from presidential results. Office resources, campaign funds, and access to television and other media continue to increase. The result should be a growing separation of presidential and House election results as members insulate themselves from the vagaries of fluctuations in presidential results.[14]

The difficulty is that about the time the presumed disassociation between presidential and House results became conventional wisdom, the relevant trends reversed. Figure 3.3 presents three indicators of the extent of separation of presidential and House results. One is the correlation (multiplied by 100) between Republican presidential and House results across House districts for each year of a presidential election.[15] From 1900 through 1948 the correlations were high, fluctuating between 80 and 90. When a presidential candidate did well, a House candidate from the same party also did well. From 1900 through the 1940s stability and continuity prevailed.

Then in the 1950s the correlation began to systematically decline, dropping to .15 in 1964, .30 in 1972, and .27 in 1976. The decline reflected a separation of presidential and House results within districts. This separation can be measured by calculating the absolute differences in vote percentages for presidential and House candidates. Because some presidential–House difference scores will be positive and others will be negative, they may cancel each other out in an averaging process and understate the separation occurring. For that reason the mean of absolute differences, with no sign for specific scores,

---

[14] Herrnson, *Congressional Elections*, 25.
[15] Democratic results are essentially the same except for 1948, when the correlation dropped dramatically because Southern states deserted the party over Truman's civil rights positions.

is used. Beginning in 1948 this difference increased. Another indicator is the percentage of House districts in which the party winning the presidential and House vote within the district differed. By the 1970s it was common to have split-outcomes in 30 percent of House districts. By 1984, 46 percent of House districts had split-outcomes.

Just as this disconnection seemed well established, the trends began to reverse.[16] The correlation between presidential and House results began to increase in 1980. The absolute difference between presidential and House results began to decline in the 1990s. The percentage of House districts with split-outcomes declined from its high in 1984 to 12.8 in 2004 and 19.1 in 2008. The association between presidential and House results is now increasing. The candidate-centered view does not contain an explicit prediction that the trend should be toward greater separation, but the expectation is *not* that the relationship between the two results should increase. Something has been happening to bring election results for these two offices closer together.

The data in Figure 3.3 involve all districts and might be seen as flawed because the argument is that it is the presence of incumbents that has altered the relationship between presidential and House elections. Given that concern, Figure 3.4 presents the same indicators for only those races involving incumbents. The patterns involving only incumbents are essentially the same as that for all contests.

This evidence leaves us with several facts. There was not a general increase in incumbency vote percentages or in the percentage of safe seats in the 1960s. Whatever change that did occur was enjoyed by Republicans and not Democrats; it was partisan and not general in nature. The separation of presidential and House results was temporary, and is now close to levels in the early 1900s. These are facts in need of an explanatory framework.

A Restoration?

The 1996 election suggested that the relationship between presidential and House election results was returning to the levels occurring at the beginning of

---

[16] Gary C. Jacobson, "Party Polarization in National Politics: The Electoral Connection," in Jon R. Bond and Richard Fleisher, Editors, *Polarized Politics* (Washington, DC: CQ Press), 9–30; Gary C. Jacobson, "Reversal of Fortune: The Transformation of U.S. House Elections in the 1990s," in David W. Brady, John F. Cogan, and Morris Fiorina, Editors, *Continuity and Change in House Elections* (Palo Alto, CA: Stanford University Press, 2000), 21–24. There was some evidence that national factors were playing a greater role in House elections: David W. Brady, Robert D'Onofrio, and Morris P. Fiorina, "The Nationalization of Electoral Forces Revisited," in David W. Brady, John F. Cogan, and Morris P. Fiorina, Editors, *Continuity and Change in House Elections* (Palo Alto: Stanford University Press, 2000), 130–148. For an analysis skeptical of any nationalization of the individual-level sources of voting for the two offices see Richard Born, "National Forces and the U.S. House Vote, 1980–2004: The Uncertain Progress of Nationalization," *Congress and the Presidency*, Vol. 35, No. 1 (Spring 2008), 87–103.

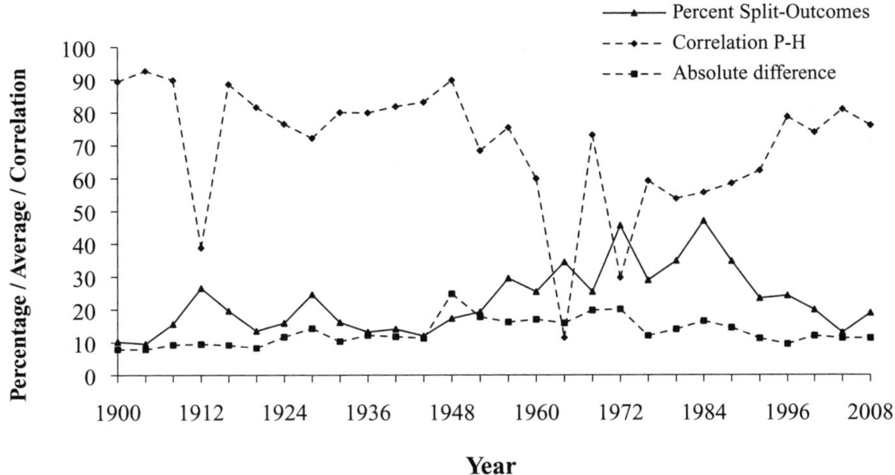

FIGURE 3.4. Republican Presidential–House Election Relationships, 1900–2008, Incumbent Districts Only

the century. Whatever had disrupted this relationship appeared to have passed. Perhaps the decades of the 1960s and 1970s were simply a time of turmoil. The 1960s were widely seen as a decade of social disruption.[17] The parties were losing some control over the presidential nomination process.[18] It might be possible to regard the decline in the relationship as just temporary and reflecting the instability of the 1960s.[19]

The difficulty with the view that we are returning to normalcy is that systematic and sustained changes in the political geography of American politics have occurred. The geographical bases of support for the parties are not what they were in the past.[20] The South had been Democratic but was now predominantly Republicans.[21] The Northeast had been heavily Republican but was now

[17] Maurice Isserman and Michael Kazin, *America Divided: The Civil War of the 1960s* (New York: Oxford University Press, 2004); Alan Petigny, *The Permissive Society: America, 1941–1965* (New York: Cambridge University Press, 2009); Bernard Von Bothhmer, *Framing the 1960s: The Use and Abuse of a Decade from Ronald Reagan to George W. Bush* (Amherst: University of Massachusetts Press, 2010).

[18] Cohen, Karol, Noel, and Zaller, *The Party Decides.*

[19] Warren E. Miller (updated by Kenneth Goldstein and Mark Jones), "Party Identification and the Electorate at the Beginning of the Twenty-First Century," in L. Sandy Maisel, Editor, *The Parties Respond: Changes in American Parties and Campaigns* (Boulder, CO: Westview Press, 2002), 79–98. There is a history of scholars presuming that there is an equilibrium in American politics, and results just fluctuate around that: Charles Sellers, "The Equilibrium Cycle in Two-Party Politics," *Public Opinion Quarterly*, Vol. 29, No. 1 (Spring 1965), 16–38.

[20] Gary Miller and Norman Schofield, "Activists and Partisan Realignment in the United States," *American Political Science Review*, Vol. 97, No. 2 (May 2003), 245–260.

[21] Merle Black and Earl Black, *Politics and Society in the South* (Cambridge, MA: Harvard University Press, 1987); Merle Black and Earl Black, *The Rise of Southern Republicans* (Cambridge,

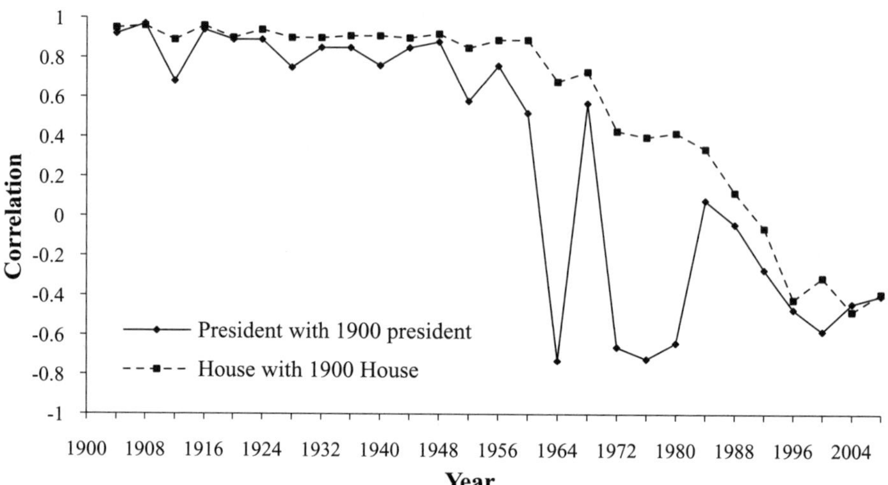

FIGURE 3.5. Correlation of Republican Presidential and House State Percentages 1904–2008 with 1900 State Percentages

heavily Democratic.[22] The extent to which recent levels of electoral support are associated with past levels is shown in Figure 3.5. In this case Republican state-level results for each year are correlated[23] with results from 1900.[24] Presidential elections from 1904 are correlated with 1900. Then the state-level results from 1908, 1912, 1916, and so forth are correlated with 1900. The point is to assess the extent of geographical stability of relative support levels over time, using 1900 as a baseline. For House election results, they are aggregated to the state level. District-level results cannot be correlated over time because districts are redrawn each decade. Aggregating to the state level reduces variation in House results but allows some assessment of change.

MA: Harvard University Press, 2002); Byron E. Shafer and Richard Johnston, *The End of Southern Exceptionalism: Class, Race, and Partisan Change in the Postwar South* (Cambridge, MA: Harvard University Press, 2006).

[22] Reiter and Stonecash, *CounterRealignment*.

[23] This correlation tracks the relative position of states over time and how stable they are. The overall Democratic vote may rise or fall over time, but the correlation tracks the stability of the *relative* positions of states to their 1900 position. Results for 1900–1996 are taken from Rusk, *A Statistical History of the American Electorate*, 158–170. The results for 2000–2008 are taken from the FEC results presented on their Web page: http://www.fec.gov/pubrec/.

[24] This approach has been used by several scholars: Gerald Pomper, "Classification of Presidential Elections," *Journal of Politics*, Vol. 29, No. 3 (August 1967), 545–547; Walter Dean Burnham, "American Voting Behavior and the 1964 Election," *Midwest Journal of Political Science*, Vol. 12, No. 1 (February 1968), 8; and Arthur C. Paulson, *Realignment and Party Revival: Understanding American Electoral Politics at the Turn of the Twenty-First Century* (Westport, CT: Praeger, 2000), 23–34.

The important issue is the extent of geographical continuity of party electoral bases over time. To what extent is the base of recent years equivalent to that of earlier years? For Republican presidential candidates the relative position of states was fairly consistent through the 1948 election, with the correlation of state percentages with 1900 results generally varying between .7 and .9. In the 1952–1960 elections it declined but remained positive. Then the correlation of 1964, 1972, 1976, and 1980 with 1900 turned sharply negative. The 1968 results were complicated by the votes going to George Wallace, a matter that will be discussed in chapter 7. In the 1960s and 1970s the states relatively supportive of Republicans in 1900 were now the least supportive. By the 1990s and 2000s the states least supportive in 1900 were now the most supportive. Over a century the political geography of presidential elections has changed dramatically.

House election results retained a positive association with 1900 results much longer than presidential results. Although presidential results developed a largely negative relationship with 1900 beginning in 1964, House results did not develop a negative relationship with 1900 until 1992. Changes in House results lagged presidential results by several decades. That lag is important for understanding the presidential–House relationship and will be discussed at length later.

Summary: Doubts about Premises and Conclusions

Together these results suggest significant problems with conventional conclusions about incumbents and the presidential–House election connection. The conventional view has been that the relationship between the two sets of elections has declined because House incumbents have been able to create a "personal" vote such that their vote percentages can diverge from the presidential outcome in House districts. The problems begin with the premises. First, House incumbents have not been able to increase their average vote percentages in the last 60 years. Second, their average divergence (in absolute percentage points) from presidential results rose but has declined in the last two decades. The increased incumbency effect / candidate-centered interpretation suggests the divergence should at least remain the same, and not decline. It should also be noted that the empirical issue of whether House members pulled away from presidential results or presidential candidates pulled away from the vote percentages of House candidates and or incumbents has never been examined. Third, the increase in safe seats was experienced only by Republicans; it is not a general change. Fourth, there are fewer split-outcomes in House districts. Fifth, and most important, the evidence indicates that the correlation between presidential and House results has been increasing over the last three decades.

Further, the return of the relationship between these results is not a return to prior patterns. The geographical bases of the parties have undergone a major transition and reversal compared to the early part of the century. Major changes have occurred, and those changes pulled the results apart and then brought them back together. It is difficult to accept any interpretation of change built around a notion that incumbents are reducing their relationship to the presidential vote.

There is something fundamentally lacking with the interpretation of the relation of presidential–House election results that has dominated the last several decades. The candidate-centered interpretation might have seemed useful in explaining the decline in this relationship, but none of the factors relevant to that explanation – member resources or campaign funds – have declined, so that framework has little utility for explaining the reversal of trends. We need another framework. An alternative framework, focusing on party pursuits, will be presented in chapter 4. Before doing that, however, it will be useful to assess the theoretical presumptions that underlie the existing interpretation.

Frameworks and Consequences

The evidence just reviewed suggests that partisanship is now affecting both presidential and House results. The individual-level evidence indicates that those who identify with a party are now, after a decline in the 1960s and 1970s, more inclined to vote for their party.[25] Party voting in Congress is steadily increasing.[26] Yet even as these trends continue, congressional elections are regularly characterized as "candidate-centered." Are these trends of increased partisanship compatible with a framework that sees elections as candidate-centered?[27] The argument to be presented here is that they are not. Academics have developed a framework and derived interpretations from it that have drawn us away from incorporating the role of parties in creating the changes of the last several decades. Before moving to an argument about what is driving the change of recent decades, it is important to review the interpretation of elections that has dominated the last 40 years.

Any critique of current interpretations must begin with the "candidate-centered" claim. The essential problem with this characterization is that it is an assertion without specificity. It is a blanket interpretation that provides no

---

[25] Bartels, "Partisanship and Voting Behavior, 1952–1996"; and Stonecash, *Parties Matter*.

[26] Donald C. Baumer and Howard J. Gold, *Parties, Polarization, and Democracy in the United States* (Boulder, CO: Paradigm, 2010), 119–143.

[27] For examples of analyses that see these trends as compatible, see David W. Brady and Kara Z. Buckley, "Governing by Coalition: Policymaking in the U.S. Congress," in L. Sandy Maisel, Editor, *The Parties Respond: Changes in American Parties and Campaigns*, Fourth Edition (Boulder, CO: Westview, 2002), 244–251; Eric McGhee, "National Tides and Local Results in US House Elections," 722; John H. Aldrich, *Why Parties?* (Chicago: University of Chicago Press, 1995); and John H. Aldrich, *Why Parties? A Second Look* (Chicago: University of Chicago Press, 2011), 165.

claims that would allow its verification or refutation. It is elastic in that it provides no guidelines as to when elections begin to shade from being party- to candidate-centered. Is the extent of this measured by the percentage of split-outcome districts, by the average difference of a House candidate from presidential votes, or by the ability to produce less change in a House percentage when a presidential vote shifts? Or is it measured at the individual level as the percentage of partisans who defect from their party's candidate? Does defection of more than 15 percent constitute a candidate-centered outcome or does it have to be 20 percent? Does it matter if the defection occurs in a competitive district or one with lopsided partisanship? There are no guidelines for whether or how much the phenomenon is present. The statement that campaigns are candidate-centered is difficult to refute.

It is that elusive content that has allowed the characterization to continue even as partisanship has steadily increased in recent elections. There is no doubt that presenting *candidates* to the electorate is central to campaigns now, but how do we separate voting for the candidate from voting for the party when presidential and House results covary fairly strongly, when party members vote together in Congress, and when partisan voters strongly support their party candidates? This ambiguity of what constitutes a candidate-centered outcome makes a more detailed critique of this claim very difficult.

It is possible, however, to review the accumulation of research perspectives and findings that provide the basis for the assertion that elections are candidate-centered. A combination of interpretations and findings provide support for this claim. Several matters have been particularly important in leading to this conclusion. The essential idea of candidate-centered politics is that a candidate can pull a vote away from the partisan vote in the district. That presumes some stable partisanship in the district. Yet there has been considerable change in American politics, so there must be some notion of how change occurs, but one that will still provide a stable district partisanship. The ideas that have answered these questions while still providing a basis for candidate-centered politics involve the combination of party identification, normal votes, and critical realignment. Together they provide a framework, but they also largely remove the study of gradual change and the role of parties as creators of change.

The Foundation: A Stable Party Identification and a Normal Vote

A fundamental building block for many analyses of American politics is individual party identification. This concept began as the "Michigan model" of voters.[28] This portrait of voters assumed that voters developed fairly strong attachments to parties, but those attachments were largely affective, based on

---

[28] This characterization occurred because the first major studies of voting behavior were conducted out of the University of Michigan.

social identities and not issues.[29] There was a relatively stable division of voters between the parties, and the attachment of voters to the parties was stable. Changes in voter attachments were not regarded as likely or important.[30] The role of issues was modest in providing a basis for these divisions. Ideological conflicts within society were declining,[31] class divisions were also seen as declining[32] and few voters were ideological.[33] Given the limited role of issues, the strong attachments were seen as affective or enduring emotional attachments that are formed early in life and are unlikely to change.

Despite all the change that has occurred in American politics, the acceptance of this view of party attachments has remained strong. You and "your" social group are either Republican or Democratic and remain so without much ideological thought.[34] The importance of the view that party identification is stable is indicated by the resistance to the idea that it can change gradually, either at the individual or aggregate level.[35] Some have suggested that voters are continually assessing party positions[36] and that gradual changes occur in party identification based on issues.[37] This notion that individuals change their identification has been challenged as largely measurement error.[38] Others suggested that aggregate partisanship might fluctuate over time in response to

---

[29] Campbell, Converse, Miller, and Stokes, *The American Voter*, 120–167; Philip E. Converse and Gregory Markus, "Plus ça Change...; The New CPS Election Study Panel," *American Political Science Review*, Vol. 73, No. 1 (March 1979), 32–49.

[30] Gerald M. Pomper, "The Impact of *The American Voter* on Political Science," *Political Science Quarterly*, Vol. 93, No. 4 (Winter 1978–1979), 625; For a critique of this conclusion, see Jeffrey M. Stonecash, "Political Change and Party Identification: Stability versus Change and the Exclusion of Parties." Presented at the 2011 Midwest Political Science Association Meetings, Chicago, Illinois, March 30–April 3, 2011.

[31] Daniel Bell, *The End of Ideology* (New York: Collier Books, 1962).

[32] Robert R. Alford, *Party and Society: The Anglo–American Democracies* (Westport, CT: Greenwood Press, 1963).

[33] Campbell et al., *The American Voter*, 188–215.

[34] Donald P. Green, Bradley Palmquist, and Eric Shickler, *Partisan Hearts and Minds: Political Parties and the Social Identities of Voters* (New Haven, CT: Yale University Press, 2002).

[35] For different perspectives on generational changes, see Richard M. Merelman, "Electoral Instability and the American Party System," *Journal of Politics*, Vol. 32, No. 1 (February 1970), 115–139; Warren E. Miller, "Generational Changes and Party Identification," *Political Behavior*, Vol. 14, No. 3 (September 1992), 333–352; and Stonecash, *Parties Matter*, 112–128.

[36] Fiorina, *Retrospective Voting in American National Elections*.

[37] Alan I. Abramowitz and Kyle L. Saunders, "Ideological Realignments in the U.S. Electorate," *Journal of Politics*, Vol. 60, No. 3 (August 1998), 634–652; Alan Abramowitz, "Ideological Realignment among Voters," in Jeffrey M. Stonecash, Editor, *New Directions in American Political Parties* (New York: Routledge, 2010), 126–147.

[38] Donald P. Green and Bradley Palmquist, "Of Artifacts and Partisan Instability," *American Journal of Political Science*, Vol. 34, No. 3 (August 1990), 872–902; Donald P. Green and Bradley Palmquist, "How Stable Is Party Identification," *Political Behavior*, Vol. 16, No. 4 (December 1994), 437–66.

events and conditions.[39] That suggestion has generated strong opposition and assertions that gradual or secular change does not occur.[40]

This presumption of general stability is crucial for forming expectations about district-level votes. If voters are stable, and there is a known partisan composition within a district, then we can assume there is a "normal vote" within a district, or a likely partisan vote in the absence of short-term forces.[41] The predictability of individual behavior should translate into predictable aggregate or district behavior. There are likely to be fluctuations away from the normal vote based on short-term factors, but there is still a normal vote.[42] Given a normal vote, the focus could then shift to the role of short-term factors that could push the district vote away from being "normal."[43] These factors could be current issues, the economy,[44] changes in congressional[45] or presidential

[39] Michael MacKuen, Robert S. Erikson, and James A. Stimson, "Macropartisanship," *American Political Science Review*. Vol. 83, No. 4 (December 1989), 1125–1142; Stimson, MacKuen, and Erikson, "Dynamic Representation"; Michael MacKuen, Robert S. Erikson, and James A. Stimson, "Question Wording and Macropartisanship," *American Political Science Review*, Vol. 86, No. 2 (June 1992), 475–481; Robert S. Erikson, Michael B. MacKuen, and James A. Stimson, "What Moves Macropartisanship? A Response to Green, Palmquist, and Shickler," *American Political Science Review*, Vol. 92, No. 4 (December 1998), 901–912.

[40] Paul R. Abramson and Charles W. Ostrom, "Macropartisanship: An Empirical Assessment," *American Political Science Review*, Vol. 85, No. 1 (March 1976), 181–192; Paul R. Abramson and Charles W. Ostrom, "Response," *American Political Science Review*, Vol. 86, No. 2 (June 1992), 475–486; Donald P. Green, Bradley Palmquist, and Eric Shickler, "Macropartisanship: A Replication and Critique," *American Political Science Review*, Vol. 90, No. 4 (December 1998), 883–899; Green, Palmquist, and Shickler, *Partisan Hearts and Minds*; Janet Box-Steffensmeier and Renee M. Smith, "The Dynamics of Aggregate Partisanship," *American Political Science Review*, Vol. 90, No. 3 (September 1996), 567–580; Michael F. Meffert, Helmut Norpoth, and Anirudh V.S. Ruhl, "Realignment and Partisanship," *American Political Science Review*, Vol. 95, No. 4 (December 2001), 953–962; and James E. Campbell, "Explaining Politics, Not Polls: Reexamining Macropartisanship with Recalibrated NES Data," *Public Opinion Quarterly*, Vol. 74, No. 4 (Winter 2010), 1–27.

[41] Converse, "The Concept of a Normal Vote."

[42] Angus Campbell, "Surge and Decline: A Study of Electoral Change," in Angus Campbell, Philip E. Converse, Warren E. Miller, and Donald E. Stokes, Editors, *Elections and the Political Order* (New York: John Wiley, 1966), 40–62; James E. Campbell, "A Revised Theory of Surge and Decline," *American Journal of Political Science*, Vol. 31, No. 4 (November 1987), 965–979; and John R. Petrocik, "An Expected Party Vote: New Data for an Old Concept," *American Journal of Political Science*, Vol. 33, No. 1 (February 1989), 44–66.

[43] Angus Campbell, "A Classification of the Presidential Elections," in Angus Campbell, Philip E. Converse, Warren E. Miller, and Donald E. Stokes, Editors, *Elections and the Political Order* (New York: John Wiley, 1966), 63–77.

[44] Gerald H. Kramer, "Short-Term Fluctuations in U.S. Voting Behavior, 1896–1964," *American Political Science Review*, Vol. 63, No. 1 (March 1971), 131–143; and Tufte, "Determinants of the Outcomes of Midterm Congressional Elections."

[45] Richard Born, "The Shared Fortunes of Congress and Congressmen: Members May Run from Congress, but They Can't Hide," *Journal of Politics*, Vol. 52, No. 4 (November 1990), 1223–1241.

approval,[46] wars, campaign spending,[47] the quality of challengers,[48] the number of seats held by a party above its "normal" number,[49] or the voting behavior of incumbents.[50]

Critical Realignment and Change

With a focus primarily on how short-term deviations from a normal vote occur, the dominant framework had one significant difficulty to grapple with. Change presented a conceptual problem. If districts have stable votes, and House candidates are successfully increasing their deviation from that base, how could long-term changes be explained? There clearly have been significant changes in partisan loyalties within regions and districts over time. How does stability exist while there is evidence of considerable change?

The answer was apparently through critical realignment.[51] During the 1950s V. O. Key presented two models of change. One emphasized that change might happen gradually,[52] and the other emphasized that change happened through

[46] Samuel Kernell, "Presidential Popularity and Negative Voting: An Alternative Explanation of the Midterm Congressional Decline of the President's Party," *American Political Science Review*, Vol. 71, No. 1 (March 1977), 44–66. For analyses of Senate elections, see Barbara Hinckley, "Incumbency and the Presidential Vote in Senate Elections: Defining Parameters of Subpresidential Voting," *American Political Science Review*, Vol. 64, No. 3 (September 1970), 836–842; Alan I. Abramowitz and Jeffrey A. Segal, "Determinants of the Outcomes of U.S. Senate Elections," *Journal of Politics*, Vol. 48, No. 2 (May 1986), 433–439; and Albert D. Cover, "Presidential Evaluations and Voting for Congress," *American Journal of Political Science*, Vol. 30, No. 4 (November 1986), 786–801.

[47] Gary C. Jacobson, "The Effects of Campaign Spending in Congressional Elections," *American Political Science Review*, Vol. 72, No. 2 (June 1978), 469–491; Gary C. Jacobson, "Money and Votes Reconsidered: Congressional Elections, 1972–1982," *Public Choice*, Vol. 47, No. 1 (1985), 7–62; Robert S. Erikson and Thomas R. Palfrey, "Campaign Spending and Incumbency: An Alternative Simultaneous Equations Approach," *Journal of Politics*, Vol. 60, No. 2 (May 1998), 355–373.

[48] Jacobson and Kernell, *Strategy and Choice in Congressional Elections*; Krasno and Green, "Preempting Quality Challengers in House Elections."

[49] Richard A. Waterman, "Comparing Senate and House Electoral Outcomes: The Exposure Thesis," *Legislative Studies Quarterly*, Vol. 15, No. 1 (February 1990), 99–114.

[50] David W. Brady, Brandice Canes-Wrone, and John F. Cogan, "Differences in Legislative Voting Behavior between Winning and Losing House Incumbents," in David W. Brady, John F. Cogan, and Morris P. Fiorina, Editors, *Continuity and Change in House Elections* (Palo Alto, CA: Stanford University Press, 2000); Brandice Canes-Wrone, David W. Brady, and John F. Cogan, "Out of Step, Out of Office: Electoral Accountability and House Members' Voting," *American Political Science Review*, Vol. 96, No. 1 (March 2002), 127–140; and Janet M. Box-Steffensmeier, David C. Kimball, Scott R. Meinke, and Katherine Tate, "The Effects of Political Representation on the Electoral Advantages of House Incumbents," *Political Research Quarterly*, Vol. 56, No. 3 (September 2003), 259–270.

[51] Campbell et al., *The American Voter*, 531–53; Pomper, "The Impact of *The American Voter* on Political Science," 624.

[52] V. O. Key, "Secular Realignment and the Party System," *Journal of Politics*, Vol. 21, No. 2 (May 1959), 198–210.

critical realignments.[53] The essence of the latter idea is that parties develop electoral bases, and these bases become stable. Society changes and new issues emerge, but parties, given their established bases, find it difficult to respond. Eventually the new issue acquires high salience among voters, and party candidates stake out new positions in an effort to respond.[54] A significant percentage of voters respond and abruptly shift their partisan allegiances, and a new political alignment emerges. These assumptions are summarized by Burnham as follows:

Critical realignments... have arisen out of a growing – and inherent – dissynchronization between the capacities, routines and official ideologies of political elites and the organizable political effects at the mass base of relatively uncontrollable change in a capitalist society. They are the ultimate empirical demonstration of two propositions about American electoral politics.

First, once established, a dominant political alignment, its associated elites and their activities will continue to function in a routinized way indefinitely unless acted upon by some overwhelming external force.

Second, the adjustments of policy outputs and interest representation which American pluralists have celebrated in our parties and other institutions operate within strictly limited areas at the margins.

No established political elite is prepared to incorporate demands the effective realization of which is incompatible with its fundamental interests or with the existing rules of the game.[55]

The crucial assumption is that parties find it difficult to monitor gradual social change and adjust to it. Social change proceeds faster than political change, and the disjuncture eventually results in a critical realignment. Parties are largely seen as reacting to change and not as entities that monitor social

---

[53] V. O. Key, "A Theory of Critical Elections," *Journal of Politics*, Vol. 17, No. 1 (February 1955), 3–18.

[54] As an example of this presumed dynamic – that the electorate moves and parties struggle to respond – see Patricia A. Hurley, "Partisan Representation, Realignment, and the Senate in the 1980s," *Journal of Politics*, Vol. 53, No. 1 (February 1991), 3–33. She notes: "Realignments, then, are simultaneously driven by mass opinion and behavior and elite behavior: the connection between opinion and policy moves from mass to elite and from elite to mass during realigning periods. The electorate, dissatisfied with politics as usual, sends large numbers of new members to Congress, creating a new majority or a greatly reduced margin of control for the existing majority. The pump is then primed for realignment, but it will only follow if the advantaged congressional party continues to provide policy dissatisfaction to its existing identifiers as well as to the independents" (5). Notice that partisan support shifts and then politicians are seen as trying to catch up and respond. Parties are not actively seeking voters but are trying to respond to voter dissatisfaction.

[55] Walter Dean Burnham, "Revitalization and Decay: Looking Toward the Third Century of American Electoral Politics," *Journal of Politics*, Vol. 38, No. 3 (August 1976), 148.

change and formulate plans to respond to change and win the support of particular segments of the electorate.[56]

For reasons that are unclear, many scholars appear to have embraced critical realignment as more useful than secular realignment as a way to interpret politics.[57] Indeed, it appears that for many scholars, references to realignment came to mean critical realignment. Why that occurred is not clear, but two matters appear to be important. Several prominent scholars[58] embraced the framework as a useful way of interpreting political change.[59] Perhaps most important is that the critical realignment interpretation is very compatible with the Michigan model, which presumes stable, affective attachments.[60] Party

---

[56] Sundquist, *Dynamics of the Party System*, 29; Burnham, "American Politics in the 1970s," 307. This is stated most clearly in Everett Carll Ladd with Charles D. Hadley, *Transformations of the American Party System* (New York: W. W. Norton, 1975): "Parties, elections and voting are all seen, in a fundamental sense, as dependent variables. They exist as parts of the political system which is, precisely, a subunit of the larger social system. As such, they are much more acted upon that acting upon" (22).

[57] Making inferences about what academics were thinking as they conducted studies is clearly a chancy matter. I cannot remotely know what anyone was thinking. These observations are based on a reading of the articles appearing in journals at the time. The conclusions are based on the issues and literature cited in framing analyses and the kinds of data and information used. For example, in the literature during the 1970s, in explaining electoral trends, it was common to cite the work of E. E. Schattschneider, Walter Dean Burnham, and James Sundquist. These scholars were advocates of the critical realignment interpretation of political change. The presumption is that in citing these works academics were drawing on this interpretation because they found it more useful for explaining change. The conclusion is also based on how academics reacted to analyses that raised questions about the presumed conversion that occurs in a critical realignment. In 1979 Kristi Andersen in *The Creation of a Democratic Majority* (Chicago: University of Chicago Press, 1979) presented an analysis of major urban areas and argued that much of the change might be due to the mobilization of previously unengaged voters. That was met with criticisms that conversion must explain changes that occurred: Sundquist, *Dynamics of the Party System*, 229–239; Robert S. Erikson and Kent L. Tedin, "The 1928–1932 Partisan Realignment: The Case for the Conversion Hypothesis," *American Political Science Review*, Vol. 75, No. 4 (December 1981), 951–962. The desire to preserve an explanation of abrupt change has been strong.

[58] E. E. Schattschneider, *The Semisovereign People: A Realist's View of Democracy in America* (New York: Holt, Rinehart and Winston, 1960); Walter D. Burnham, *Critical Elections and the Mainsprings of American Politics* (New York: W. W. Norton, 1970); Sundquist, *Dynamics of the Party System*; and Patricia A. Hurley, "Partisan Representation and the Failure of Realignment in the 1980s," *American Journal of Political Science*, Vol. 33, No. 1 (February 1989), 240–261.

[59] Another indication of preoccupation with critical realignment is the volume of research about it and the enduring debate about its relevance. The studies and the debate about this perspective are illustrated in the collection of papers in Byron E. Shafer, Editor, *The End of Realignment* (Madison: University of Wisconsin Press, 1991), suggesting that the concept is of limited utility. In contrast Nardulli argues that the concept is useful but there has been far more regional variation in realignments than previously recognized. Peter F. Nardulli, "The Concept of Critical Realignment, Electoral Behavior, and Political Change," *American Political Science Review*, Vol. 89, No. 1 (March 1995), 10–22.

[60] This connection is articulated in Helmut Norpoth and Jerrold G. Rusk, "Electoral Myth and Reality: Realignments in American Politics," *Electoral Studies*, Vol. 26 (June 2007), 392–403.

identification is stable until some major events alter it. Critical realignments occur, and then party attachments again become stable and relatively enduring for individual identities.

This framework seemed helpful for making sense of history. The argument that history was defined by bursts of intense political conflict that created persistent alignments fit with the view that major changes occurred in 1860, 1896, and 1932.[61] Textbooks organize history into eras of specific "party systems" that persist following a critical realignment.[62] Scholars argue for the value of this classification scheme and seek to rebut criticisms of critical realignment.[63]

Critical realignment provides an explanation for presuming relatively stable normal votes within districts while allowing for change. A set of normal votes exists across districts. Then social change builds, parties do not respond well, and realignment occurs. The realignment creates a new set of normal votes within districts. It is possible to acknowledge change without having to deal with the consequences of long-term gradual change. This presumption that stability largely prevailed at any one time made it possible to conduct cross-sectional analyses of House voting at the district level, focusing on deviations from that normal vote.

The Missing Realignment and Theoretical Innovation

At about the time that critical realignment appeared to be widely accepted, the theory encountered the problem that the next expected realignment did not occur. By the 1960s it had been 30 years since a critical realignment had occurred. The conditions seemed ripe for one. The old issues of class and labor-management conflict seemed to be of less relevance.[64] As these issues faded in significance, voters were losing interest in parties and new issues were not yet

---

[61] David W. Brady, "A Reevaluation of Realignments in American Politics: Evidence from the House of Representatives," *American Political Science Review*, Vol. 79, No. 1 (March 1985), 28–49.

[62] Frank J. Sorauf, *Party Politics in America* (Boston: Little, Brown, 1968); and Richard A. Waterman, "Institutional Realignment: The Composition of the U.S. Congress," *Western Political Quarterly*, Vol. 43, No. 1 (March 1990), 81–92.

[63] The primary criticism of this framework was presented by David R. Mayhew, *Electoral Realignments: A Critique of an American Genre* (New Haven, CT: Yale University Press, 2002). His criticism has drawn counter analyses arguing that the political world can be organized around major realignments in 1896, 1932, and a staggered realignment beginning in 1968. See James E. Campbell, "Party Systems and Realignments in the United States, 1868–2004," *Social Science History*, Vol. 30, No. 3 (Fall 2006), 359–386. Others argue that there is clear evidence of periodic and regular changes in party dominance: Samuel Merrill III, Bernard Grofman, and Thomas L. Brunell, "Cycles in American National Electoral Politics: Statistical Evidence and an Explanatory Model," *American Political Science Review*, Vol. 102, No. 1 (February 2008), 1–17.

[64] Although that conclusion has dominated, the evidence does not indicate that class is of less relevance in American politics. Jeffrey M. Stonecash, *Class and Party in American Politics* (Boulder, CO: Westview, 2000); and Jeffrey M. Stonecash, "Class in American Politics," in

sufficiently salient or capitalized upon by politicians to create a new alignment. The framework provided an explanation for the decline in individual party identification and the declining correlation of partisan voting across states over time.[65] Partisanship was declining and the party system was decomposing until something came along to replace it.[66] Despite the expectation, it was difficult to find evidence of a critical realignment, although Burnham did try.[67]

The questions became: Why was realignment not occurring, and what did it its nonoccurrence mean for House elections? The answers were that something had changed in American politics to reduce the role of parties and partisanship. Parties and partisanship were declining, and voters were less attached to parties.[68] House members now had access to polling to help them anticipate changes in voter sentiment and adjust their own positions.[69] Incumbents had more resources to present themselves to voters.[70] As the traditional party organization declined, campaign organizations took on new forms comprised of pollsters, consultants, and direct mail companies. These new mechanisms of getting messages to voters were responsive to candidates and not party organizations. They gave House candidates autonomy and more control over their electoral fortunes.[71]

Given that a critical realignment was unlikely to occur, analyses could then presume the existence of normal votes within districts, and focus on the ability of House candidates to move the vote away from that.[72] The study of incumbency became "'the central connective thread' running through the entire literature on Congress."[73] The notion that campaigns and election results were driven by individual candidates became "the dominant theoretical foundation for much of the contemporary research examining the U.S. Congress."[74] The result was a shift away from studying the presidential–House relationship as

Jeffrey M. Stonecash, Editor, *New Directions in American Politics* (New York: Routledge, 2010), 126–147.

[65] Walter D. Burnham, "American Politics in the 1970s: Beyond Party?," in William N. Chambers and Walter Dean Burnham, Editors, *The American Party Systems: Stages of Political Development*, Second Edition (New York: Oxford University Press, 1975).

[66] Walter D. Burnham, "The Changing Shape of the American Political Universe," *American Political Science Review*, Vol. 59, No. 1 (March 1965), 7–28; Burnham, "American Politics in the 1970s, 277–307.

[67] Walter Dean Burnham, "American Voting Behavior and the 1964 Election," *Midwest Journal of Political Science*, Vol. 12, No. 1 (February 1968), 1–40.

[68] William Crotty, *American Parties in Decline*, Second Edition (Boston: Little, Brown, 1984).

[69] John G. Geer, "Critical Realignments and the Public Opinion Poll," *Journal of Politics*, Vol. 53, No. 2 (May 1991), 434–453.

[70] Mayhew, *The Electoral Connection*.

[71] Aldrich, *Why Parties? A Second Look*, 281–285.

[72] For example, see Wattenberg, *The Rise of Candidate – Centered Politics*; and David Menefee-Libey, *The Triumph of Candidate-Centered Politics* (New York: Chatham House, 2000).

[73] King and Gelman, "Systematic Consequences of Incumbency in U.S. House Elections," 110.

[74] Jamie L. Carson and Jeffrey A. Jenkins, "Examining the Electoral Connection across Time," *Annual Review of Political Science*, Vol. 14 (June 2011), 25–46. This conclusion is expressed

well as the subsequent outpouring of studies of House incumbents previously reviewed. The primary analytical focus became cross-sectional analyses that assess the short-term ability of candidates to move their vote away from either the base vote in a district or the presidential vote. Some defined the presidential vote as probably the best indicator of that base partisan vote,[75] whereas others used presidential popularity.[76]

The focus on cross-sectional analyses and short-term factors also fit with notions of how presidential effects occur. The concern became how much a presidential vote ran ahead of the House vote, assuming that probably meant that the president had pulled the House vote for his party's candidates higher than it otherwise might be.[77] Given that assumption, the influence of a presidential candidate was measured by the percentage of districts in which the winning president ran ahead of the partisan vote in districts for that year.[78] Although measures varied, the focus was on how presidential campaigns affected House votes *within* one year.[79]

There were also considerable efforts to consider the impact of presidents in midterm elections. Some examined just the relationship between gains and losses in House results,[80] whereas others focused on the relationship between presidential and subsequent elections. Presidential elections create

by others. See Wood, *The Myth of Presidential Representation*, 123; and Baumer and Gold, *Parties, Polarization, and Democracy in the United States*, 107–108.

[75] William M. Leogrande and Alana S. Jeydel, "Using Presidential Election Returns to Measure Constituency Ideology: A Research Note," *American Politics Quarterly*, Vol. 25, No. 1 (January 1997), 3–18.

[76] Dennis M. Simon, Charles W. Ostrom, Jr., and Robin S. Marra, "The President, Referendum Voting and Subnational Elections in the United States," *American Political Science Review*, Vol. 85, No. 4 (December 1991), 1177–1192.

[77] Moos, *Politics, Presidents, and Coattails*, 10; James E. Campbell, "Predicting Seat Gains from Presidential Coattails," *American Journal of Political Science*, Vol. 30, No. 1 (February 1986), 165–183; and James E. Campbell and Joe E. Summers, "Presidential Coattails in Senate Elections," *American Political Science Review*, Vol. 84, No. 2 (June 1990), 513–524.

[78] Moos, *Politics, Presidents, and Coattails*; Froman, *Congressmen and Their Constituencies*, 66; Leroy N. Rieselbach, *Congressional Politics* (New York: McGraw-Hill, 1973), 52; Born, "Reassessing the Decline of Presidential Coattails," 63–64. In contrast, others asked how House electoral success affected presidential results. David Broockman, "Do Congressional Candidates Have Reverse Coattails? Evidence from Regression Discontinuity Design," *Political Analysis*, Vol. 17, No. 4 (Autumn 2009), 418–434.

[79] Burnham, "Insulation and Responsiveness in Congressional Elections;" Charles Press, "Presidential Coattails and Party Cohesion," *Midwest Journal of Political Science*, Vol. 7, No. 4 (November 1963), 320–335; Cummings, *Congressmen and the Electorate*; Edwards, "The Impact of Presidential Coattails on Outcomes of Congressional Elections," 100; Calvert and Ferejohn, "Coattail Voting in Recent Presidential Elections," 408; Ferejohn and Calvert, "Presidential Coattails in Historical Perspective," 131; Born, "Reassessing the Decline of Presidential Coattails"; James E. Campbell, "Presidential Coattails and Midterm Losses in State Legislative Elections," *American Political Science Review*, Vol. 80, No. 1 (March 1986), 45–63; Gary C. Jacobson, *The Politics of Congressional Elections*, 164.

[80] Bruce I. Oppenheimer, James A. Stimson, and Richard W. Waterman, "Interpreting U.S. Congressional Elections: The Exposure Thesis," *Legislative Studies Quarterly*, Vol. 11, No. 2 (May 1986), 227–247; and Richard W. Waterman, Bruce I. Oppenheimer, and James A. Stimson,

higher turnout because of the greater attention given to those elections. That stimulus can help presidential winners bring in more peripheral voters, sway their vote to other contests, and win more seats for their party. The issue then becomes how much turnout declines in the following election among those only motivated to vote for the winning presidential candidate, costing the president's party seats, and creating a "surge and decline" of partisan support.[81] These analyses were still, however, largely focusing on short-term presidential effects.

What all these analyses have in common is a focus on the short-term effects of presidents and their campaigns on House elections.[82] This focus is on finding explanations for deviations from some normal or base vote. The scatter-plots in Figures 3.6 and 3.7 illustrate the situations that received so much attention: They represent the relationship between presidential and House percentages in 1900 and 1972. In 1900 the vote for the president was strongly associated with the House vote. By 1972 the association had declined a great deal, and the vote for the Democratic presidential candidate in a district had little to do with what the House candidate received. Given the remarkable diversity of House

"Sequence and Equilibrium in Congressional Elections: An Integrated Approach," *Journal of Politics*, Vol. 53, No. 2 (May 1991), 372–393.

[81] Angus Campbell, "Surge and Decline: A Study of Electoral Change," 1966, 40–62; Barbara Hinckley, "Interpreting House Midterm Elections: Toward a Measurement of the In-Party's 'Expected' Loss of Seats," *American Political Science Review*, Vol. 61, No. 3 (September 1967), 694–700; Albert Cover, "Surge and Decline in Congressional Elections," *Western Political Quarterly*, Vol. 38, No. 4 (December 1985), 606–619; Campbell, "Explaining Presidential Losses in Midterm Congressional Elections"; Campbell, "Presidential Coattails and Midterm Losses in State Legislative Elections"; James E. Campbell, "The Presidential Surge and Its Midterm Decline in Congressional Elections, 1868–1988," *Journal of Politics*, Vol. 53, No. 2 (May 1991), 477–487; James E. Campbell, "The Presidential Pulse and the 1994 Midterm Congressional Election," *Journal of Politics*, Vol. 59, No. 3 (August 1997), 830–857; and James E. Campbell, *The Presidential Pulse of Congressional Elections*, Second Edition (Lexington: University Press of Kentucky, 1997). A similar approach was taken in assessing the impact of presidential campaigning on Senate elections: Jeffrey E. Cohen, Michael A. Krassa, and John A. Hamman, "The Impact of Presidential Campaigning on Midterm U.S. Senate Elections," *American Political Science Review*, Vol. 85, No. 1 (March 1991), 165–178.

[82] The concern here is with district-level results. There also have been numerous studies seeking to assess the extent of straight-ticket voting under the presumption that voting for a presidential candidate might incline an individual to also vote for the House candidate of the same party. Some of the early individual level studies are Warren E. Miller, "Presidential Coattails: A Study in Political Myth and Methodology," *Public Opinion Quarterly*, Vol. 19, No. 4 (Winter 1955), 353–368; Jacobson, "Presidential Coattails in 1972"; Calvert and Ferejohn, "Coattail Voting in Recent Presidential Elections"; Lyn Ragsdale, "The Fiction of Congressional Elections as Presidential Events," *American Politics Quarterly*, Vol. 8, No. 4 (October 1980), 375–398; Alan I. Abramowitz, "Economic Conditions, Presidential Popularity, and Voting Behavior in Midterm Congressional Elections," *Journal of Politics*, Vol. 47, No. 1 (February 1985), 31–43; and Paul Gronke, Jeffrey Koch, and J. Matthew Wilson, "Follow the Leader? Presidential Approval, Presidential Support, and Representatives' Electoral Fortunes," *Journal of Politics*, Vol. 65, No. 3 (August 2003), 785–808.

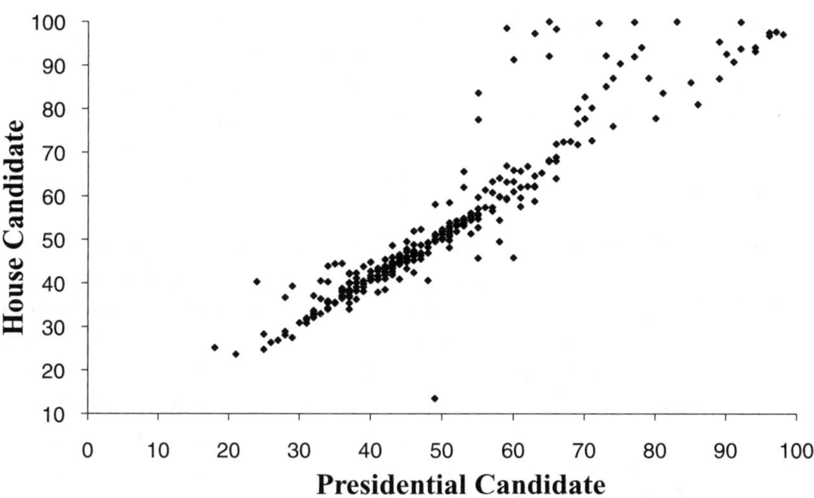

FIGURE 3.6. Relationship of Democratic Presidential and House Vote Percentages, 1900

votes for any specific presidential vote percentage, the focus became explaining the divergences.

The 1972 situation also suggests the basis for the concern about the separation of presidential and House results on the ability of presidents to work with a coherent majority in Congress. As the 1973 congressional session began it would be hard to imagine that members of the House saw their vote percentage as being tied to that of the presidential contest. Not only did Richard Nixon

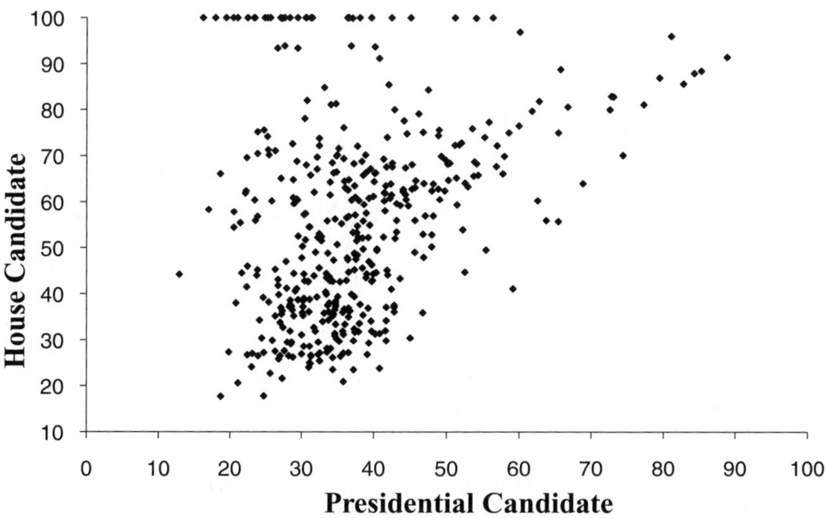

FIGURE 3.7. Relationship of Democratic Presidential and House Vote Percentages, 1972

not have a majority of Republicans in the House, but he could not count on Republicans supporting him because of the limited connection of their vote to his. The presumption was that House candidates had achieved the ability to disconnect the voting for them from voting for the president.

Explaining Change

The consequence of this candidate-centered framework has been to largely remove social and electoral change and the role of political parties in reacting to and creating change, matters to be discussed shortly. But this framework still has had a significant problem to address. Changes in partisan alignments are occurring in American politics. Voters' partisan attachments are increasingly divided by race,[83] class,[84] ideology,[85] and religious attachment.[86] Within Congress, legislators are increasingly divided. The dilemma is how to maintain a candidate-centered interpretation of politics while political divisions are steadily growing. If everyone is operating independently, how does polarization occur?

The way to avoid the role of parties in creating divisions is to characterize the change occurring as "sorting."[87] Politicians are pursuing their own agendas, perhaps without much connection to the concerns of voters.[88] Candidates are sorting themselves between parties. They arrive in Congress with their own views, and constitute a collection of individuals with more-or-less similar positions. Parties presumably play little role in creating the voting records that members compile.[89] The possibilities that their voting records are very much a product of shifting party strategies and may reflect party unity as much as

---

[83] Edward G. Carmines and James A. Stimson, *Issue Evolution* (Princeton, NJ: Princeton University Press, 1989); and Kerry L. Haynie and Candis S. Watts, "Blacks and the Democratic Party: A Resilient Coalition," in Jeffrey M. Stonecash, Editor, *New Directions in American Political Parties* (New York: Routledge, 2010), 93–109.

[84] Stonecash, *Class and Party in American Politics*; Larry M. Bartels, *Unequal Democracy: The Political Economy of the Gilded Age* (Princeton, NJ: Princeton University Press); and Stonecash, "Class in American Politics."

[85] Alan I. Abramowitz, *The Disappearing Center: Engaged Citizens, Polarization, and American Democracy* (New Haven, CT: Yale University Press, 2010), 34–61.

[86] Geoffrey C. Layman, "'Cultural Wars' in the American Party System," *American Politics Quarterly*, Vol. 27, No. 1 (January 1999), 89–121; Geoffrey C. Layman, *The Great Divide: Religious and Cultural Conflict in American Party Politics* (New York: Columbia University Press, 2001); and Laura R. Olson, "Religion, Moralism, and the Cultural Wars: Competing Moral Visions," in Jeffrey M. Stonecash, Editor, *New Directions in American Political Parties* (New York: Routledge, 2010), 148–165.

[87] Fiorina, *Cultural War*, 61–70.

[88] Fiorina, with Abrams, *Disconnect*.

[89] Keith Krehbiel, "Where's the Party?"; and Keith Krehbiel, "Paradoxes of Parties in Congress," *Legislative Studies Quarterly*, Vol. 24, No. 1 (February 1999), 31–64.

ideology are given little attention.[90] Voters in turn are eyeing the polarization among national elites and either re-sorting themselves between the parties or changing their political opinions to accommodate their partisanship.[91] The emphasis in these interpretations is on individualized and independent choices by politicians and voters. Everyone is assessing what is happening and making choices that lead to polarization. Parties are not central to the process. Change can occur and be explained without a role for parties as actors trying to create this change.

In summary, the candidate-centered view is built around a presumption of normal partisan votes in districts. In the past the normal vote in the district somewhat constrained the vote percentage candidates could get. There were occasional critical realignments that disrupted the prior normal vote but also produced a new one. This dynamic broke down in the 1960s as the influence of party organizations declined. House candidates acquired a greater ability to determine voter sentiment, and the means to get appropriate images and messages to voters. This allowed them to create a personal vote that yields a vote percentage higher than the normal vote. That produces a greater deviation from the presidential vote (presumably closer on average to the normal vote) and reduces the correlation between presidential and House votes. Since the 1960s the political alignments and polarization that have developed are a result of candidates and voters autonomously sorting themselves out.

The Limitations of the Prevailing Framework

The development of this framework has had three (and perhaps more) significant consequences for our ability to understand change. First, it diminishes concern for the extent to which there are national issues of concern to voters, candidates, and parties that would animate parties to organize and seek new constituencies as a basis of power. Second, as a corollary it largely removes political parties as actors that might be creating change. Third, it directs our attention to cross-sectional analyses that make seeing change difficult. Together these three make it much less likely that we would direct our attention to the changing relationship between presidential and House results.

---

[90] For a discussion and critique of these ideas, see Frances E. Lee, *Beyond Ideology* (Chicago: University of Chicago Press, 2009), 24–73.

[91] Mathew Levendusky, *Partisan Sort* (Chicago: University of Chicago Press, 2009). He argues that "voters typically shift their ideology to fit with their party identification; ideology-driven party exit (changing one's party to fit with one's ideology) occurs in only a narrow set of circumstances" (3). This suggests a limited role for parties. Party identification is seen as stable, and voters change their opinions to accommodate their party identification. What is missed in this is the possibility that party leaders are playing a central role in persuading voters that issues are connected. For an argument that parties are seeking to connect issues, see E. J. Dionne, *They Only Look Dead* (New York: Touchstone, 1997).

The Substantive Concerns of Voters: The Divide about Government

Although the 1960s–1970s were seen by many as a time of dealignment, in retrospect it is clear that another interpretation is possible. While there was political turmoil, there was also a fundamental battle developing about the role of government. As will be discussed in later chapters, liberals had wanted to expand many government programs, and in the 1960s they did so. They also wanted programs such as affirmative action and busing. Government was seen as capable of playing a positive role in expanding opportunities for many. In the 1970s inequality began its steady increase, and many liberals were very supportive of various programs to counter poverty and provide opportunity.[92]

In sharp contrast conservatives were increasingly troubled about the size of government, the reliance of citizens on government, the extent of redistribution occurring, and the apology by liberals for practices and behaviors conservatives found very troubling.[93] The response was the rise of the conservative movement to oppose the role that government was assuming in society.[94] That movement has grown steadily since the 1960s.

The result has been the development of a fundamental division about what role government should play in society. Liberals continue to believe that government can contribute to improving conditions, and that these actions do not harm freedom of individuals in society. Conservatives are quite different in opposing an expanded role for government, and increasingly argue that the actions of government are harming society.

The candidate-centered framework and sorting do not necessarily exclude the role of such a fundamental division emerging, but the emphasis of the former interpretation is on individuals operating independently. The notion of candidates operating independently does little to suggest there is a common set of concerns driving their actions. The notion of sorting conveys the sense that individuals are simply rearranging where they sit in the distribution of opinions and party identification. There is no sense that a fundamental division is developing.[95] Further, the notion that party identification is a result of voters changing their opinions about issues to accommodate their party identification provides little sense that democracy is driven by some fundamental concerns of the electorate. Rather, we have voters rearranging their opinions

---

[92] G. Calvin Mackenzie and Robert Weisbrot, *The Liberal Hour: Washington and the Politics of Change in the 1960s* (New York: Penguin Press, 2008); Nolan McCarty, Keith T. Poole, and Howard Rosenthal, *Polarized America: The Dance of Ideology and Unequal Riches* (Cambridge, MA: MIT Press, 2006).

[93] Mark D. Brewer and Jeffrey M. Stonecash, *Split: Class and Cultural Divides in American Politics* (Washington, DC: CQ Press, 2007).

[94] This literature is growing, but as examples, see Perlstein, *Before the Storm*; and Lisa McGirr, *Suburban Warriors* (Princeton, NJ: Princeton University Press, 2002).

[95] As an example see Fiorina, *Cultural War?*

to accommodate the cues of party leaders. There is little focus in all of this on the development of a fundamental debate.

The Neglected Party Role amid Polarization

Following the 1960s the evolving interpretation of political parties increasingly presented them as passive in shaping the candidates emerging to represent the party.[96] The conventional assessment was that they had lost control of candidates and the positions the candidates took. The emergence of primaries meant that parties could not control nominations. The increasing spread of civil service meant the parties had fewer patronage workers to draw on. The adoption of the office-block ballot made it easier for voters to split their ticket and for candidates to create a personal constituency.[97]

The result was a declining role for the party,[98] which had less influence in the political process.[99] The party was adapting by becoming a service provider, supporting candidates by providing money, mailing lists, and access to consultants.[100] We were presented with a general image of party organizations as being without basic political principles, apparently passively supporting the candidates who emerged from the individual calculations of those deciding to run for office.[101] The candidate-centered view of parties and campaigns carries with it the presumption that any long-term goals and strategies of national party organizations, presidential candidates, or congressional organizations do not play a significant role in seeking to alter long-term partisan voting patterns.

---

[96] A dissent to this view was presented by Schlesinger, who argued: "It should be clear by now that the grab bag of assumptions, inferences, and half-truths that have fed the decline-of-party thesis is simply wrong" (1152). Joseph A. Schlesinger, "The New American Political Party," *American Political Science Review*, Vol. 79, No. 4 (December, 1985), 1152–1169.

[97] John F. Bibby, "State Party Organizations: Strengthened and Adapting to Candidate-Centered Politics and Nationalization," in L. Sandy Maisel, Editor, *The Parties Respond: Changes in American Parties and Campaigns* (Boulder, CO: Westview Press, 2002), 19–46.

[98] Joel H. Silbey, "From 'Essential to the Existence of Our Institutions' to 'Rapacious Enemies of Honest and Responsible Government': The Rise and Fall of American Political Parties, 1790–2000," in L. Sandy Maisel, Editor, *The Parties Respond: Changes in American Parties and Campaigns* (Boulder, CO: Westview Press, 2002), 1–18.

[99] Burnham, "The Changing American Political Universe."

[100] The view that parties are service providers has become widespread. A summary of this view is presented in Herrnson, *Congressional Elections*, 87–131.

[101] For reviews of the role of consultants in this progression, see David A. Dulio, *For Better or Worse: How Political Consultants Are Changing Elections in the United States* (Albany: SUNY Press, 2004); David A. Dulio, "The Impact of Political Consultants," in Stephen C. Craig and David B. Hills, Editors. *Electoral Challenge: Theory Meets Practice*, Second Edition (Washington, DC: CQ Press, 2011), 243–270; and Sean A. Cain, "Political Consultants and Party-Centered Campaigning? Evidence from the 2010 U.S. House Primary Election Campaigns." Presented at the 2012 Southern Political Science Association Meetings, New Orleans, Louisiana, January.

In this view parties, to the extent they are relevant at all, are just the collection of individuals who arrived in legislatures with more or less similar views.[102] The polarization among members of Congress was presumably a result of individualized sorting among candidates.

The difficulty with this interpretation is that it largely ignores the substantive concerns and subsequent organizational activities of parties that played a role in the developing alignment that is the basis of the partisan divisions that have emerged.[103] This role begins with the concerns of individuals and groups within parties that prompted them to organize and seek representation of their concerns. The substantive division over the role of government was a force prompting liberals and conservatives to be more active.[104] Each party was engaged in struggles over what views would dominate in establishing public policy. Activists and groups were pressuring their parties. Parties in turn listened, and recruited groups. The dynamic changed the composition of each party.[105]

As the process of altering party compositions evolved, each party sought to recruit candidates representing the changed views. This process of selecting candidates to represent this party is no longer one in which party leaders just select candidates. But the party, as broadly conceived, does play a significant role.[106] It may not look like it did in the early 1900s, but there is an ongoing interaction among party leaders, interest groups, donors, activists, and the party base that affects which candidates emerge.[107] For some candidates, the word goes out that they are widely supported, and donations and workers follow. For others there is less political support and fewer opportunities for a campaign. Incumbents and party organizations raise substantial amounts of

---

[102] The most prominent case of this argument is Krehbiel, "Where's the Party?"

[103] Jeffrey M. Stonecash, "Political Science and the Study of Parties: Sorting Out Interpretations of Party Response," in Mark D. Brewer and L. Sandy Maisel, Editors, *The Parties Respond*, Fifth Edition (Boulder, CO: Westview Press, 2012).

[104] For an overview of this lengthy struggle, see Jacob S. Hacker and Paul Pierson, *Winner-Take-All Politics: How Washington Made the Rich Richer – and Turned Its Back on the Middle Class* (New York: Simon and Schuster, 2010).

[105] Geoffrey C. Layman, Thomas M. Carsey, John C. Green, Richard Herrera, and Rosalyn Cooperman, "Party Polarization, Party Commitment, and Conflict Extension among American Party Activists," *American Political Science Review*, Vol. 104, No. 2 (May 2010), 324–346.

[106] Thomas A. Kazee and Mary C. Thornberry, "Where's the Party: Congressional Candidate Recruitment and American Party Organizations," *Western Political Quarterly*, Vol. 43, No. 1 (March 1990), 61–80; Marty Cohen, David Karol, Hans Noel, and John Zaller, "Political Parties in Rough Weather," *The Forum*, Vol. 5, No. 4 (2008); and Cohen et al., *The Party Decides*.

[107] L. Sandy Maisel, Cherie Maestas, and Walter J. Stone, "The Party Role in Congressional Competition," in L. Sandy Maisel, Editor, *The Parties Respond: Changes in American Parties and Campaigns* (Boulder, CO: Westview Press, 2002), 121–138; and John J. Coleman and Jeffrey M. Stonecash, "Political Parties versus Preferences: An Assessment," revision of a paper originally delivered at the 2004 Midwest Political Science Association Meetings, Chicago, Illinois, April 15–18.

money and manage to move it around to support desired candidates.[108] These interactions yield a set of candidates and evolving positions of the parties.

Perhaps most important, this dynamic is not just a product of lots of individual sorting. Parties contain individuals and groups who are continually assessing where the party is and what direction it might take. Particularly when parties lose or are continually in the minority, they seek to assess what they need to do to reverse this situation. There are regular efforts to determine where to allocate resources so the party can expand its base.[109] Some are part of internal party organization activities as party leaders assess past results and seek to plan for the future.[110] Other times in an effort to persuade others, arguments about where the party is and where it might go are presented as essays or books.[111]

[108] Ray La Raja, "Political Parties in an Era of Soft Money," in L. Sandy Maisel, Editor, *The Parties Respond: Changes in American Parties and Campaigns* (Boulder, CO: Westview Press, 2002), 163–188. He notes: "For the first time in the history of American parties, national organizations control much of the campaign activity in federal elections down through the party hierarchy" (177); Eric S. Heberlig and Bruce A. Larson, "Redistributing Campaign Funds by U.S. House Members: The Spiraling Costs of the Permanent Campaign," *Legislative Studies Quarterly*, Vol. 30, No. 4 (November 2005), 597–624.

[109] Paul S. Herrnson, "National Party Decision-Making, Strategies, and Resource Distribution in Congressional Elections," *Western Political Quarterly*, Vol. 42, No. 3 (September 1989), 301–323; Robin Kolodny and Diana Dwyre, "Party-Orchestrated Activities for Legislative Party Goals," *Party Politics*, Vol. 4, No. 3 (July 1998), 275–295; and Robin Kolodny, *Pursuing Majorities: Congressional Campaign Committees in American Politics* (Norman: University of Oklahoma Press, 1998).

[110] Philip Klinkner, *The Losing Parties: Out-Party National Committees, 1956–1993* (New Haven, CT: Yale University Press, 1994); Paul S. Herrnson, "National Party Organizations at the Dawn of the Twenty-First Century," in L. Sandy Maisel, Editor, *The Parties Respond: Changes in American Parties and Campaigns* (Boulder, CO: Westview Press, 2002), 60–62.

[111] Any attempt to list all the publications making an argument as to what direction a party might pursue would fill pages. To cite just a few of the prominent ones, within the Republican Party there have been those who argued that the party should move more conservative and pursue the South, as argued by Kevin Phillips, *The Emerging Republican Majority*. Some have argued that the party should appeal to religious conservatives: Richard Viguerie, *The New Right: We're Ready to Lead* (Falls Church, VA: Viguerie Co, revised edition 1981). There are also those who have argued that the party should be careful about how much it is identified with social conservatives and fundamentalists who are opposed to science and reliance on knowledge: David Brooks, "The Class War before Palin," *The New York Times*, October 10, 2008: A33; and Charlie Cook, "Learn or Languish: The GOP's Focus on Social, Cultural, and Religious Issues Cost Its Candidates Dearly among Upscale Voters," NationalJournal.com, November 15, 2008. The advice to the Democratic Party has been extensive, particularly as it lost what seemed a solid majority in the last several decades. These essays express such views as that the party became too focused on race to those arguing that class and inequality of opportunity need to be given more attention. Examples of the former are Richard Scammon and Ben Wattenberg, *The Real Majority* (New York: Coward-McCann, 1970); Thomas B. Edsall and Mary D. Edsall, *Chain Reaction: The Impact of Race, Rights, and Taxes on American Politics* (New York: W. W. Norton, 1991); and Gordon MacInnes, *Wrong, for All the Right Reasons: How White Liberals Have Been Undone by Race* (New York: New York University Press, 1996). The latter is exemplified by David Paul Kuhn, *The Neglected Voter: White Men and*

The important matters in understanding the nature and role of parties are what processes are seen as relevant, what questions are asked, and where that directs our attention. To some the role of parties begins with the arrival in office of those elected. The presumption is that candidates emerge with their own views. There is then a collective action problem of reaching agreement.[112] To others the sum of party activities is vastly larger and informal. In this view the "collective action" problem is much larger, encompassing reading public opinion, listening to and interacting with activists and groups, formulating plans, recruiting candidates, and marshaling resources to pursue some evolving notion of what government should be doing. It is amorphous and hard to capture but it exists. The candidate-centered interpretation directs our attention away from these party activities.

In retrospect it is not surprising that the efforts of parties as entities trying to shape their future would be neglected. As the turmoil of the 1960s–1970s developed, the academic literature gave little attention to organized party efforts to create change. The presumption was that parties did not differ much and were not doing anything to pursue a clear agenda. A 1950 APSA committee on parties concluded that parties were not that different from each other.[113] Voters were seen as having stable but affective attachments to parties.[114] There was individual and aggregate stability of partisanship resulting in normal votes within constituencies.[115] The geographical bases of the parties were long-standing and relatively stable. The South had been reliably Democratic for over a century, and despite the disruption that occurred in 1948 many still regarded the South as solidly Democratic.[116] The Northeast had been solidly Republican for a long time, and despite some losses during the 1930s, it was still predominantly Republican in the 1950s.[117] There might be short-term deviations from this normal vote in presidential years, but there would probably be a return to normality in midterm elections.[118] The emphasis was on party dealignment and

---

the Democratic Dilemma (New York: Palgrave Macmillan, 2007). Others argue that the party should not focus on the South. Thomas F. Schaller, *Whistling Past Dixie: How Democrats Can Win without the South* (New York: Simon and Schuster, 2006). The debates within each party are reviewed in Brewer and Stonecash, *Dynamics of American Political Parties*, 145–199.

[112] This view is summarized in Aldrich, *Why Parties? A Second Look.*

[113] American Political Science Association, Committee on Parties, "Toward a More Responsible Two-Party System," *American Political Science Review*, Vol. 44, No. 3, Part 2, Supplement (September 1950), v–96. For a valuable history of this argument, see Taylor E. Dark III, "Liberals, Labor, and Party Government," *Polity*, Vol. 43, No. 3 (July, 2011), 358–387.

[114] Campbell et al., *The American Voter.*

[115] Converse, "The Concept of a Normal Vote."

[116] Philip E. Converse, "On the Possibility of Major Political Realignment in the South," In Angus Campbell, Philip E. Converse, Warren E. Miller, and Donald E. Stokes, *Elections and the Political Order* (New York: John Wiley), 212–242.

[117] Reiter and Stonecash, *Counter Realignment*, ch. 4.

[118] Campbell et al., "Surge and Decline," 1966.

a growing incumbency effect, both of which left little role for organized party activity.[119]

The primary role seen for parties was how to operate within specific elections. The role of national party organizations in considering and pursuing long-term change received far less attention.[120] Analyses of presidential elections generally focused on candidate strategies within a given electoral context.[121] The concern was: How much were presidential candidacies able to move certain groups of voters for that election? How much did the events of that time frame affect vote choices? The result has been little focus on change. "The approach most political scientists have taken to studying the presidency for almost fifty years has given us only limited purchase on presidents as agents of systematic change." "What escapes investigation is the possibility that presidents are out to change the rules of the game itself."[122]

---

[119] There were some exceptions that hinted that changes in the parties might be playing a role. The work by Carmines and Stimson, *Issue Evolution*, focuses on the dynamics of voter reaction to party change, but even in those analyses party evolutions seems to be largely an external factor voters just react to, not an entity pursuing a coalition. See Edward G. Carmines, Steven H. Renten, and James A. Stimson, "Events and Alignments: The Party Image Connection," in Richard Niemi and Herbert Weisberg, Editors, *Controversies in Voting Behavior* (Washington, DC: CQ Press, 1984); Edward G. Carmines, John P. McIver, and James A. Stimson, "Unrealized Partisanship: A Theory of Dealignment," *Journal of Politics*, Vol. 49, No. 2 (May 1987), 376–400; and Carmines and Stimson, *Issue Evolution*.

[120] As an example of an exception see Klinkner, *The Losing Parties*. As he notes: "For all the relevance of out-parties, political science has been rather neglectful in its treatment of them, particularly for the United States" (4).

[121] Most of the presidency literature appears to be about the institutional growth of power. There is also an enormous number of books that deal with specific presidential elections. They range from journalistic accounts, such as Theodore H. White, *The Making of the President, 1964* (New York: Atheneum, 1965), to insider accounts of specific campaigns, to academic analyses of specific elections, such as Kate Kenski, Bruce W. Hardy, and Kathleen Hall Jamieson, *The Obama Victory: How Media, Money, and Message Shaped the 2008 Election* (New York: Oxford, 2010). There are also works that review the strategies for individual campaigns: Nelson W. Polsby and Aaron Wildavsky with David A. Hopkins, *Presidential Elections: Strategies and Structures of American Politics*, Twelfth Edition (New York: Rowman & Littlefield, 2008); and Paul F. Boler, *Presidential Campaigns*, Revised Edition (New York: Oxford University Press, 2004). These usually treat each campaign largely as a set of decisions and events separate from other presidential elections.

[122] Daniel J. Galvin, *Presidential Party Building: Dwight D. Eisenhower to George W. Bush* (Princeton, NJ: Princeton University Press, 2010), 10. As he notes, "What, then, if we assume that the contours of the system are not a given, but are in each instance, a main object of contestation?" (11). For example, a reading of the major journals during these two decades reveals very few references to the notion that within the Republican Party conservatives were mobilizing to try to push the party in a more conservative direction. The candidacy of Barry Goldwater was generally seen as an aberration in the party nomination process. In contrast, a reading of the *National Review* over the 1950s and 1960s provides numerous stories and essays in which the debate among conservatives about how to seize the party and push it more conservative is very clear. Those stories are documented in Reiter and Stonecash, *Counter Realignment*.

For House elections the primary concern became how much members could increase their visibility and vote percentages. The rise of the view that House campaigns were candidate-centered has led to much less attention among academics on how *congressional parties* seek to expand their electoral bases and mobilize candidates and resources to do so.[123] The primary emphasis has been on how candidate traits and resources within elections create variations in outcomes. When party actors are incorporated, the focus is generally on their strategies for coping with or exploiting short-term conditions.

The essential problem with prevailing approaches is that parties do make plans. Those plans may emerge from the national organization, or the presidential or congressional wing. There are efforts to target voters the party wishes to attract and who will be compatible with the direction that party wants to go.[124] Party leaders engage in strategic positioning, an activity has received far less attention than it should. What is missing from almost all of these studies is some consideration of the possibility that the patterns occurring are part of a long-term realignment sought by dominant factions within each party. Parties do have plans for pursuing voters they wish to attract and represent, and those efforts create change.[125] Those efforts need to be incorporated into analyses.

The Limitations of Short-Term Analyses

The third effect of the candidate-centered framework is that it leads to a reliance on cross-sectional analyses that tend to focus on short-term factors as a source of outcomes. What current issues affect vote choices? How experienced is each candidate? How many resources does each candidate have? How did the national economy in a given year affect the partisan vote for House candidates?[126] How was the changing swing ratio affecting the relationship

Including the logic of party pursuits expressed in Phillips's *The Emerging Republican Majority* would diminish the credibility of a candidate-centered approach to analysis.

[123] There are some excellent studies that track changes in the regional bases of the congressional parties, but the connection to presidential results receives little attention. See as examples David W. Rohde, *Parties and Leaders in the Postreform House* (Chicago: University of Chicago Press, 1991); and Polsby, *How Congress Evolves*.

[124] The literature on this is growing. See D. Sunshine Hillygus and Todd G. Shields, *The Persuadable Voter* (Princeton, NJ: Princeton University Press, 2008); Mark D. Brewer and Jeffrey M. Stonecash, *Split: Class and Cultural Divides in American Politics* (Washington, DC: CQ Press, 2006); Mellow, *The State of Disunion*, and Karol, *Party Position Change in American Politics*.

[125] As an example, see John R. Petrocik, "Realignment: New Party Coalitions and the Nationalization of the South," *Journal of Politics*, Vol. 42, No. 2 (May 1987), 347–375.

[126] Kramer, "Short-Term Fluctuations in U.S. Voting Behavior, 1896–1964"; Tufte, "Determinants of the Outcomes of Midterm Congressional Elections"; and, Donald R. Kinder and D. Roderick Kiewiet, "Economic Discontent and Political Behavior: The Role of Personal Grievances and Collective Economic Judgments in Congressional Voting," *American Journal of Political Science*, Vol. 23, No. 3 (August 1979), 495–527.

between presidential and house votes across districts as candidate-centered politics developed? What changes were occurring in the swing-ratio, or the relationship between the national vote percentage for a party and the percentage of seats won in a year or across years?[127] The general presumption of these analyses appears to be that there is stability of voter loyalties in districts. The issue for analysis is how much candidates or events might move the vote from that base.

Although these cross-sectional analyses have produced valuable studies of what affects outcomes in specific elections, the focus has three significant limitations. It assumes an essentially stable electoral base such that deviations from some normal vote can be seen as something to be explained by current conditions. It confines the effects of presidential campaigns to current elections, when presidential campaigns may have much grander aspirations than just the current situation. It largely ignores the issue of whether parties may have strategies that are long-term in nature. As will be discussed in the next chapter, reconsidering each of these presumptions presents the possibility of a very different analysis and understanding of the relationship between presidential and House elections over time. But first the nature and implications of these presumptions deserves some development.

Perhaps the most important matter is the presumption that there is essentially a stable electoral alignment and that the focus can be on deviations from that stability.[128] As stated by McKuen et al., "The dominant paradigm posits a stable self-maintaining party system that changes character only in sudden transfigurations." They voiced their objection to this presumption, noting:

We have considerable evidence that the ideological and social bases of the party division shift continually. We add our voice to those who argue that our theoretical challenge transcends that of cataloguing electoral history into periods of realignment and periods of partisan stability. We must focus more clearly on the constancy of change.[129]

---

[127] Tufte, "The Relationship between Seats and Votes in Two-Party Systems;" Ferejohn, "On the Decline of Competition in Congressional Elections"; Richard G. Niemi and Patrick Fett, "The Swing Ratio: An Explanation and an Assessment," *Legislative Studies Quarterly*, Vol. 11, No. 1 (February 1986), 80; Jacobson, "The Marginals Never Vanished;" Brady and Grofman, "Sectional Differences in Partisan Bias," Ansolabehere, Brady, and Fiorina, "The Vanishing Marginals and Electoral Responsiveness," 30.

[128] As an example of such a presumption, in Robert S. Erikson, "The Puzzle of Midterm Loss," *Journal of Politics*, Vol. 50, No. 4 (November 1988), 1011–1029, Erikson states "the post-WWII period supposedly is one of stable equilibrium with a fairly constant normal vote" (1018). This leads to the presumption that a century of congressional elections can be analyzed without any reference to historical change. Arjun Wilkins, "Electoral Security of Members of the U.S. House." Presented at the 2011 Midwest Political Science Association Meetings, Chicago, IL, April 2011.

[129] MacKuen, Erikson, and Stimson, "Macropartisanship," 1139.

The stability presumption makes it difficult to incorporate long-term change. As Cooper and Brady expressed it in commenting on the analysis of Congress:

Static analysis assumes change or movement within a closed system, where conditions of equilibrium prevail, and thus encourages the development of theories grounded in cross-sectional analysis. In contrast, diachronic analysis assumes that change is ever unfolding and thus is primarily concerned with the interaction of variables over extended periods of time.[130]

If the focus of analyses is on a series of cross-sectional analyses, done year by year, it becomes very difficult to include or see change over time.[131] It also becomes difficult to include the impact of presidential and party strategies if their effect is gradual and long-term. If a presidential candidate or congressional party is pursuing an electoral base that is different from their prior base, the effects of change may be difficult to see.[132] Why such a pursuit might take place will be discussed in the next chapter, but first it may help to pursue the limits of cross-sectional analyses if change is involved.

A cross-sectional analysis focuses on explaining deviations from some expected pattern within a given year, as if those deviations are a product of conditions and behaviors within that year. To return to Figures 3.6 and 3.7, in 1900 there are few significant deviations of House vote percentages from presidential results, whereas in 1972 there are many significant deviations. For 1900 the presumption is that there is little to explain in terms of how House candidate behaviors could have pulled their vote away from the presidential vote because the deviations are limited. For 1972 the votes of House candidates differ significantly from that for presidential results. If the presidential vote is taken as roughly expressing the base partisan vote of a district, the presumption is that the actions of candidates can be analyzed to explain the deviations.

As an alternative, consider the possibility that a presidential candidate seeks to change his or her electoral base. A presidential candidate may assess recent elections and see a strong association between presidential and House results,

---

[130] Joseph Cooper and David W. Brady, "Toward a Diachronic Analysis of Congress," *American Political Science Review*, Vol. 75, No. 4 (December 1981), 988–1006.

[131] This is the case even if the cross-sectional analysis includes lagged years. If states change steadily but cumulatively in their partisan voting, as occurred in the 1960s and after, a series of cross-sectional analyses of state-level results with prior years included will create the impression of considerable stability. For an example of that, see Larry M. Bartels, "Electoral Continuity and Change, 1868–1996," *Electoral Studies*, Vol. 17, No. 3 (September 1998), 275–300.

[132] The tendency in some analyses is to see outcomes in a given year as a set of strategic locations by candidates as they try to gauge what positioning will help them win. Democratic candidates in a conservative district may move to the right so as to fit in the district. This maneuvering may separate a House vote from the presidential vote. This may be valid within a year, but long-term changes get lost in such an analysis. See Bernard Grofman, William Koetzle, Michael McDonald, and Thomas L. Brunell, "A New Look at Split-Ticket Outcomes for House and President: The Comparative Midpoints Model," *Journal of Politics*, Vol. 62, No. 1 (February 2000), 34–50.

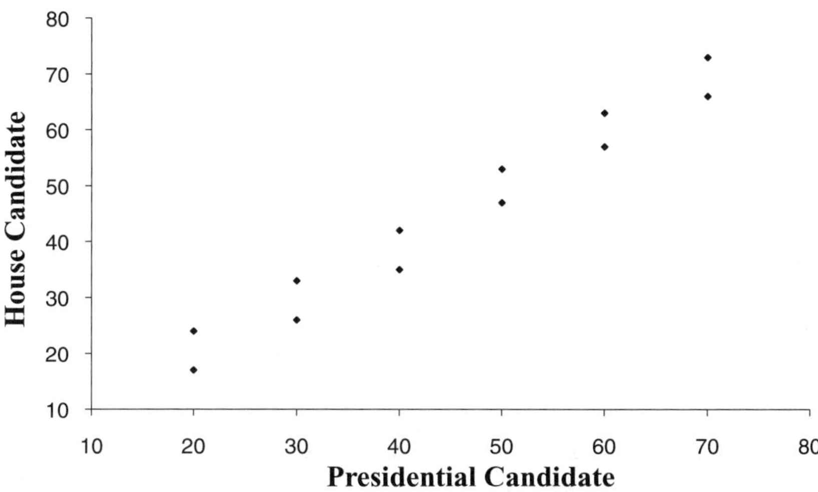

FIGURE 3.8. Republican Presidential and House Vote Percentages, 1900

as shown in Figure 3.8. But this base may not constitute a majority, or it may be ideologically incompatible with developing party goals. Assume a Republican presidential candidate then seeks to win votes in areas where the party previously did not do well (the lower left quadrant). If the presidential candidate is successful, then for the districts in the lower left corner of a scatter-plot the Republican presidential vote would increase and move toward the middle of the scatter-plot. But this move may not be accompanied by strong Republican candidates running for the House seat, thus resulting in the same low Republican House vote that has historically occurred. The result would be as shown in Figure 3.9. The four districts in the lower left quadrant may move to higher levels of support for the presidential candidate without the House percentage moving in those districts. Also assume the Republican presidential candidate retains the historical base of the party as indicated in the upper right quadrant.[133] If this pattern occurs for numerous districts in the lower left quadrant, then there will be less of a relationship between presidential and House results.

The important matter is how the voting for House candidates changes, or does not change. House incumbents may well be able to persist with their prior level of partisan support for several elections even as the presidential vote shifts over time. If the presidential vote shifts before the House vote, the connection between the two votes will decline, and the association between the presidential

---

[133] If the presidential candidate decides to focus less on areas where the party has historically done well (the upper right quadrant), and those areas are less supportive than normal, then eventually the presidential vote in those districts in the upper right quadrant might shift to the left. But for the sake of this example, assume that the traditional base does not change immediately.

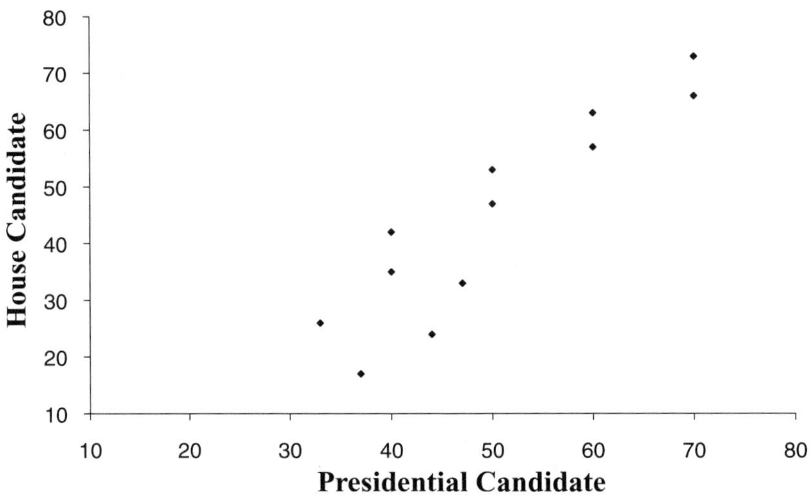

FIGURE 3.9. Republican Presidential and House Vote Percentages, after Changes

and House vote would decline. If we use presidential results as a baseline,[134] the changes occurring will create greater deviations of House percentages from some predicted relationship. For any current election the correlation between results would decline, suggesting dealignment or candidate-centered politics. Although it can be seen that way, it can also be seen as the consequence of changes in House elections lagging behind presidential results.

The deviations from the presidential vote within any given year are likely to be even more random than is shown in Figure 3.9. Most incumbents will continue and maintain their general level of support for some time even as the underlying partisanship is shifting. Others will retire, and open seat results may accord more with current presidential results. If change is occurring, cross-sectional analyses of presidential–House election results have a very difficult time incorporating that change. In those analyses deviations are treated as a reflection of *current* conditions when they may have more to do with differential rates of change of results by office.[135]

---

[134] Leogrande and Jeydel, "Using Presidential Election Returns to Measure Constituency Ideology." In this case the presidential vote in that year may be taken as a reflection of the general partisanship of that district relative to others.

[135] For examples of incorporating historical change in analyzing the rise of divided Senate delegations, see Brunell and Grofman, "Explaining Divided U.S. Senate Delegations, 1788–1996," and Gary M. Segura and Stephen P. Nicholson, "Sequential Choices and Partisan Transitions in U.S. Senate Delegations: 1972–1988," *Journal of Politics*, Vol. 57, No. 1 (February 1995), 86–100. The former presumes divided delegations reflect lagged realignment, whereas the latter presumes they reflect short-term current conditions.

TABLE 3.1. *State-Level Republican Presidential and House Results over Time*

	Presidential Results				House Results		
1900 %	n	1940	1972	Change	1940	1972	Change
0–44	13	25.6	67.9	42.3	17.5	42.4	23.1
45–51	9	42.2	65.8	23.6	41.2	50.7	9.5
52–55	10	46.5	59.4	12.9	50.1	49.0	−1.1
56+	13	49.6	56.9	7.3	53.6	51.6	−3.0

Although this may be an interesting hypothetical point, is there evidence that differential rates of change of the presidential–House result occur and are relevant to analyses? It is not possible to compare House districts across extended periods because the districts change with reapportionment. The only way to compare partisan voting in presidential and House races over time is to aggregate House election results to the state level and compare state percentages across time. Table 3.1 does that for Republican voting results. States are grouped according to their Republican presidential partisanship in 1900. Then the results for 1940 and 1972 (the year of a low relationship between presidential and House results) are presented. From 1900 to 1940 the relative partisan position of states in presidential and House results remained essentially the same. States that were heavily Republican in 1900 were heavily Republican in 1940 for both offices. By 1972 things had changed a great deal: The states that had the lowest Republican percentage in 1900 and 1940 had the highest percentage in 1972. The states with low percentages in 1900 moved from relatively low to relatively high over time.

The important matter is how House results changed. They followed the pattern of presidential results, but the net changes were much less. Those states with the lowest Republican House percentages in 1900 had the greatest gain, but by considerably smaller amounts. House Republican percentages lagged presidential results. This lag in state results is probably more erratic across House districts because some incumbents retire and are replaced by candidates from the other party, and other incumbents persist. The consequence is that by 1972 it is very likely that the scatter-plot relationship shown in Figure 3.7 was a reflection of some current conditions, but also of long-term transitions that were only beginning. Presidential results were changing faster than House results. Explaining deviations of House votes from presidential votes in 1972 with current conditions may produce some empirical findings, but it is not clear that a cross-sectional analysis is appropriate. Voting for both offices was changing but at different speeds, and capturing that in a cross-sectional analysis is difficult.

This situation of a historical disjuncture between presidential and House election results is not a fluke of just 1972. As will be reviewed later, 1972 presidential results were indicative of future changes in voting for that office, but House election results took some time to catch up.[136] The South continued to become more Republican, with House results lagging.[137] The Northeast was shifting from Republican to Democratic, with those changes coming gradually.[138] It is not impossible to consider trends in district voting, but the logic of cross-sectional analyses makes it difficult to incorporate the changes of the second half of the 20th century. The issue is how might we think about electoral change over time and how it affects the presidential–House relationship?

---

[136] Mark D. Brewer and Jeffrey M. Stonecash, "Changing the Political Dialogue and Political Alignments: George Wallace and His 1968 Presidential Campaign." Presented at the 2009 Midwest Political Science Association Meetings, April, 2009.

[137] Earl Black and Merle Black, *Politics and Society in the South* (Cambridge, MA: Harvard University Press, 1987); Merle Black and Earl Black, *The Rise of Southern Republicans* (Cambridge: Harvard University Press, 2002).

[138] Reiter and Stonecash, *Counter Realignment*.

4

Explaining Change

The Role of Party Pursuits

Explaining electoral change as a result of party pursuits begins with the factors that might prompt party candidates to seek change. The decision to pursue change is likely to be driven by the electoral math facing candidates or parties and by concerns with ideology and social trends. Further, there must be some substantial percentage of party members who support such efforts. It need not be a majority, but for a sustained effort to achieve change there must a substantial percentage.

Presidential Candidates: When parties begin campaigns they seek to win a majority. The "wing" of the party that faces the simplest problem is that of presidential candidates. A candidate either wins or loses, and if a campaign is to be run, the focus must be on what will produce a majority in the Electoral College. Presidential candidates invariably begin a campaign with an assessment of what base they can probably rely on and what voters they might be able to win. These calculations can be done with a short-term focus on just the upcoming election or with a long-term focus on pursuing an expanded or different electoral base. Our attention in politics is usually drawn to the short-term strategies of presidential candidates seeking to win the support of specific groups.[1] The concern here is with the long-term and what would prompt candidates to seek to change an electoral base. The process of assessing political prospects may be the same, but the difference is whether the goal is just the next election or more enduring changes. Presidential candidates are very important in any process of change. They are the most visible representative of their party and the most capable of projecting an altered image to the electorate.[2] Presidential

---

[1] Polsby, Wildavsky, and Hopkins, *Presidential Elections*, Twelfth Edition; and Boler, *Presidential Campaigns*.

[2] Stuart E. Macdonald and George Rabinowitz, "The Dynamics of Structural Realignment," *American Political Science Review*, Vol. 81, No. 3 (September 1987), 779; Ronald B. Rapoport,

candidates cannot change a party's electoral base alone, but they can play a major role.

There are three main factors that might prompt a presidential candidate to pursue a strategy that focuses on changing the policy positions, image, and electoral base of his or her party. First, in assessing his or her prospects a candidate must consider the historical record of elections. If a party has lost most recent presidential elections, any campaign plan must involve finding a way to expand the party's electoral appeal beyond its existing base.[3] Repeated losses force very serious assessments of strategy.[4] Second, a candidate may be motivated by a belief that the party must change its ideological position. A candidate may sincerely believe in a set of views different from those currently dominant in the party or that the party does not present a viable alternative to the other party and must change. Third, the candidate may perceive that social changes either make it imperative to alter the party's position or provide an opportunity to pursue a different base. The three of these may combine to make change highly likely.

Candidates or sitting presidents generally begin the assessment of their prospects by counting on the historical electoral base of the party. They may also include other voters the party has won in some prior elections. They must first decide whether this total is sufficient to win. If it is insufficient, then they must decide who else might be attracted.[5] Then they have to consider how this possible constituency is distributed spatially across the states and the realities of the Electoral College.[6] A candidate cannot win without a majority in the Electoral College. That forces a candidate to calculate which combination of state victories would be necessary to create a majority.[7]

Election results provide the simplest feedback to a party. To the extent that a party receives the same support over several elections, it confirms its situation. If a party consistently wins a majority, this suggests it can continue with what it is doing. To a party consistently in the minority, the results indicate it must

"Partisan Change in a Candidate-Centered Era," *Journal of Politics*, Vol. 59, No. 1 (February 1997), 185–199.

3   Theodore Lowi, "Toward Functionalism in Political Science: The Case of Innovation in Party Systems," *American Political Science Review*, Vol. 57, No. 3 (September 1963), 570–583; James, *Presidents, Parties and the State*, 11–12; Galvin, *Presidential Party Building*, 20–21.

4   Cohen et al., *The Party Decides*, 91–92.

5   As Dan Wood argues, the presumption here is that presidents do not represent everyone, despite such rhetoric, but they seek a partisan base plus whatever additional base is necessary to win: B. Dan Wood, *The Myth of Presidential Representation* (New York: Cambridge University Press, 2009).

6   Stonecash, "The Electoral College and Democratic Responsiveness."

7   Two works in particular present compelling and articulate theoretical frameworks for understanding the factors that would prompt a presidential candidate to seek to expand his or her electoral base and to carefully assess how to do so while coping with the Electoral College. See James, *Presidents, Parties, and the State*; and, Cohen, Karol, Noel, and Zaller, *The Party Decides*. I gratefully borrow heavily from their conceptual approach to political calculations.

TABLE 4.1. *Party Success in Presidential Elections by Years, 1900–2004*

Years	Party and Campaigns Won	Democratic % of		Republican % of	
		Popular Vote	Electoral College	Popular Vote	Electoral College
1900–1928	R – 6 / 8	40.1	39.3	50.2	60.7
1932–1964	D – 7 / 9	52.6	66.0	45.8	34.0
1968–2004	R – 7/10	44.9	36.5	49.3	63.5

Note: The percentages shown are averages of the national percentages for the years indicated. The elections included stop with 2004 because the focus is on how past results shape candidate calculations. The 2008 results are not included because they will affect the 2012 calculations, an election outside the scope of this analysis.

reassess its situation. This feedback is particularly important for presidential candidates. A history of losses means that replicating past electoral bases will produce another loss.

There are three eras over the last century during which presidential candidates began a campaign facing the reality of prolonged minority status for their party and a realization that its existing base was insufficient to win a majority. This was true for Democrats in the early 1900s, Republicans in the 1930s–1950s, and Democrats from 1968 to 2004. These situations prompted the party to seek a broader base not just for the immediate election but for the future. These patterns of sustained losses have been central to American presidential campaigns and calculations. If winning and losing fluctuated randomly from campaign to campaign, driven by differences in short-term candidate strategies, any candidate could begin with the sense that the focus could be on careful planning for exploiting short-term factors in the impending campaign. Presidential campaigns, however, have involved periods of enduring differences in party strength. Table 4.1 indicates the strings of party victories that have occurred over the last century. From 1900 to 1928 Republican presidential candidates won six of the eight presidential campaigns. Further, Republicans could easily have regarded the two losses as anomalies. In 1912 Theodore Roosevelt, a prior Republican president, became dissatisfied with the Republican Party and ran as a third-party candidate. He took significant votes from the Republican candidate, which allowed Woodrow Wilson to win with less than a majority of the vote. Wilson then ran as a sitting president in 1916 and won a close election.

From 1932 to 1964 Democrats won seven of nine presidential contests. The two elections won by a Republican were those by Dwight Eisenhower, a general from World War II with a very positive personal image. Democrats dominated the Congress, and the party had a majority of party identifiers in the nation in the 1950s. Republican presidency wins could be rationalized as reflecting Eisenhower's popularity, and thus requiring no fundamental change in the Democrats' policies. Then Republicans won 7 of the 10 contests held from

1968 through 2004. Democrats generally did well in the House, but the party was struggling to win the presidency. There were clearly strings of elections in which one party dominated the presidency. The results suggested the need for the party of the losing presidential candidates to consider its limitations and who it might be able to attract to win the presidency.

If a presidential candidate thinks that the existing likely electoral base is inadequate for a victory, he or she faces the immediate short-term need to find states where the party has not lost badly in recent elections, and then find a way to appeal to groups that have not been voting for the party. These could be "disaffected groups either within one's own party, the major-party opposition, or attached to third-party organizations." These groups, however, cannot just be anywhere. The challenge is to find states where the margin has been close and where there is a sufficient concentration of those who might be appealed to, and then pursue those voters and allocate resources "where a marginal increase may mean the difference between defeat and victory."[8]

The next consideration for candidates considering change is what policy positions should define a candidacy. A candidate may either believe in positions different from those that have defined the party or conclude that it is necessary for practical reasons to shift policy positions. Or the candidate may be responding to a faction within the party that is relatively liberal or conservative and that argues that the party is not providing a clear contrast in policy positions. That faction may contend that the party has to provide a clear alternative if it is to escape minority status.

Although election results or ideological convictions may propel change, the process of pursuing change and attracting voters is not likely to be a simple progression. Changes in voter loyalties, either to a party or away from it, are sometimes difficult to anticipate. A presidential candidate and his or her campaign staff may well misjudge the likelihood of retaining the existing base while trying to attract new voters. Uncertainty is an ever-present and much unappreciated aspect of these decisions. Harry Truman and his advisors thought that the South would not defect if he supported civil rights, but they were wrong.[9] In the early 1960s conservative Republicans did not think the candidacy of Barry Goldwater could cost them Northeast states, but they were wrong.[10] In the 1970s and 1980s Democrats appeared to assume they could balance the demands of minorities and white males and maintain their majority, but the erosion of support among white males was greater than they expected.[11]

---

8 James, *Presidents, Parties and the State*, 14–16.
9 Harvard Sitkoff, "Harry Truman and the Election of 1948: The Coming of Age of Civil Rights in American Politics," *Journal of Southern History*, Vol. 37, No. 4 (November 1971), 597–616; and James, *Presidents, Parties and the State*, 6.
10 Reiter and Stonecash, *Counter Realignment*, 62–73.
11 Edsall and Edsall, *Chain Reaction*.

In the 1980s–2000s Republicans sought to attract social conservatives and appeared to assume they could continue to retain the more affluent and more educated, but their pursuit cost them votes among the latter.[12] Anticipating the durability of older party attachments as party candidates seek new constituents is not easy. It may also be hard to move voters from their traditional loyalties. There are numerous studies that suggest that voters' party identifications are slow to change.[13] Pursuit of an altered electoral base may take several election cycles to achieve.[14] Although there is uncertainty, a presidential candidate faced with a sustained insufficient electoral base may simply have no choice but to pursue an altered electoral base and hope that past party attachments are strong enough that the base will stay with the party while an altered appeal is presented to voters.[15]

These efforts to change a party's base are likely to create internal conflicts over what policies should be pursued. One faction of the party may be convinced that the direction of the party needs to change, but sense that the existing base is unwilling to support different policy goals. This may set off an internal battle for control and policy direction as the dissatisfied seek to change the party base and deemphasize the goals of its older base.[16]

There have been several cases of efforts by factions to challenge the existing base of the party. Democrats in the early 1900s were experiencing conflict because the non-Southern wing wanted more national legislation, and the Southern wing was opposed to an active national government. When Franklin D. Roosevelt won in 1932, he did so with an expanded electoral base different from what the party had attracted, and he realized that he had to pursue policies that would retain that base in a reelection bid.[17] By the late 1950s the liberal wing of the Democratic Party was more actively pushing for liberal programs and was willing to oppose its Southern wing.[18] During the 1950s and 1960s the conservative wing of the Republican Party was frustrated at how moderate

---

[12] Rebekah Liscio, Jeffrey M. Stonecash, and Mark D. Brewer, "Unintended Consequences: Republican Strategy and Winning and Losing Voters," in John C. Green and Daniel J. Coffey, Editors, *The State of the Parties*, Sixth Edition (New York: Rowman & Littlefield, 2010), 255–270.

[13] Green at al., *Partisan Hearts and Minds*.

[14] For an analysis of such a pursuit and how difficult it is to identify a new coalition, see Robert Mason, *Richard Nixon and the Quest for a New Majority* (Chapel Hill: University of North Carolina Press, 2004).

[15] James, *Presidents, Parties and the State*, 12 and 17.

[16] James, *Presidents, Parties and the State*, 3, 12, and 17.

[17] Lizabeth Cohen, *Making a New Deal: Industrial Workers in Chicago, 1919–1939* (New York: Cambridge University Press, 1990); and David Plotke, *Building a Democratic Political Order: Reshaping American Liberalism in the 1930s and 1940s* (New York: Cambridge University Press, 1996).

[18] Arthur G. Stevens Jr., Arthur H. Miller, and Thomas E. Mann, "Mobilization of Liberal Strength in the House, 1955–1970: The Democratic Study Group," *American Political Science Review*, Vol. 68. No. 2 (June 1974), 667–681.

the party was and wanted to move in a more conservative direction even if it alienated some moderates in the Northeast.[19]

With regard to motivations, then, the likelihood of pursuing change will be prompted by two conditions. A party is more likely to pursue a changed electoral base when the evidence from prior elections indicates that the existing base will not produce a majority. A party is also more likely to experience pressures for change when it is has a faction with differing views and is frustrated by the unwillingness of the existing base to support policies the faction wants. The combination of minority status and a faction with strong convictions that the party has to change direction to attain a majority and that it should stand for the "right" policies will create pressures to expand and change the electoral base of the party.

In summary, presidential candidates begin a race by assessing the historical record of how well their party has done overall, where they have done well, and where they might gain votes. They must also consider how current events and social change may be altering the political landscape. A candidate may have a string of losses but see social change as presenting an opportunity to do better where the party has not traditionally done well. Social change, to be discussed shortly, may be eroding the candidate's situation or creating opportunities to pursue another base that might be larger or more compatible with emerging policy preferences within the party. These calculations are never simple.

The Congressional Party: Although presidential candidates have a fairly clear goal – winning an election – the nature and goals of a congressional "party" are not nearly as simple. The first complication with the notion of a congressional party is the extent of diversity within the party among those holding office. The greater the diversity, the less the ability to act in a coherent and unified way, and the less the ability to project a clear image to the electorate. To the extent a congressional party has internal homogeneity, it can think about acting coherently and creating the mechanisms to do so and present a clear policy image to voters.[20]

Just as with presidential candidates, a congressional party is likely to consider the base it has, where it wishes to take the party in the future, and what electoral base it might prefer to have. It may focus on where the party may wish to gain seats because the party is in the minority within a house of Congress or for ideological reasons. If a party is in the minority within one or both houses

---

[19] Reiter and Stonecash, *Counter Realignment*, ch. 4.

[20] Rohde, *Parties and Leaders in the Postreform House;* John H. Aldrich and David W. Rohde, "The Consequences of Party Organization in the House: The Role of the Majority and Minority Parties in Conditional Party Government," in Jon Bond and Richard Fleisher, Editors, *Polarized Politics: Congress and the President in a Partisan Era* (Washington, DC: CQ Press, 2000), 31–72; and David Rohde and John Aldrich, "Consequences of Electoral and Institutional Change: The Evolution of Conditional Party Government in the U.S. House of Representatives," in Jeffrey M. Stonecash, Editor, *New Directions in American Political Parties* (New York: Routledge, 2010), 234–250.

of Congress, it will presumably be more inclined to seek to expand its electoral base. That desire is likely to be tempered by the issue of how much the existing party members would have to change party policy positions to accommodate new members. If the new members would not be considerably different from existing members, the inclination to pursue new members should be high. If, however, the constituencies to be pursued have a different set of concerns from existing ones, there are likely to be tensions with existing members when it comes to seeking change. Existing party members may be in a minority, with all its attendant frustrations, but they can continue as members of Congress, retain their existing beliefs, and still have some prestige and influence within the institution. The idea of pursuing and attracting a new electoral base that is alien to the values of the existing majority is likely to create considerable tension and hesitation among existing party members.[21]

The initiative to engage in changing a congressional party's primary concerns may fall to the party leadership, which may be more inclined to see the need to broaden and expand the party base by pursuing new constituents with different preferences. Recognizing the likelihood of remaining in the minority, the leaders may even be inclined to "act both cohesively and contrary to the preferences of a majority of the rank and file."[22] To the extent the effort to attract new members with differing views is successful, it is likely to accentuate the tensions and conflicts within the party. Indeed, if the balance within the party is tipped, it may transform the policy positions of the party.

For example, as will be reviewed later, during the 1920s Democrats were in the minority and knew they had to expand their base outside the South to achieve a majority. There were some efforts to appeal to northern labor constituencies,[23] but many southerners were uneasy about Catholics and were reluctant to pursue ethnic urban voters in the North.[24] Benefiting from the political effects of the Great Depression, the party won many seats in northern urban areas. The altered composition of the party created internal policy tensions. In the 1950s and 1960s there was a further increase in the presence of non-Southern moderates and liberals, which eventually altered the dominant concerns within the party.

Republicans experienced their own rebalancing. During the 1950s conservatives within the Republican Party wanted to pursue southern conservatives, but the moderate wing of the party in the North was very uneasy about such an objective. The conservatives were frustrated by the moderation of the party

[21] Andrew J. Polsky, "The 1996 Elections and the Logic of Regime Politics," *Polity*, Vol. 30, No. 1 (Autumn 1997), 160.

[22] James, *Presidents, Parties and the State*, 20.

[23] Elizabeth Sanders, *Roots of Reform: Farmers, Workers, and the American State* (Chicago: University of Chicago Press, 1999), 173–177 and 340–386.

[24] David Burner, *The Politics of Provincialism: The Democratic Party in Transition* (New York: Alfred Knopf, 1968).

and wanted to change its composition and its policy positions.[25] The process of change was lengthy, but eventually the party's composition and its policy positions changed to become more conservative.

This issue of what party positions to adopt becomes pressing when a party previously in the minority finds itself in the majority because of the addition of members with different concerns. If a party moves from sustained minority status to majority status, two imperatives will push it to grapple with what positions to adopt. If the new members come from areas the party has previously not won, the pressures will be particularly strong. Viewing their party's electoral history in their districts, these new members are likely to argue for the need to present a different party image if they and the party majority are to survive. They are likely to view their situation as precarious and will argue for the need for the party to present different policies that will help new members secure reelection. Although existing members may not be enthusiastic about supporting different policies, grudging support is likely to emerge from both the leadership and from rank-and-file members, if only to try and retain a majority. The transition from minority to majority status brings power and the ability to achieve desired personal and party goals. Those newly in the majority are likely to be supportive of the needs of the new members for the simple expediency that responding to these needs will keep the party in power.[26] Whether the older members agree to the policy positions of the new members is likely to be a more contentious issue. If the new contingent steadily increases as a part of the party, it will put even more pressure on the leadership to shift the policies of the party.

For example, by 1935 the northern wing of the Democratic Party was firmly established as a much larger portion of the party, and was able to push a party that was historically in favor of limited government and states' rights to enact legislation to support an activist national government.[27] By the 1960s the liberal wing of the Democratic Party had grown even more and was able to push for more liberal legislation. Within the Republican Party the rise of the conservative wing from the 1960s through the 2000s steadily pushed the party to adopt more conservative policies.

Change does not come without consequences. As a party's positions and images change, this can create a negative view of the party among the older base. The new policy stances may alienate older supporters and prompt some voters to consider voting for the other party. Perhaps most important for this analysis are the responses of House members from the areas previously held by the party. If the presidential "wing" of the party is pursuing a new electoral base in different areas with new policy positions, and many House members are following that change, the resulting disjuncture of constituencies

---

[25] Reiter and Stonecash, *Counter Realignment*, chs. 4 and 5.
[26] James, *Presidents, Parties, and the State*, 28–29.
[27] James, *Presidents, Parties, and the State*, 12–15.

and uncertainty is likely to prompt many candidates to seek to pursue as much autonomy of organization and image as possible. The process of change is likely to prompt some members to seek to survive by separating their image from that of the shifting party. This will create at least for a time the phenomenon of "candidate-centered" politics that has received so much attention. This became particularly important in the 1960s and 1970s when a major change was occurring. This was also a time when the means of being autonomous – polling, direct mail, television ads – became more widespread.[28] The result will be some separation of presidential–House election results.

This emergence of campaigns in which House candidates try to separate their image from the shifting party image will persist until the process of party change eventually results in members from the older geographical base being replaced by the other party. Bringing election results for presidential and House contests together may take some time, but if there is a consistent base sufficient to support a new direction for the party, House candidates will emerge in the new areas, and results are likely to come together. The occurrence of candidate-centered campaigns will be a temporary matter until some unity of interests and of results occurs.

Social Change and Shifting Political Contexts

Finally, the pursuit of a majority coalition by either the presidential or congressional wing becomes much more complicated when demographic, social, and economic changes are occurring within the nation. What appears to be a stable political context as a strategy is developed may shift and disrupt the logic of political calculations. The interests involved and what they want may be changing. Where groups reside may be changing. New groups may emerge that change existing assessments of political strategy. How an issue is seen may be changing.

The Northeast was once dominated by manufacturing industries and unions who were very supportive of free trade. As competition from non-union manufacturing in the Sunbelt and other nations took business away from the North, a decline in manufacturing jobs began during the 1950s and 1960s. Unions, an important part of the Democratic coalition, became worried about the loss of jobs and became less supportive of free trade policies. As a major part of their coalition found their needs changing, Democratic presidential and House candidates had to struggle with whether to shift their positions from supporting free trade to opposing it. The decline in manufacturing meant fewer unskilled jobs and resulted in a need for welfare in the Northeast.[29] Democrats were facing shifting interests.

---

[28] For an extensive review of these changes, see Aldrich, *Why Parties? A Second Look*, 255–323.
[29] Mellow, *The State of Disunion*.

Population shifts can also prompt reconsideration of strategies. Internal migration and population growth have increased the relative importance of the South and West in the Electoral College. To the extent these states are less liberal, Republicans might assume there is a greater base for their ideas, and Democrats have to assess whether their identity as supporters of a "safety net" are as relevant in states growing economically. Republicans viewed the steady population growth occurring in the Sunbelt in the 1950s and 1960s and thought there was a new conservative electorate that they could attract.[30] The movement of the black population prompted reconsideration of Democratic strategies. Prior to the 1950s most blacks lived in the South and could not vote. Blacks left the South after World War II in search of freedom, better jobs, and the right to vote, and created a new liberal base in Northern cities for Democrats to seek to attract.[31] Immigration in the last two decades has brought many Hispanics to states and created a new constituency that parties have to decide how to appeal to.

New issues emerge and how issues are seen changes. As the 1950s evolved, racial conflict became a much more significant issue. After *Roe v. Wade*, abortion grew as an issue and the parties gradually had to develop responses.[32] Republicans became sympathetic to anti-abortion policies because they wanted to gain votes in the South and among those with strong religious attachments.[33] As the ERA (Equal Rights [for women] Amendment) was considered, the issue of how women should be treated changed from focusing on paternalistic protection of women in the workplace to granting them rights. As that change occurred, the parties gradually switched their views of how to relate to women, with Democrats supporting women's rights and Republicans – the original sponsors of the ERA – opposing the focus on rights.[34] The focus of education debates has also shifted. In the 1960s–1970s the issue was inequality in resources among schools and segregation. Then the issue shifted to whether schools were effective in changing the performance of students. Republicans were able to emphasize how well schools were doing rather than the class background of students or how much money they had.[35]

In addition to long-term changes such as those just discussed, each party also faces the persistent need to deal with short-term factors. A well-thought-out strategy may have to be set aside to react to an unexpected immediate matter

[30] Phillips, *Emerging Republican Majority.*

[31] Nicholas Lemann, *The Promised Land: The Great Black Migration and How It Changed America* (New York: Vintage, 1992).

[32] Karol, *Party Position Change in American Politics.*

[33] Hillygus and Shields, *The Persuadable Voter*, 107–144.

[34] Christina Wolbrecht, *The Politics of Women's Rights: Parties, Positions, and Change* (Princeton, NJ: Princeton University Press, 2000).

[35] Christina Wolbrecht and Michael Hartney, "Race and Resources versus Excellence and Exams: Explaining Changing Party Positions on Education Policy." Presented at the 2012 Southern Political Science Association Meetings, New Orleans, January, 2012.

that is likely to dominate an upcoming election. The economy may decline, and the focus has to shift to economic matters. A scandal may dominate the news. The opposing party may support a war or an expanded health-care bill, creating a perceived opportunity to criticize that party before an election. Parties are continually trying to balance short-term and long-term goals.

The Communication of Shifting Positions

If a presidential candidate, party faction, or congressional party does seek to change its electoral base, it then faces the task of conveying altered policy positions to voters. There are multiple means of communicating altered positions. This might be done by indicating sympathy for the concerns of a group that feels its concerns have been neglected. Presidents Truman and Kennedy sought to convey concern for blacks and civil rights issues before the national party became strongly identified with this issue. When Ronald Reagan ran for president, and during his first few years, he spoke of the culture of life, which conveyed to social conservatives that he understood their concerns.

Candidates might also run ads indicating their concern for particular social problems with the goal of connecting with groups concerned with these issues. Legislators may sponsor legislation to establish their concern for an issue, and then call attention to that legislation in campaigns to indicate their identification with the concerns of particular groups. A party may publish a platform endorsing particular positions. If it controls one house of Congress, it may enact legislation to convey its positions, even knowing that the legislation is unlikely to pass both houses and be accepted by the president. To establish a position, it may strongly oppose or even filibuster legislation sponsored by the other party.

Although the mechanisms of signaling shifting positions are clear, the message may not always be. The clarity of the message will depend on the extent to which the party is homogeneous in its composition.[36] If the party is in the process of changing and contains a diverse set of actors sending out different position messages, the "party" message will be muddled. In the 1960s and 1970s the Democratic Party in Congress contained both members supportive of and opposed to civil rights legislation. For some time voters had a difficult time sorting out just how liberal the party was on this issue. From the 1970s through the 1990s the Republican Party contained numerous members who were not anti-abortion.[37] It was only gradually that the party became unified on this issue such that the message to social conservatives was clear, and these voters strongly supported the Republican Party.

The ability of a party to convey that it is shifting its positions is further complicated by the inattention of many voters. Voters in general do not follow

---

[36] Rohde and Aldrich, "Consequences of Electoral and Institutional Change."
[37] Brewer and Stonecash, *Split*, 127–130.

politics closely.[38] Many rely on shortcuts in interpreting party and candidate positions,[39] and the shortcut of a party label may be outdated and less accurate as change proceeds. Getting a message widely disseminated has become harder because the media have become more fragmented over time.[40] If a party's positions are changing gradually, and media outlets have become more diverse with each one having a smaller audience and voters being only sporadically attentive, conveying a message of a shift in policy positions to all of the electorate takes longer. Those who are attentive may change relatively quickly, but others may change with a considerable lag.[41] As a party becomes more unified and the positions of members become more uniform, the perception that positions have changed should follow, but only gradually. The process of establishing a clear party image can be very difficult as change proceeds.

Implications

If the logic just outlined is what drives parties, then we should see specific implications. First, for minority status to prompt change, there should be clear and sustained electoral evidence that a party lacks a majority. Temporary setbacks are unlikely to persuade a party that it has a fundamental problem. For example, when Republicans lost in 1912, it would be easy to conclude that the problem was the presence of Teddy Roosevelt and his third-party effort, and that the effect of his actions would not persist. When Republicans lost badly in 1964 and 2006–2008 in House elections, it would be easy to rationalize that their presidential candidate in 1964 and the actions of President George W. Bush were the problem, and once these individuals were removed from prominence the party would recover. The 1994 Democratic loss of the House surprised most observers, and after that election many were not convinced that the Democratic Party needed a fundamental reassessment. It is prolonged status in the minority that is likely to make a party reconsider its situation.

Second, if this status is recognized, there should be some indication that the party has recognized its problem and has diagnosed who it should or might attract. There should be evidence that it has analyzed where it might gain votes and formulated a plan to attract those voters. There should be evidence of discussions of how to pursue change.

---

[38] John Zaller, *The Nature and Origin of Mass Opinion* (New York: Cambridge University Press, 1992); and Michael Delli Carpini and Scott Keeter, *What Americans Know about Politics and Why It Matters* (New Haven, CT: Yale University Press, 1996).

[39] Samuel Popkin, *The Reasoning Voter* (Chicago: University of Chicago Press, 1994).

[40] Markus Prior, *Post-Broadcast Democracy* (New York: Cambridge University Press, 2007), 94–137.

[41] Larry M. Bartels, "Uninformed Votes: Information Effects in Presidential Elections," *American Journal of Political Science*, Vol. 40, No. 1 (February 1996), 194–230; and Ryan Claassen, "Political Awareness and Partisan Realignment: Are the Unaware Unevolved?," *Political Research Quarterly*, Vol. 64, No. 4 (December 2011), 818–830.

Third, if the party has a strategy and is pursuing specific sets of voters, for it to continue with the strategy there should be some evidence that the plan is working. There should be indications that the party is succeeding in attracting voters it was previously not winning and has targeted. The progress may be slow, and there may be periodic setbacks as the party copes with unanticipated trends and events. Those setbacks may create anxieties and debate about the plan, and slow down efforts to continue with it. A specific presidential candidate may have doubts about or disagree with the plan and reduce emphasis on it. Over several elections, however, there should be evidence that the plan is attracting the desired voters.

Party changes in policy positions are unlikely to occur without resistance because the pursuit of new voters is likely to involve altering the party's policy priorities. The greater the differences between the old and new electoral bases, the greater the ensuing tensions are likely to be. Although an older base may support pursuit of new voters if it will bring a majority and the power that comes with it, there is still likely to be some reluctance and resistance to the agenda of the new wing of the party. Even if the new wing argues that the new agenda must be pursued to maintain a majority, the older base is still likely to resist. The consequence is that as a party shifts its composition we are likely to see the older base be less inclined to support the new party policy direction.

Finally, because presidential candidates face the immediate issue of the Electoral College, they are more likely to lead change. They must adapt if they are to have a chance of winning. There may well be instances in which legislative leaders recognize the need to act, as Newt Gingrich did prior to 1994, but presidential candidates are likely to lead. As change proceeds, incumbents are likely to work very hard to create personal images that allow them to survive changing partisan sentiments in their districts.[42]

The important matter for the relationship between presidential and House results is that election results for the two offices are unlikely to proceed together in a coordinated fashion. Presidential candidates, House party organizations, and individual House candidates are likely to operate independently of each other as change proceeds. It is this independence that will likely result in separation of presidential–House results. Presidents may be capable of creating broad changes in their electoral bases, but House election results are likely to lag as voters only gradually change all their allegiances, and as incumbents seek to hold on to their seats as long as they can, even while the local political context is changing. Separation will occur until results for the two offices come together.

There are then four conditions that in combination can prompt change that may pull presidential–House results apart. First, is a party in the minority? Is

---

[42] Scott Basinger and Helmut Norpoth, "Incumbency and Realignment: Partisan Change in House Elections." Presented at the 2007 Midwest Political Science Association Meetings, Chicago, Illinois, April, 2007.

this status persistent, and does it exist in both presidential and House elections? Second, is this status recognized by the party? Third, do party leaders identify voters they might be able to attract to gain a majority?[43] Does the party, even if the process is filled with contending views and uncertainty of information, formulate a plan about how to attract these new voters? Fourth, do presidential candidates lead in the pursuit of new voters, or does the congressional wing lead? If the wings of the party proceed somewhat independently, then these actions can create differences in electoral voting patterns and pull apart presidential and House election results. If presidential change leads, then we should expect that presidential results pull away from House results, rather than House results pulling away from presidential results.

The concern of the following chapters is to examine how the parties responded to strings of electoral losses and how their responses affected the relationship between presidential and House elections.

[43] Karol, *Party Position Change in American Politics*.

PART II

EXPLAINING A CHANGING RELATIONSHIP

5

The Democratic Pursuit of the North

In the years following the 1896 election, the nation was dominated by Republicans.[1] Democrats had to expand their electoral base to have a chance to be the majority party. To begin with presidential elections, over half of the nation's Electoral College votes came from the North, and Republicans won a very high percentage of them (Table 5.1). Roughly one-fourth came from western states, and Republicans also did well there. The dominance of Republicans put enormous pressure on Democrats to change their appeal and expand their electoral base.

As the table indicates, Democrats did very well in the South, winning an average of 67.6 percent of the popular vote and 90.4 percent of the Electoral College votes within that region. The party won only 14.2 percent of Electoral College votes within the North and 34.1 percent within the remainder of the nation. It was a party with its base in the South and with a record of only limited success outside that region. It was also a party regularly losing presidential elections.

The challenge was to boost the party's vote percentage within specific states. Almost all states allocate their Electoral College votes on a winner-take-all basis. That rule distorts the strength and weakness of a party. Elections could be close within states, but one party could still have margins sufficient to win enough states to win the Electoral College votes. To indicate the situation

---

[1] Just how rapidly this Republican dominance developed is not a settled issue. The argument that there was a significant and relatively abrupt change is presented by Walter Dean Burnham, *Critical Elections and the Mainsprings of American Politics* (New York: W. W. Norton, 1970). There are others who argue that the evidence suggests a much more modest increase. See Mayhew, *Electoral Realignments: A Critique of an American Genre*; Alan Ware, *The Democratic Party Moves North* (New York: Cambridge University Press, 2006); and Jeffrey M. Stonecash and Everita Silina, "Reassessing the 1896 Realignment," *American Politics Research*, Vol. 33, No. 1 (January 2005), 3–32.

TABLE 5.1. *Democratic Fortunes, 1900–1928*

Averages for 1900–1928 for:	North	South	Other
Percent Nation's EC votes in:	50.5	25.6	26.1
Percent Democratic popular votes won in:	35.5	67.6	39.5
Percent of EC votes won by Democrats in:	14.2	90.4	34.1
Percent of Democratic EC votes from:	9.5	71.5	27.8

Note: The results in this table and the next two represent the averages for each indicator for the years shown. For example, within any year in the North, there are 17 state percentages. The average is then calculated for that year of the 17 state percentages. Then the average of those averages for the nine elections from 1900 to 1928 is calculated. The emphasis is on state percentages and their average instead of the total vote within a region because the Electoral College creates a focus on states and the percentage within a state. The North consists of all states from Maine to West Virginia, and then west to Minnesota and Illinois. The South consists of the 11 states from Virginia down to Florida, across to Texas, and up to Kentucky.

of Democrats by region, Table 5.2 presents more detailed information. Two matters are important for the party's situation. First, its regional problems were consistent over time. It never did well in the North, where the highest percent of the popular vote won was 45.7 in 1916. It did somewhat better in the West, but it still received above 50 percent only once, in 1916.

Perhaps just as important is that there were very few states in both regions where the margin of loss was close enough that the party could presume a carefully planned campaign might bring victory. As a rough indicator of the possibilities a party might capitalize on, the table indicates the number of states in which the margin of loss for the Democratic was less than 10 percentage points. In those cases, with a maximum 55–45 difference, the party would only need to increase its vote percentage by five and reduce the other party's percentage by an equivalent amount to shift the outcome and win the state. As the table indicates for the North and West, there were not many states with a margin less than 10 percentage points. This situation made it imperative that the party fundamentally change and increase its appeal in the North and West.

Pressure for change might also have come from House Democrats. Table 5.3 summarizes the electoral situation of Democrats in the House. As in presidential elections, Democrats did very well within the South, regularly winning at least 70 percent of the popular vote and over 90 percent of the seats. The one exception, the decline in 1928, will be discussed later. Within the North the party was not in good shape. It never reached 42 percent of the popular vote, and it won more than 25 percent of the seats within that region only in 1912 when a third party materialized. If the party assessed its possibilities by targeting all the districts where Republicans won with less than 55 percent of the vote, even adding these seats to those already held would not produce a majority of the seats within the North in most years. The prospects in the West were

TABLE 5.2. *The Democratic Presidential Situation, 1900–1928*

	Year							
	1900	1904	1908	1912	1916	1920	1924	1928
North (18 states)								
Total electoral votes	231	247	247	268	268	268	268	268
% EC Democrats won	0	0	0	61.2	13.4	0	0	8.6
Number of states won	0	0	0	12	3	0	0	2
Number lost by <10 %	7	1	0	1	12	1	2	3
Average popular vote %	39.7	34.3	36.3	38.3	45.7	31.0	26.3	40.0
South (11 states)								
Total electoral votes	117	124	124	130	130	130	130	130
% EC Democrats won	100	100	100	100	100	90.8	90.8	42.3
Number of states won	11	11	11	11	11	10	10	5
Number lost by <10 %	0	0	0	0	0	1	1	3
Average popular vote %	66.7	70.7	68.0	70.6	73.7	65.8	68.8	56.5
West (no. of states)	16	16	18	19	19	19	19	19
Total electoral votes	99	105	112	133	133	133	133	133
% EC Democrats won	41.4	11.4	31.3	42.9	82.7	9.0	16.5	8.5
Number of states won	7	2	6	7	16	2	3	2
Number lost by <10 %	3	1	3	1	2	1	3	1
Average popular vote %	48.9	33.1	43.5	41.4	53.4	36.0	28.6	39.8
% EC votes from South	74.1	91.2	78.0	37.0	47.1	90.8	84.2	61.1
Party winning	R	R	R	D	D	R	R	R

TABLE 5.3. *The Democratic House Situation, 1900–1928*

	Year							
	1900	1904	1908	1912	1916	1920	1924	1928
North								
Number seats – total	195	211	211	232	232	232	232	232
Average popular vote %	41.8	36.0	40.9	41.2	41.6	31.8	35.1	40.1
% seats Democrats won	21.0	12.3	24.6	60.2	25.0	7.3	20.3	20.8
% R won <55%	25.8	27.7	31.3	38.2	38.8	20.7	13.4	13.0
% Democrats from region	26.5	19.0	30.2	47.8	28.7	13.0	25.7	28.9
South								
Number seats – total	82	86	86	90	90	90	90	90
Average popular vote %	70.8	75.8	76.9	81.1	77.3	75.6	83.2	79.3
% seats Democrats won	91.5	93.0	89.5	94.4	84.4	90.0	94.4	82.2
% R won <55%	0	2.3	7.0	3.3	10.0	5.6	1.1	11.1
% Democrats from region	48.4	58.4	44.8	29.2	37.6	61.8	46.5	44.6
West								
Number seats – total	80	89	94	113	113	113	113	113
Average popular vote %	48.6	46.2	52.3	51.9	52.6	41.6	49.1	48.0
% seats Democrats won	48.8	34.8	45.7	59.3	60.2	29.5	45.1	38.9
% R won <55%	26.3	24.7	28.7	33.6	13.4	19.7	14.2	13.3
% Democrats from region	25.2	22.6	25.0	23.0	33.7	25.2	27.9	26.5
% of all House seats won	43.4	35.5	44.0	67.1	46.4	30.2	42.1	38.3

somewhat better. The party was consistently close to winning a majority of the popular vote, and it was closer to winning a majority of the seats.

The broad pattern for both Democratic presidential and House candidates was the same. The party had a solid base in the South. It did better in the West than in the North. The challenge was to expand its base beyond the South.

Party Response

The process by which a "party" grapples with its status and formulates a response is not simple. If the party was in the majority, some may be inclined to see a setback as temporary due to short-term events, and they may not see a need for change. Others may see signs of an eroded situation but disagree about how to respond. There are always differing interpretations about why voters turned to the other party, and corresponding disputes about what must be done. Some argue it is the messenger and others argue it is the message. Although the process may be messy, parties consistently in the minority at least face clarity of their situation. Democrats were largely in the minority from 1900 through 1928. What was their response? In what follows, no effort is made to chronicle all the efforts made. That detail would be overwhelming. The focus here is the general response of Democrats to being in the minority and how this affected the presidential–House relationship from 1900 to 1928.

Although some see the election of 1896 as involving a significant and dramatic shift in partisan support to Republicans, the evidence about that is not clear, and this ambiguity affected the party's response.[2] Burnham has been the primary advocate of the view that an abrupt and enduring shift to Republicans occurred in 1896.[3] The evidence, however, suggests that there was not great change, and that any move to Republicans developed gradually in subsequent years.[4]

In the 1896 William Jennings Bryan lost the popular vote 51.1 percent to 46.9 percent and the Electoral College 271 to 176. The Democratic loss in the presidential race in 1896 was by only 4.2 percentage points. In House elections the major damage experienced by the party had been in 1894, when a significant economic depression was under way. From 1892 to 1894 Democrats lost the majority and 114 seats. In 1896, House Democrats improved their situation, picking up 35 seats. After the 1896 election Republicans held 211 seats and

---

[2] As we get farther away from historical events it is tempting to impose interpretations of party systems and define eras as if the conditions simply favored one party over another. This is reinforced by the argument that voters attach themselves to a party and resist change. The result is that there is a pattern in textbooks of classifying eras as apparently stable, with little change during the era. As this review indicates, it is often not that clear.

[3] Burnham, *Critical Elections and the Mainsprings of American Politics*.

[4] Mayhew, *Electoral Realignments*; and Stonecash and Silina, "Reassessing the 1896 Realignment."

Democrats 142. In 1898 the House situation again improved for Democrats, with the party picking up 25 seats. The results did not yet indicate the party was in trouble and in need of a fundamental shift of its base. The party had a solid base in the South and was steadily gaining House seats since the major setback of 1892, increasing from 93 in 1894 to 124 in 1896 and 161 in 1898. There were encouraging signs for Democrats.

Given those conditions, it was easy for Bryan to argue that he deserved another chance to beat McKinley and to draw on the base of the party to secure the nomination. He did get two more chances, running against McKinley in 1900 (getting 45.5 percent of the popular vote) and 1908 (getting 43.0 percent of the popular vote). In 1904 Alton Parker ran and received 37.6 percent of the popular vote. Between 1898 and 1908 the percentage of the national vote received by House Democrats varied from 41.0 (1904) to 47.0 (1898). The party was close a few times, but consistently in the minority.

Although Bryan represents an example of a party repeating its appeal, there were efforts by the party to expand its base. The difficulty was in getting the efforts to produce results. As early as the late 1800s Democrats were trying to create a coalition encompassing those harmed by the transition to an industrial economy. The logic was that the party could create a majority comprised of the South; western farmers unhappy with high railroad costs, low prices for crops, and high mortgage costs; and urban workers seeking legislation supportive of improving their working conditions and wages.[5] During the late 1800s Democrats regularly sponsored legislation to increase the money supply so some inflation would occur, which would reduce the real costs of paying back bank loans that required a fixed payment.[6] The party sought to support labor unions so urban workers in the North might organize and bargain for better work conditions. The issue of the money supply faded after 1896, but over the next two decades the party continued to sponsor legislation that would try to regulate large corporations and working conditions, and to support the ability of unions to form and function.[7] However, the party's efforts to expand its base were not successful. From 1896 through 1908 the party continued to derive the bulk of its support from the South.

As often happens in politics, events the party did not plan for helped them. In the 1910 and 1912 elections Democrats were finally successful because Teddy Roosevelt became unhappy with his party and created a third party, sometimes called the Progressive or Bull Moose Party. He wanted the party to focus more on various reforms, and he wanted to lead that effort as their presidential candidate. He did not win the party nomination and chose to form another party.[8]

---

[5] Sundquist, *Dynamics of the American Party System.*

[6] Richard Bensel, *The Political Economy of American Industrialism, 1877–1900* (New York: Cambridge University Press, 2000).

[7] Sanders, *Roots of Reform,* 267–313 and 340–386.

[8] Sundquist, *Dynamics of the American Party System,* 180–181.

Candidates were recruited for the 1910 congressional elections. The result was that many votes that probably would have gone to Republican candidates went to these third-party candidates and Democrats achieved a majority (226–167) for the first time since the 1892 elections. In 1912 Roosevelt ran as a third-party presidential candidate, again taking many probable Republican votes, and Democrat Woodrow Wilson won the presidency. Democrats also gained 53 seats, increasing their majority to 279–145.

The challenge that Democrats and Woodrow Wilson faced was to interpret their majority and try to maintain it. The party had been trying to expand its electoral base outside the South without much success. Now a split within the Republican Party and its consequences in 1910 and 1912 had given them an opportunity. It was hard to avoid the realization that the party was in power only because of a split within the Republican Party.

The issue the party faced was what appeals might get areas that put Democrats in office in 1910 and 1912 to continue to vote for the party. The emphasis of Democrats for decades had been on an agenda of regulating railroad costs, limiting the power of corporations, and increasing the money supply. They also wanted to reduce the tariff imposed on goods brought into the United States. Republicans, with a base in the North, were opposed to these efforts. Railroads, corporations, and banks were based in the North and generated jobs. The tariff generated the bulk of the national government's revenues, and was what shielded many northern factories from foreign competition. The South, which wanted extensive trade in cotton, was opposed to the effects of the tariff on the region's ability to secure international trade for its products. Although all these policies catered to the party's base, they did little to attract support outside the base.

The 1910 elections finally provided the party with the expanded base it had been seeking. In 1906 the party was in the minority (163–222) in the House with only 46 seats in the North. Twenty-eight percent of their seats were in the North. In 1908 they had 52 seats in the North and had 172 seats to the 219 Republicans held. The 1910 elections produced a majority (222 Democrats to 166 Republicans) with 42 percent of their seats (94) from the North. Of the 94 seats won in the North, 33 were won with the Democrat receiving less than 50 percent of the vote. Retaining those seats would not be easy.

The party realized it had to stake out some policy positions that would attract voters, and the congressional party took steps to do so. In an effort to appeal to northern workers, for several years Democrats had been proposing legislation to regulate labor conditions, but the party was in the minority and was unable to enact its proposals. In 1909 Democrats proposed an individual income tax for those with high incomes, which Republicans rejected. After the party acquired a majority in 1910 it enacted a number of programs intended to bolster support among labor groups in the North. In 1912 it passed legislation to give postal workers the right to organize, and it established the eight-hour workday for federal employees.

The 1912 election brought the Democrat further gains. Woodrow Wilson won the presidency, and Democrats increased their number of seats in the House from 230 to 291 and in the Senate from 44 to 51. This allowed the party in 1913 to enact the federal income tax, with only the most affluent paying the tax.[9] The elections of 1910 and 1912 put Democrats in power, but the results also indicated how vulnerable the party's position was. In the North, Wilson's average popular state vote was only 38.3 percent, and Democratic House candidates averaged only 41.2 percent. The party had not really improved its electoral support. In the West, Wilson won an average of 41.4 percent and House candidates won 51.9 percent. The party had to recognize that the two preceding elections were not expressions of pro-Democratic support. The efforts of Teddy Roosevelt in recruiting candidates in 1910–1912 and his candidacy in 1912 had drained votes away from Republicans. If the party was to retain seats in 1914 and the presidency in 1916, it had to continue to take steps to win the votes that were going to Roosevelt's progressive supporters.

The political situation during these years embodies the conditions discussed in the prior chapter that create change in a party's focus. Democrats had been regularly losing presidential elections. They had not held the majority in the Senate going back to the 1870s. From 1897 through 1911 the party was in the minority in the House. The party could not use its new majority to just respond to its historical base: It had to seek to expand its base. The recognition of this need for change occurred to President Wilson as well as party members within Congress. As Sanders comments, in explaining the tensions but also imperatives facing congressional Democrats:

The reasons for the agrarian Democrats' persistence in the labor agenda was obvious: the northern urban Democrats from labor districts backed the farmers' program even when it was not in *their* interest to do so, and without support from other regions, the state-expansionist agrarians could not hope to control the national government. Whenever the commitment [to the labor agenda] faded under the pressure of the party's minority conservative faction (as in 1904), the dismal electoral results provided a sharp reminder of where the most promising strategy lay (1999: 341).

The congressional party knew it had to reach beyond its base, and sought to do so. Following the 1910 elections Democrats were able to win control of the House, but not the Senate. The party in the House used its majority power to pass several bills to signal to northern labor that Democrats were sympathetic to their concerns.

The farmer's party [Democrats] used its partial control of the legislature as a "dress rehearsal for the rise to power that was now anticipated. The agrarians would demonstrate to the country – and in particular to labor – that this was the genuine party of reform. The result was a great outpouring of labor proposals, including bills sharply

---

[9] Sanders, *Roots of Reform*, 224–227.

limiting injunctions in labor disputes, providing jury trials in contempt cases, prohibiting Justice Department prosecutions of labor under the antitrust laws, legalizing unions in the postal service, creating a Department of Labor in the cabinet and giving it power to mediate labor disputes, . . . [and] enacting at long last the eight-hour limitation on all federal government contracts and on river and harbor work.[10]

Many of these bills did not become law, but the legislation was a response to the realization that the party had to expand its base beyond the South if it was going to win a majority. The goal was to signal concern to the voters whom the party wanted to attract.

In 1912 the fortunes of House Democrats improved, and Democrat Woodrow Wilson won the presidency, but the party's success was largely due to the candidacy of Teddy Roosevelt and the House candidates he recruited. The problem for Wilson was that he won a majority of votes only in the South. He won the Electoral College votes of many northern states, but only by small margins. The situation was not good for Democrats.[11]

The existence of a Democratic majority in Congress, like Wilson's presidential victory itself, had been predicated on the rupture of the Republican Party and the formation of the Progressive Party. Prospects for the organizational longevity of the new party were dim, and a reunited Republican Party threatened the Democrats with a return to out-party status. Constructing a stable Democratic majority in this unsettled environment required the active solicitation of traditionally non-Democratic votes. Wilson hoped to contain the erosion of his artificially inflated congressional majority with an explicit appeal to Progressives and progressive Republicans.[12]

Wilson's concern was that if Democrats did not enact legislation responding to progressive concerns, those who had voted for Teddy Roosevelt and his candidates in 1912 would return to the Republican Party and endanger Wilson's chances in 1916.[13] In response, Wilson advocated legislation desired by Progressives to regulate corporations. They wanted a regulatory system that granted discretion to a regulatory commission. Obtaining support from the southern wing for this was difficult because the agrarian wing distrusted eastern experts and wanted specific statutory language to limit corporations. Wilson was able to make the argument that the traditional base had to compromise if the party wanted to remain in the majority, and the party eventually enacted the Federal Trade Commission Act of 1914, which relied upon the expertise of commissioners and staff.[14]

These years demonstrated some essential matters about parties and the connection between presidential and House results. Democrats recognized that they were the minority party and that they had to expand their electoral base.

---

[10] Sanders, *Roots of Reform*, 342–343.
[11] James, *Presidents, Parties, and the State*, 131–137; Ware, *The Democratic Party Heads North*.
[12] James, *Presidents, Parties, and the State*, 124 and 188.
[13] James, *Presidents, Parties, and the State*, 167 and 186–187.
[14] James, *Presidents, Parties, and the State*, 162–182.

TABLE 5.4. *Democratic Vote Percentages in House Districts, by Region, 1912–1924*

	Year			
	1912	1916	1920	1924
Region[15]				
Northeast				
President	39.4	45.6	29.1	26.5
House	41.2	40.7	32.1	36.4
Midwest				
President	36.8	46.1	28.7	21.8
House	39.7	41.7	29.9	31.6
South				
President	70.6	74.0	66.2	70.1
House	83.0	78.4	76.2	84.0
Other (largely West)				
President	42.1	51.2	36.1	31.0
House	45.2	47.0	35.7	42.6
National correlation	.90	.89	.88	.88

They were in power because of conflicts among Republicans, and they had to act to appeal to the disaffected within the other party. They also perceived that their electoral fates were tied together. The Democratic label defined the presidential and congressional wings, and the party needed to recognize that and create a policy identity that would help both wings attract votes in new areas. The Democratic Party, after years as the minority party, was seeking to change its status by supporting policies not desired by or helpful to its traditional electoral base.

The Limits of Party Efforts

The regional splits in partisan loyalties in the United States had been in effect since the 1870s, and they proved difficult to alter. As Table 5.4 indicates, the party's efforts yielded no improvement of its electoral fortunes in regions where it needed to gain votes. The efforts to appeal to Progressives who had bolted the Republican Party did not bring the Democratic Party greater support in the Northeast or in the Midwest in 1916. Woodrow Wilson was able to marginally improve his vote percentages in enough states to barely win the 1916 presidential election, but he did not get to 50 percent in the Northeast

[15] Northeast is Maine, New Hampshire, Vermont, Massachusetts, Rhode Island, Connecticut, New York, New Jersey, Delaware, and Pennsylvania. The Midwest is Ohio, Indiana, Illinois, Michigan, Wisconsin, and Minnesota. The South is Virginia, North Carolina, South Carolina, Georgia, Florida, Alabama, Mississippi, Louisiana, Texas, Tennessee, and Kentucky. The remaining states are Other.

TABLE 5.5. *Average Democratic House Percentage in Districts by Woodrow Wilson's Percentage in 1912 Presidential Election*

		Year							
Wilson % 1912	N	1912	1914	1916	1918	1920	1922	1924	Change
<40	173	35.7	34.5	38.1	34.1	26.2	35.5	28.5	−7.2
40–44	62	45.9	45.2	46.7	45.6	37.2	44.1	41.1	−4.8
45–49	76	46.8	46.8	45.6	46.3	37.9	48.9	48.2	1.4
50 or more	122	82.3	82.9	77.9	86.9	74.7	82.5	81.6	.7

or Midwest. The party had made specific efforts to appeal to northern labor in urban areas, but there was virtually no change in Democratic voting for the president or House candidates in large cities.[16]

The stability of the results within regions and the inability of either wing to change its degree of electoral support resulted in stability of the relationship between presidential and House results.[17] The correlation remained around .90 from 1912 through 1924. The party was finding it difficult to change its base, and both presidential and congressional wings faced the same situation: Their electoral support was tied together and largely confined to the South.

The failure of the party to make progress is shown in Table 5.5. If Democrats were to make progress from their 1912 situation, they needed to improve in districts where Wilson did not do well in 1912. From 1912 through 1924 Democrats lost support in districts in which Wilson received less than 45 percent. In those where he got 45–49 percent, Democratic House candidates improved their situation by 1.4 percentage points. The party was making no progress where it needed to do so. The correlation of Democratic House vote percentages of 1912 with 1924 was .86.

[16] Samuel J. Eldersveld, "The Influence of Metropolitan Party Pluralities in Presidential Elections since 1920: A Study of Twelve Key Cities," *American Political Science Review*, Vol. 43, No. 6 (December 1949), 1189–1206; and Carl N. Degler, "American Political Parties and the Rise of the City: An Interpretation," *Journal of American History*, Vol. 51, No. 1 (June 1964), 41–59.

[17] Although the relationship of results within each year remained strong, this does not mean that the results for specific districts were stable or that changes from 1912 to 1916 for both House and presidential candidates moved together. The results move together, but there is also considerable randomness in the covariance of district changes for the two offices. For the years of 1912 through 1928 it is possible to track changes over time because Congress did not reapportion after the 1920 census, so districts were the same over time. For changes within districts from 1912 to 1916 for the two offices, the correlation is .46. For 1916 to 1920 the correlation is .32, and from 1920 to 1924 the correlation is .40. From 1912 to 1924 the correlation is .41. These correlations indicate considerable deviation from districts moving together. Despite that, the overall correlation remains high because the mean scores for regions differed so much from the South that differences in presidential and House changes within districts did not disrupt the large differences in partisan support between regions. Those large differences between regions created enough dispersion of scores to maintain the high correlation of results even as there was variability in changes within regions.

From the late 1800s through the late 1920s the Democratic Party was the minority party in the United States. The party recognized this and pursued policies to attract voters outside its base in the South, but its efforts produced essentially no gains. Even when the party acquired power following the 1910 and 1912 elections, its percentages in presidential and House elections did not increase much.

Why were party efforts unsuccessful, and why did presidential and House results remain tied together? The goal of Democrats was to expand their base, with many thinking that advocating for labor would increase their support among northern urban labor. There were already some northern cities with a substantial Democratic component, and Democrats thought they could expand that base. Despite their efforts, three factors limited the success of their appeal. The party carried with it a historical image that was probably not appealing to urban labor. Democrats positioned themselves on cultural issues in a way that made the party unappealing. The party was also seeking to appeal to a constituency that was probably not yet engaged in the political process such that they might have responded.

Although the Democratic Party of the early 1900s was substantially rural and Southern, the party also had a base in northern cities. That seemingly strange combination was a legacy of the early 1800s and the positions of the parties in that era. The Republican Party was Protestant and not receptive to Catholic immigrants. The Jeffersonian legacy of the Democratic Party was that government intrusion into lives should be limited. The contrast prompted many immigrants to opt for identification with the Democratic Party when they first entered the country, creating substantial pockets of Democratic support in northern cities.[18] The 1920 census indicated that for the first time a majority of Americans lived in cities. There was a potential to increase support in these growing areas and expand the party's base.

The difficulty the party faced was its historical image of concerns. Parties build up images of whom and what they represent. From the 1870s through the early 1900s the Democratic Party had a southern agricultural base. The bulk of its representatives and presidential candidates came from a world that bore little resemblance to that known to northern urban dwellers. The party's support of limited government appealed to some Catholic immigrants who wanted government to stay out of their lives. But the South was also a part of the nation that was seeking to curtail who could participate in democracy.[19] It was presenting the North with candidates such as William Jennings Bryan, a moralistic fundamentalist who was intolerant of immigrant ways. As Burner has argued, the approach of the party was not just to help those in cities, but to save them from themselves.

---

[18] Burner, *The Politics of Provincialism*, 15.

[19] J. Morgan Kousser, *The Shaping of Southern Politics: Suffrage Restriction and the Establishment of the One-Party South, 1880–1910* (New Haven, CT: Yale University Press, 1974).

By the 1920s, then, the Democratic Party had laid for itself in the hinterland a solid progressive foundation, and progressive in the tradition of Bryan. Somewhere in the process, moreover, the country Democracy was acquiring more and more clearly a tone that had always been present in the progressive movement itself – a tone of moralism, the style of the Jeremaid.

The aims of the rural faction became larger than the economic and political; it sought no less than the rescue of traditional American virtue, and that virtue it identified with the countryside, which must now resist the corruption of the cities – their political machines, their saloons, their strange religious faiths.[20]

The historical image of the party as focused on rural concerns was reinforced by the party's stance on some specific issues of the day during the early 1900s involving Prohibition, labor policy, and immigration legislation. The much discussed recent "cultural wars"[21] are not new to American politics. The transition in where Americans were living and who populated cities was troubling to "old-stock" Americans.[22] The late 1800s and early 1900s was also a time when there was extensive immigration, and many were Catholics. The development of urbanization and the rising presence of immigrants in cities raised issues of whether English should be required, whether Catholic schools would be discouraged,[23] whether alcohol should be banned,[24] and whether legislation should be enacted to restrict or stop further immigration from parts of Europe.[25]

In this context, Democrats adopted positions on several specific issues that surely conveyed to northern urban immigrant populations a sense that the Democratic Party was no more sympathetic to their concerns than the Republican Party. In 1917 Congress passed the Eighteenth Amendment, which would ban the sale of alcohol. Democrats voted for the ban as strongly as Republicans. The amendment was ratified by enough states in 1919, but the issue remained highly salient in subsequent years because there were numerous battles over how much to enforce the law. The strongest support for enforcement came out of the South, where the Democrat Party was based. The opposition to alcohol

---

[20] Burner, *The Politics of Provincialism*, 11.

[21] James Davison Hunter, *Culture Wars: The Struggle to Define America* (New York: Basic Books, 1991); and Fiorina, with Abrams and Pope, *Culture War? The Myth of a Polarized America*.

[22] Robert H. Wiebe, *The Search For Order, 1877–1920* (New York: Hill and Wang, 1967).

[23] These early cultural wars are analyzed in Paul Kleppner, *The Cross of Culture: A Social Analysis of Midwestern Politics, 1850–1900* (New York: The Free Press, 1970); and Richard Jensen, *The Winning of the Midwest* (Chicago: University of Chicago Press, 1971).

[24] Ann-Marie E. Szymanski, *Pathways to Prohibition: Radicals, Moderates, and Social Movement Outcomes* (Durham, NC: Duke University Press, 2003). As she documents, the efforts to ban alcohol were lengthy and pervasive in the nation prior to 1917.

[25] D. J. Tichenor, *Dividing Lines: The Politics of Immigration Control in America* (Princeton, NJ: Princeton University Press, 2002).

was generally seen as driven by Protestant leaders and as anti-Catholic.[26] In terms of labor policy, despite the efforts earlier in the decade of congressional Democrats to appeal to urban labor, after WWI ended in 1918 the Wilson administration proved to be unsympathetic to helping labor maintain the gains they had won as concessions to keep them working during the war effort. There were numerous strikes, and the Justice Department did not side with labor.[27] Immigration issues also did not help. In the late 1910s and early 1920s Democrats voted for numerous immigration restrictions. In 1924 majorities in both parties voted to severely restrict immigration, and set quotas for future entrance based on the percentage of the population that existed in 1890. The message was that the entrance of numerous immigrant groups since 1890 was not good for the nation and should not be continued.[28] The 1924 Democratic convention illustrated the party's dilemma. The northern wing of the party wanted to condemn the Klu Klux Klan, which was strongly anti-Catholic, but the convention, by a narrow margin, voted against the resolution.

Taken together, the party's stance on issues of Prohibition, labor, and immigration surely made it difficult for immigrants to see the Democratic Party as sensitive to their concerns. In specific and general stances, the Democrats struggled to overcome the image created by their base as they sought to expand their electoral base. The result of these policy stances was that the Democratic Party experienced limited success in expanding its base into northern urban areas during most of the 1920s. There were some signs that Democrats might expand their base, to be discussed next, but the result of the continuity of the party's base was that presidential and House election results remained closely connected through the 1920s.

---

[26] Daniel Okrent, *Last Call: The Rise and Fall of Prohibition* (New York: Scribner, 2010); and Burner, *The Politics of Provincialism*, 89.
[27] Burner, *The Politics of Provincialism*, 41–48.
[28] Burner, *The Politics of Provincialism*, 77.

6

Expanding the Democratic Base

Despite the party's persistent troubles, in 1932 the Democratic New Deal coalition emerged. The party, long reliant on a Southern base, gained votes and seats outside the South, and gained a majority that persisted for some years. Although there was considerable change in where the party won votes, the relationship between presidential and House vote percentages remained remarkably stable from the 1920s through 1944. As indicated earlier in Figure 3.4, the correlation had fluctuated between .90 and .70 (excluding 1912) between 1900 and 1928. It was .81 in 1932 and 1936, and .83 in 1940 and 1944. This era is often described as one of realignment, which presumably means a significant shift in electoral alignments.[1] Yet the correlation between voting for presidential and House candidates did not change. How does a party expand its base and bring in a significantly new electoral base while this association does not change?

Analyzing 1928–1932 Gains

The question facing Democrats in the 1920s was how to expand their base beyond the South, and to do so on a consistent basis. The issue within the party was whether to run presidential candidates who would appeal to northern urban constituencies and attract enduring support in those areas. Although in retrospect it appears clear which way the party should and would move, there was little clarity during the 1920s. The battle over what direction to take consumed the party[2] during the 1920s, until the beginning of the Great Depression in 1929 gave the party electoral gains in 1930 and 1932 it had not

---

[1] Sundquist, *Dynamics of the Party System*, 198–239.
[2] Douglas B. Craig, *After Wilson: The Struggle for the Democratic Party, 1920–1934* (Chapel Hill: University of North Carolina Press, 1992).

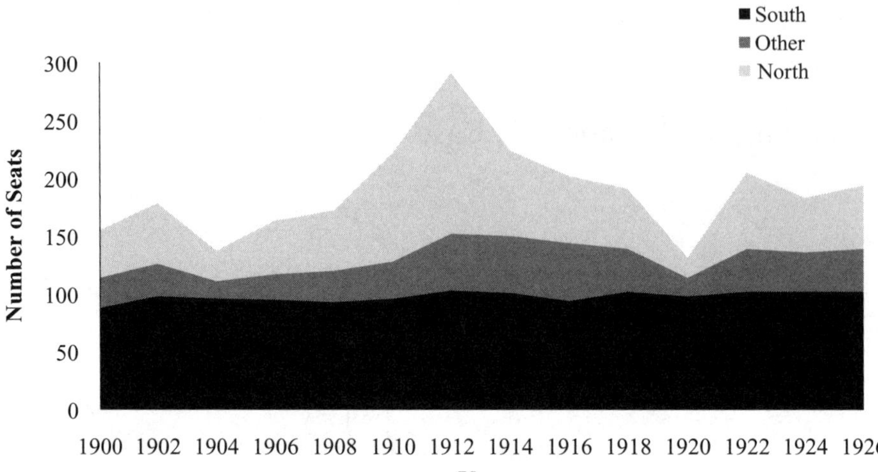

FIGURE 6.1. Democratic House Seats Won, by Region, 1900–1926

been able to achieve before. The challenge then became how to retain the newly acquired support.

The internal struggle of the party was evident in the presidential convention of 1924. In 1922 Democrats won additional House seats, with most of the gains coming in northern urban districts. These gains increased the size of the urban wing and their sense that they should receive more attention within the party.[3] The party met in 1924 in New York City with the two contending wings of the party nominating candidates. The conservative southern wing of the party supported William McAdoo, and the urban wing wanted Al Smith, the governor of New York. After 103 ballots of sustained division, with overtones of Protestant–Catholic conflict, neither candidate could secure a majority, and both candidates withdrew. John Davis was nominated as a compromise, and the party lost in 1924. The party remained at an impasse over its future direction and did not do well in the 1926 congressional elections.

The party was in a difficult situation. It was dominated by its southern base which was not sympathetic to urban concerns. There were some signs that the party could win in northern urban districts, but the southern wing was ambivalent about supporting policy initiatives that might bring more seats in the North.[4] The southern base was not large enough for the party to win the presidency or to attain majorities in either house of Congress. The problem for the Democratic Party was evident in House results. Figure 6.1 indicates the fluctuations in House results by region from 1900 to 1926. From 1900 through 1926 Democrats won about 100 seats in the South. That base was stable and

---

[3] Burner, *The Politics of Provincialism*, 103–106.
[4] Burner, *The Politics of Provincialism*, 150–157.

unlikely to change. In the states grouped as other – largely the West – the party won between 16 and 50 seats over that time. The major fluctuation in the party's success came in the North, the states stretching from Maine down to Maryland and across the Midwest. The only times the party acquired a majority or came close was when the party did well in the North. When the party did make gains in the North, it was in urban areas.[5]

Although there was some recognition that the party needed to expand, the means and commitment to do so were faltering. The positions taken by the congressional party were increasingly dominated by the conservative southern wing, which comprised the bulk of the party. The party provided a limited alternative to Republican positions.[6] From 1925 to 1927 the national party organization almost ceased to exist, indicating the weakness of its situation.

By the late 1920s some were making efforts to rejuvenate the party and try an alternative approach. The national party organization was revived, and efforts were made to prepare for the 1928 presidential election.[7] In the 1928 nomination process Al Smith prevailed and was the party's nominee. Although there were those who hoped that Smith could significantly expand the party's base in the North, his campaign did not go well. The economy was doing well, and Herbert Hoover had a positive public image, making it difficult for any Democrat to win. Smith's campaign appeal was limited by issues of his Catholicism and his lack of support for the laws enacted to enforce Prohibition.[8] It was difficult to tell if he was establishing a general urban base or just attracting Catholics who lived predominantly in urban areas.[9] Although Smith did receive increased Democratic support in some northern urban areas, the gains were not enough to win many states. The Democratic Party was still stymied.

As sometimes happens in politics, events and not plans finally brought the Democratic Party significant inroads into the North. In October 1929 the Great Depression began and Republicans, controlling the presidency and Congress, had to decide how to respond. Their general reaction was to follow the then-dominant belief in laissez-faire economics, and assume markets would eventually correct themselves. Republicans largely chose to do very little.[10] The result was that the electorate rejected the party in power and voted against the Republican Party, with Democrats the beneficiary. There is considerable disagreement about how much of the increase in this vote was because of conversion of Republicans or mobilization of previously nonvoting immigrants

---

[5] Burner, *The Politics of Provincialism*, 154.

[6] Burner, *The Politics of Provincialism*, 150–168.

[7] Burner, *The Politics of Provincialism*, 149.

[8] Burner, *The Politics of Provincialism*, 183–186.

[9] This issue is reviewed by Allan J. Lichtman, "Critical Election Theory and the Reality of American Presidential Politics, 1916–1940," *The American Historical Review*, Vol. 81, No. 2 (April 1976), 317–351.

[10] Sundquist, *Dynamics of the Party System*, 199–204.

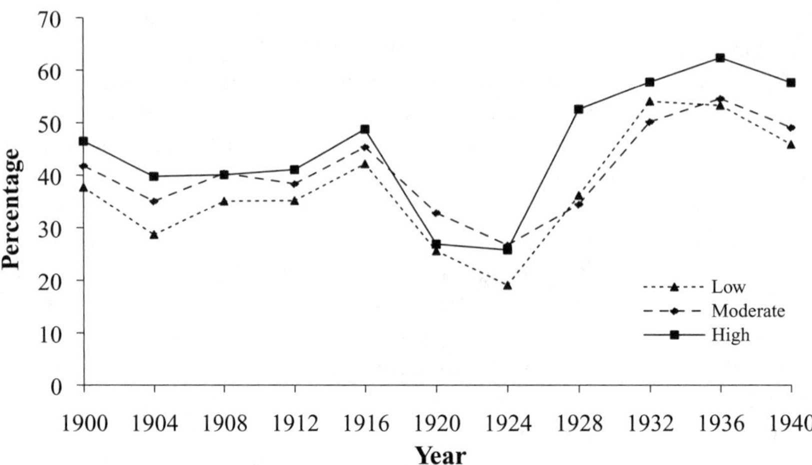

FIGURE 6.2. Democratic Presidential Percentages by Density of Northern House Districts, 1900–1940

and others,[11] but the net result was a significant increase in the percentage of people voting Democratic across the nation.

The most important changes occurred in the North. In 1928 there were 109 House districts in the nation with a density of 1,000 or more per square mile. One hundred of those districts were in the North. They constituted 43.3 percent of all House districts in the North. Figure 6.2 indicates the average presidential vote won by the density of districts within the North.[12]

In the 1920 and 1924 elections Democratic success in all three categories of districts was below that which prevailed in 1900–1916. In 1928 Al Smith received a percentage higher in the high-density districts than any presidential candidate had received since 1900. In the districts with lower density, he received support levels somewhat below those of the 1900–1916 levels. What was significant about the 1932 and 1936 elections was that they resulted in Democratic presidential voting levels in all districts higher than any years since 1900.

[11] See the analyses by Andersen, *The Creation of a Democratic Majority*, who argues that much of the change in major urban areas was due to the mobilization of previously unengaged voters, and the criticisms of that and argument that conversion of existing voters predominated. Sundquist, *Dynamics of the Party System*, 229–239; Erikson and Tedin, "The 1928–1932 Partisan Realignment."

[12] Low density is defined as fewer than 60 people per square mile, and moderate is defined as between 60 and 999 per square mile. In 1928 in the North, 13 percent of districts were in the low density category and 43.7 percent were in the middle category. In 1932 the percentages in the three categories were very similar, varying from 13.3 in the low category to 44.0 in the high category.

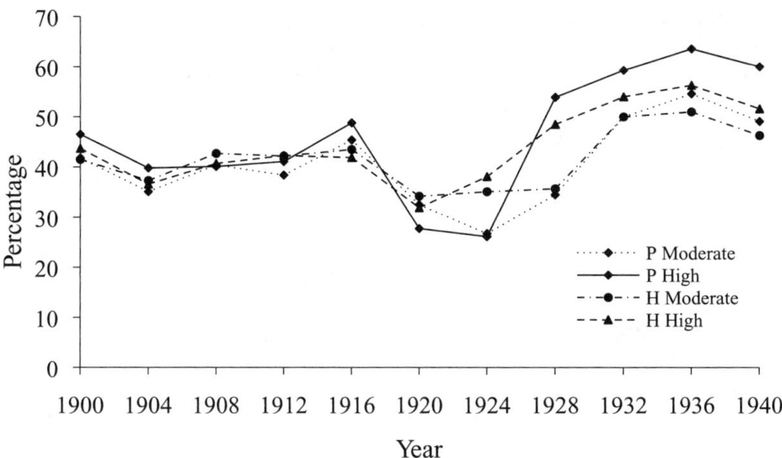

FIGURE 6.3. Democratic Presidential and House Success by District Density, North, 1900–1940

The important matter for presidents is whether they carry into office a congressional contingent with an electoral base somewhat similar to theirs. The 1932 voting shifts put a Democratic president in office. Was there a corresponding shift in the congressional vote? In this case the primary interest is in what happened in the North, because that is the area where the party was seeking expansion. There are three ways to track the correspondence between the presidential and House vote in northern districts. This might be assessed by comparing aggregate vote shifts for the two offices by types of districts. It also might be assessed by comparing the association between presidential and House votes in 1928 and 1932. These two measures are limited, however, in that they do not allow a clear comparison of how partisan fortunes changed for House members. House districts were redrawn between 1928 and 1932, and it is not possible to compare vote changes for the same districts from 1928 to 1932. A third way to track this relationship is to examine changes in presidential and House voting for those members who continued from 1928 and 1930 to 1932.

The first approach involves tracking the average percentage of the vote won in northern districts of high and moderate density (Figure 6.3). These constitute 87 percent of all northern districts. In both categories of districts the average vote moved together. In the high-density districts the presidential vote led the House vote.

The second approach to tracking the presidential–House relationship focuses on the covariation of presidential–House vote percentages across districts within 1928 and within 1932. Tables 6.1 and 6.2 indicate the presidential–House relationships in the North, the region of greatest importance to Democrats. Presidential percentages are shown to the left, and House

TABLE 6.1. *Democratic Presidential and House Votes in Northern House Districts, 1928*

Dem Pres %	N	Democratic % in House Race						P–H avg
		<40	40–44	45–49	50–54	55–59	60+	
<40	104	83	14	4	3	0	0	− 1.5
40–44	29	13	7	5	3	1	0	3.7
45–49	26	8	5	5	2	1	5	.1
50–54	4	2	0	1	1	0	4	1.0
55–59	0	0	0	0	0	0	6	3.7
60+	38	5	6	5	5	5	12	.3
N	201	111	32	20	14	7	17	

P–H average is the average difference between the presidential and House vote in House districts.

percentages are shown along the top. Not only did Smith and House Democrats do poorly in the North in 1928, but the pattern of success of Democratic House candidates largely mirrored that of Smith. Those cases in which the presidential and House percentages were essentially the same are the shaded cells. There were districts where House candidates ran ahead of the presidential vote, and districts where Smith ran ahead of the House candidates, but 108 of the 201 districts were along the diagonal where results for both offices are roughly the same.

The major difference from 1928 to 1932 was that the distribution of the Democratic vote percentages shifted up for both offices. The swing to Democrats moved together for both offices and brought many House winners to the party. The two vote percentages again largely covaried. Those cases in which the specific percentages were essentially the same are again the shaded cells. Of the 215 districts in which data exist for both offices, 105 fall along this diagonal. Roosevelt won 142 of 215 House districts. Roosevelt ran behind

TABLE 6.2. *Democratic Presidential and House Votes in Northern House Districts, 1932*

Dem Pres %	N	Democratic % in House Race						P–H avg
		<40	40–44	45–49	50–54	55–59	60+	
<40	12	9	1	1	0	0	1	− 5.0
40–44	29	10	11	7	1	0	0	3.9
45–49	32	1	4	18	8	1	0	− .6
50–54	48	2	5	8	24	5	4	1.4
55–59	36	2	2	5	9	12	6	1.5
60+	58	4	7	5	5	6	31	5.9
N	215	28	30	44	47	24	42	

TABLE 6.3. *Change from 1928 to 1932 in Democratic Presidential and House Vote Percentages for Continuing House Members, Northern House Districts*

		Change in Democratic % in House Race				
Δ Pres D %	N	−4 to 0	0–4	5–9	10+	Avg H Δ
−4–0	1	1				3.0
0–4	17	3	8	6		4.2
5–9	34	1	6	22	5	4.9
10+	29		1	5	23	5.8
N	81	5	15	33	28	

House candidates in some districts and ahead in others,[13] but the average presidential vote was much higher, and it was accompanied by greater success in House elections. In the North, Democrats increased their seats from 48 in 1928 to 76 in 1930, and then to 134 in 1932, bringing them up to more than 50 percent of the seats within the region.

Another way to assess the presidential–House association is to track changes from 1928 to 1932. Did the partisan vote for both offices move together? The ability to track change is limited by the reapportionment that occurred in 1932, the first since 1912. Many members were required to run in altered districts, making direct comparisons of the 1928 and 1932 districts impossible. Although comparing vote percentages in the same districts is not possible, it is possible to compare the vote percentages of continuing members, which is the politically relevant matter. If the same member of Congress ran in 1928 and then in 1932, the politically important comparison is whether both his vote and that for his party's presidential candidate increased. These may have increased because the member was redistricted into a more favorable district, but for a member trying to decide whether to work with a president, it is the commonality of the votes and their change that are important.

From 1928 to 1932 within the North there are 81 members of the House who won in 1928 and then ran again in 1932 and for which presidential and House percentages exist. For these continuing members, the correlation of change scores from 1928 to 1932 is .44. The specific association of change scores for these 81 are shown in Table 6.3. For most members there was an

---

[13] Although there has been concern about whether or not the presidential candidate has coattails, that seems too simplistic. A presidential candidate may present a message that increases the party vote in a district, but the House vote may lag or lead depending on the quality of the House candidate of that party. A House candidate may be inept at running a campaign and lag, making it appear that the presidential candidate has coattails. In reality the House candidate just may be a bad candidate. A House candidate may be effective and run ahead of the president, suggesting the president has no coattails. Given the ambiguity of possible outcomes, the concern here is the extent to which the two covary. When a president and his or her congressional party decide whether to work together, it is likely that it is their commonality of electoral fates that is most important.

TABLE 6.4. *Distribution of Democratic Presidential and House Vote Percentages, National Results, 1928–1932*

| | Distribution of Percentages | | | | Change 28–32: in Distribution | |
| | 1928 | | 1932 | | | |
	Pres	House	Pres	House	Pres	House
<40	41.9	39.6	2.5	8.9	−39.4	−30.7
40–44	18.1	11.3	7.0	9.4	−11.1	−1.9
45–49	12.5	11.1	7.0	13.1	−5.5	2.0
50–54	4.3	7.6	13.7	15.5	9.4	7.9
55–59	3.0	5.1	21.6	12.2	18.6	7.1
60+	20.3	25.4	48.4	41.0	28.1	15.6

increase in the presidential vote along with their vote. Of the 81 members, 64 fall along the diagonal, which reflects a close association between the gains for the two offices. For continuing House Democrats the message was that the partisan vote was for the party. Collaboration with the president was probably wise. For continuing Republicans the concern was how much to oppose Democrats.

The result of this joint movement of presidential and House election results was that the general association between the two was preserved. In simple terms, the entire distribution of Democratic presidential and House results shifted upward. Presidential results shifted up more than House results, but the general pattern was that the party's success increased across the board from 1928 to 1932 (Table 6.4), resulting in a stable correlation of results.[14] The party improved its vote percentages across the board and added states and seats in the North to its southern base.

Responding to Electoral Change

Despite the enormous gains the Democratic Party made in 1930 and 1932, its situation was by no means safe, particularly in the North. The vote of the presidential and congressional wings of the party increased together, but both wings were not in a strong situation in the North. Although Democrats won 134 seats in the North in 1932, or 59.3 percent of the seats within the region, many of these victors had only modest margins of victory. The same was true for Franklin Roosevelt. Table 6.5 indicates the distribution of the Democratic vote for House winners and the president in 1932 in the North and outside the

---

[14] Put in another way, the scatter-plot of Democratic presidential and House results shifted more toward the upper-right-hand corner of a joint plot. The slope of regressing House results on presidential percentages changed very little, going from 1.19 to 1.12. The relationship remained stable, but with more cases at higher levels for Democrats.

TABLE 6.5. *Democratic Vote for House Winners and Presidential Vote by Areas of Nation, 1932*

	N		Democratic Percentage				
		<40	40–44	45–49	50–54	55–59	60+
House Winners							
Non-North	179	0	.6	1.7	9.5	15.1	73.2
North	134	.8	1.5	9.7	36.6	18.7	32.8
President							
Non-North	202	0	0	1.5	5.5	22.8	70.3
North	223	5.4	13.0	14.4	21.5	19.7	26.0

Note: For House winners the N and percentages are for those who won. For the presidential vote, all districts are considered because the overall distribution of success across districts is relevant. Data are not available for the presidential vote for some districts.

North. Outside the North most Democratic House winners and Roosevelt won districts with substantial percentages. Only 11.8 percent of Democratic House winners outside the North received less than 55 percent of the vote. Roosevelt lost only three House districts outside the North.

In the North the party's situation was very different. Among Democratic House winners in the North, 48.6 percent won with less than 55 percent of the vote. Roosevelt received less than 55 percent in 54.3 percent of districts. Although the vote for both House and presidential Democratic candidates had moved together from 1928 to 1932, both wings of the party were not in secure positions in the North after the 1932 elections.

Democrats benefited in 1930 and 1932 from the electorate's rejection of Republicans. Both parties had to interpret the election results and decide what to do in response to the shift to electorate support. Roosevelt had not run on a clear platform because the major issue during the election was the Republican inability to do anything about the Great Depression.[15] Although in retrospect it is common to think of the 1932 shift as creating an enduring shift among voters to the Democrats, a critical realignment, the attachment to Democrats was by no means secure in 1933. What prevailed after 1932 depended on how each party responded to the existing situation.

The changes within the Democratic Party in the House in the elections of 1930 and after created pressures for the party to consider its future direction. From 1920 through 1926, Democrats averaged 176 seats and remained in the minority. On average 74 percent of their seats came from outside the North, whereas 53 percent of all House seats were in the North. The 1930 elections brought them to 216 seats, and the 1932 elections expanded their majority

[15] Sundquist, *Dynamics of the Party System,* 208–210.

TABLE 6.6. *Democratic Presidential Fortunes by Region, 1932*

	North	South	Other
Electoral College Votes			
Percent Total EC votes in:	50.8	23.7	25.4
Percent of EC votes won in:	78.1	100	100
Percent of EC votes from:	44.7	26.7	28.6
Popular Vote			
Percent popular vote won in:	51.9	80.9	64.1
States lost / total	6 / 18	0	0
States won by <10 points	4	0	1

to 313. This majority was created by winning 134 seats within the North, or 58 percent of the seats in that region. Most of these new members did not win with large margins. This new contingent presented the party with a simple dilemma: If it wanted to stay in the majority, the party had to do something to help these new members survive. The northern members came from a region less opposed to government action to respond to the Great Depression. Much as in the mid-1910s, the party was faced with the situation with what to do to retain a base it had been struggling to attract. The new base wanted policies not embraced by the older base.

Franklin Roosevelt was in a similar situation. Despite his remarkable Electoral College vote totals (472–59), his situation in the North was not strong. As Table 6.6 indicates, he won all the southern and western states, generally by large margins. The challenge for reelection involved the North. He lost 6 of the 18 states and won 4 by less than 10 points. As noted earlier, Roosevelt received less than 55 percent in 54.3 percent of House districts. Given that Democrats had traditionally not done well in the North, Roosevelt was in the same situation as his House party in having to do something to appeal to a base that was not inclined to vote Democrat.

Roosevelt and his congressional party faced a general problem and a specific one. They had to persuade the American public that government could respond and change economic conditions. They also faced the specific problem of creating a connection with northern urban voters that government was relevant to them. For many urban residents, government had never seemed very relevant as an institution that could affect their lives.[16] The challenge facing the congressional Democrats was to respond to the newfound electoral support in urban areas and create an enduring bond to the Democratic Party.[17]

---

[16] Lizabeth Cohen, *Making a New Deal: Industrial Workers in Chicago, 1919–1939* (New York: Cambridge University Press, 1990); and Plotke, *Building a Democratic Political Order*.

[17] Plotke, *Building a Democratic Political Order*; Alan Ware, *The Democratic Party Heads North*, 164, 173; M. Stephen Weatherford, "After the Critical Election: Presidential Leadership, Competition and the Consolidation of the New Deal Realignment," *British Journal of Political*

The continuation of support for Democrats in many northern districts in 1934 and 1936 was by no means certain.

As 1933 and 1934 evolved, Roosevelt was made acutely aware that his reelection prospects in some northern state depended on his policy responses. During 1934 the Progressive contingent from the Midwest states visited Roosevelt and indicated that they might run a third-party candidate against him if he did not support some of their social programs.[18] Both Roosevelt and his congressional party recognized the danger in that and enacted numerous programs responding to the Progressives' concerns – Social Security, the Works Project Administration, laws making it easier for unions to form, and nationally funded programs for unemployment compensation and Aid for Dependent Children.[19] Roosevelt also devoted considerable attention to trying to create a national party organization.[20]

The ability to retain support in areas Democrats had previously not won was helped by the decisions of Republicans. Within the party the dominant view of the proper role of government was that the national government should play only a very limited role.[21] Republicans had long held the Northeast, and as 1935 and 1936 evolved the party was sure it saw signs that it would regain that region and more.[22] Republicans generally chose to oppose Roosevelt's plans, creating a clear contrast between the two parties.[23]

The result of all these decisions and policy enactments was that Democrats retained their support in northern districts after the 1932 shift. The party suffered losses in 1938 and 1940 because of a recession in the late 1930s, but the electoral base of the party had changed, and the change persisted across the decade of the 1930s. Figures 6.4 and 6.5 indicate just how much change had occurred. Both Roosevelt and House Democrats were winning a substantial number of districts in the North. The northern delegation was now a major

---

Science, Vol. 32, No. 2 (April 2002), 221–257; and Rita Werner Gordon, "The Change in the Political Alignment of Chicago's Negroes during the New Deal," *The Journal of American History*, Vol. 56, No. 3 (December 1969), 584–603

[18] James, *Presidential Politics and the State*, 201–204.

[19] Barbara Sinclair, "Party Realignment and the Transformation of the Political Agenda: The House of Representatives, 1925–1938," *American Political Science Review*, Vol. 71, No. 3 (September 1977), 940–953; and Barbara Deckard Sinclair, *Congressional Realignment 1925–1978* (Austin: University of Texas Press, 1982).

[20] Sean J. Savage, *Roosevelt: The Party Leader, 1932–1945* (Lexington: University of Kentucky Press, 1991), 17–47 and 80–102; and Sidney M. Milkis, *The President and the Parties: The Transformation of the American Party System since the New Deal* (New York: Oxford University Press, 1993), 62–74.

[21] Sundquist, *Dynamics of the Party System*, 199–214.

[22] Clyde P. Weed, "What Happened to the Republicans in the 1930s: Minority Party Dynamics during Political Realignment," *Polity*, Vol. 22, No. 1 (Autumn 1989), 5–23; Clyde P. Weed, *The Nemesis of Reform: The Republican Party during the New Deal* (New York: Columbia University Press, 1994).

[23] Reiter and Stonecash, *Counter Realignment*, 44–54.

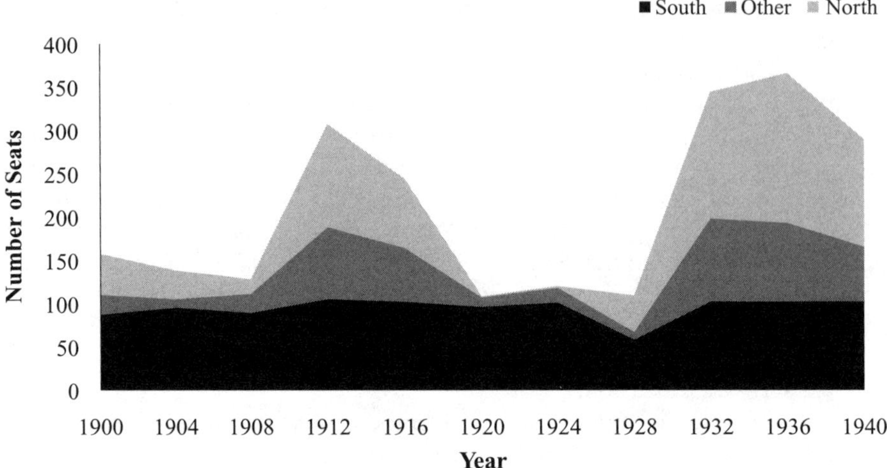

FIGURE 6.4. House Districts Won by Democratic Presidential Candidates, by Region, 1900–1940

part of the party in both presidential and House voting. Indeed, assuming the South could be retained, the northern seats were the difference between majority and minority party status. The crucial matter for the party was that its ability to retain a national majority was now clearly dependent on retaining a substantial number of northern districts.

As these political changes developed, there were no increases in the percentage of districts with split-outcomes or in the differences between presidential and House vote percentages. Figure 6.6 indicates, along with the correlation between results, how these indicators varied over time. The stability of results

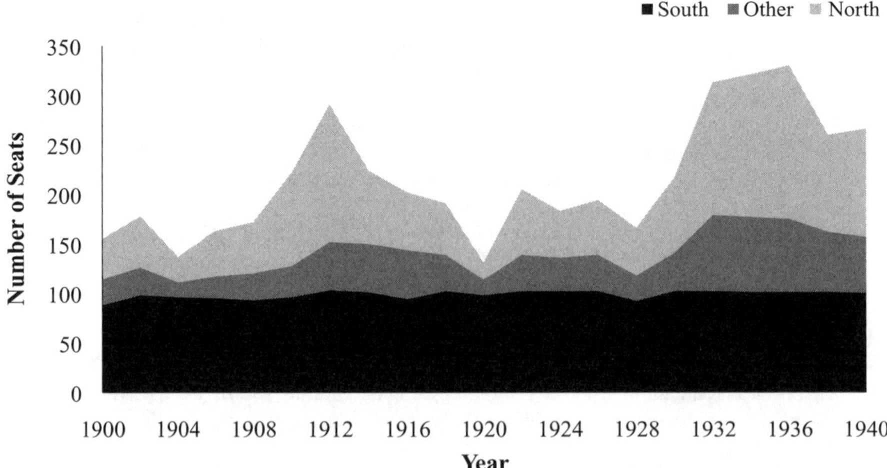

FIGURE 6.5. Democratic House Seats Won, by Region, 1900–1940

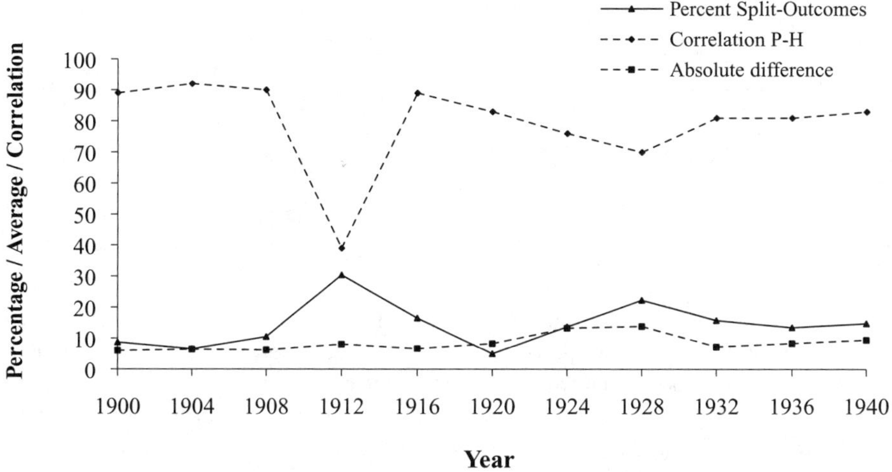

FIGURE 6.6. Presidential-House Election Results, 1900–1940, all Districts

was because presidential and House results largely moved together. The electorate rejected Republicans in 1932, carrying Franklin Roosevelt and Democratic House candidates to victory. The presidential and congressional wings largely worked together during the 1930s – with exceptions to be discussed shortly – and both wings benefited in terms of votes.

Although the votes moved together, and separating the effects of the presidential effect from party voting is difficult, the presidential vote appears to have played a significant role, particularly in the North. Southern House Democrats

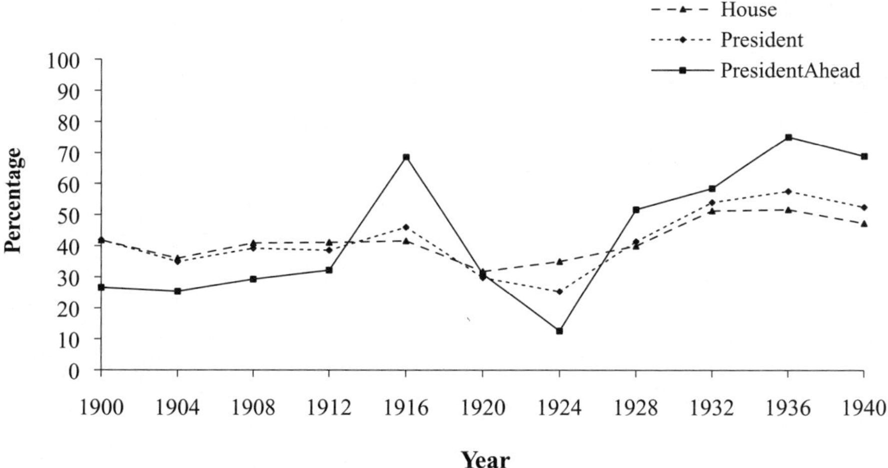

FIGURE 6.7. Northern Democratic Presidential and House Election Results, and the Percent of Districts the Presidential Vote Lead the House, 1900–1940

TABLE 6.7. *State-Level Democratic Presidential and House Results over Time*

1900 %	N	Presidential Results			House Results		
		1900	1940	Change	1900	1940	Change
0–44	21	38.8	51.6	12.8	39.8	44.1	4.3
45–49	6	46.7	51.2	4.5	47.6	50.4	2.8
50–54	5	51.9	61.1	9.2	52.7	62.3	9.6
55+	13	67.5	77.0	9.5	70.8	82.4	11.6

were so firmly ensconced that they usually did much better than their presidential candidates. The North was the problem for Democrats. As Figure 6.7 indicates, from 1900 to 1928 both Democratic presidential and House percentages were well below 50. From 1900 to 1924 Democratic presidential candidates led House candidates in only about 30 percent or less of the districts. Then in 1928 Al Smith led in more than 50 percent of districts, and in 1932 and after Roosevelt consistently led in a large majority of districts. His vote percentages were above (by modest amounts) the average House vote, and may have pulled House votes higher than House candidates alone might otherwise have achieved. Presidents have more visibility, and Roosevelt played a greater role in defining the New Deal; surely he was able to raise the vote in many districts.

The net effect of all these electoral changes was that there was a general increase in Democratic voting across the nation from 1900 to 1940. Those changes are shown in Table 6.7. The relative variations of Democratic support across states remained largely the same, but relative to 1900 levels of support within states, Democratic support was consistently higher by 1940. The result of these roughly joint changes was that the correlation between the two election results remained the same. The party added areas without losing any areas. There were tensions, to be discussed shortly, which eventually cost them the old base, but the major change of the 1930s was an expanded Democratic base.

7

Republican and Democratic Pursuits of New Constituencies

The 1930s changed the political landscape, bringing the Democratic Party majority status and a close alignment of presidential and House electoral bases. It also brought tensions within each party that would fester for many years. The within-party debates and assessments of what direction the Democratic Party should pursue were lengthy. The decision by factions within each party to seek different policies eventually led to winning new constituencies, with presidential candidates leading the way. These pursuits were fundamental in disconnecting the relationship between presidential and House results. The resulting disruption of this relationship was interpreted by many as the emergence of candidate-centered campaigns and politics by House members, but the separation of presidential and House results was really only a reflection of the lag of House results.

The concerns in this chapter are the tensions and disagreements within each party and how they prompted the changes that became evident in the 1960s and 1970s. Perhaps the most important matter leading up to the 1960s was that each party was feeling pressures to deal with the issue of whether to seek to change its electoral base. Although the Democratic New Deal coalition is often seen as dominating American politics for more than 30 years, there were tensions within the party that eventually resulted in change. For Republicans the need to consider change was more obvious: The party was largely in the minority, and had to consider how to get out of that status.

The Democratic Party

During the 1930s the Democratic Party expanded its base, winning more seats in the North. In subsequent years the party retained that added base, and those additional seats became the basis for a sustained majority in the House. As Figure 7.1 indicates, the Democrats held that majority from 1932 through

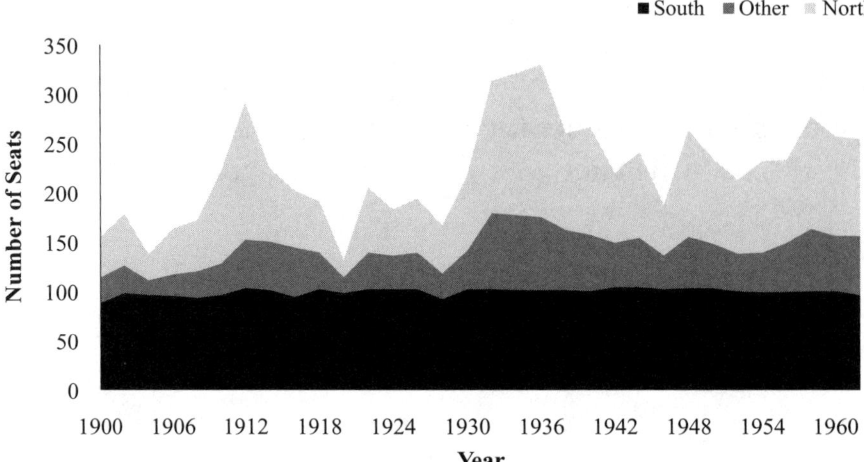

FIGURE 7.1. Democratic House Seats Won, by Region, 1900–1962

1962 except for 1946 and 1952. In each case the loss of northern seats was the reason they lost the majority. The party's ability to retain the majority remained dependent on success in the North. But that reliance created tensions that eventually resulted in changes that separated presidential and House results.

The expansion of a party's base can come with a cost if the newer base differs in preferences from the older base, and that was the case with Democrats. The northern base was more liberal than the southern delegation, and its members were pushing an agenda different from what the South wanted. The southern delegation was presented with a dilemma: The retention of northern seats kept the party in the majority, but southern members did not want to go along with northern preferences. The response of southern members was to defect from the agenda being pushed by the northern wing. The southern delegation remained in the Democratic Party because becoming Republican was still unthinkable, but they were unwilling to go along with parts of the agenda of the northern wing. In particular, the southern wing was reluctant to support legislation expanding welfare benefits,[1] making lynching a federal crime, or supporting unions.[2]

The conflict between the southern and other conservatives and the rest of the party was an abrupt emergence of a large number of moderates in the House in the 1930s.[3] As Figure 7.2 indicates, there were few moderates in

[1] Martha Derthick, *The Influence of Federal Grants* (Cambridge, MA: Harvard University Press, 1970); and Suzanne Mettler, *Dividing Citizens: Gender and Federalism in New Deal Public Policy* (Ithaca, NY: Cornell University Press, 1998).

[2] Turner, *Party and Constituency.*

[3] Jon R. Bond, Richard Fleisher, and Jeffrey M. Stonecash, "The Rise and Decline of Moderates in the House, 1876–2004." Presented at the Conference on Going to Extremes: The Fate of

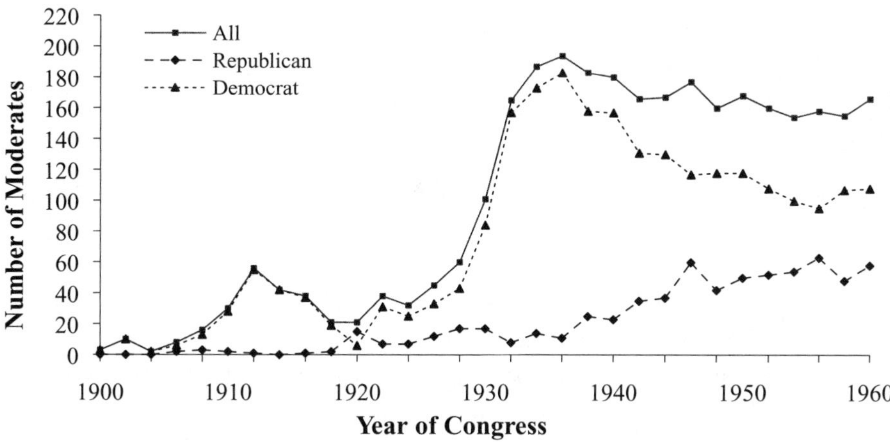

FIGURE 7.2. Moderates in the House, 1900–1960

the early 1900s. Following the 1930 and 1932 elections the number increased dramatically, with almost all of the new moderates coming from within the Democratic Party. The expansion of the Democratic Party in the 1930s created tensions between the regional wings.[4]

The relative source of the moderates changed over time and indicates the fissure within the party that became so prominent by the 1960s. In the early 1900s the northern wing of the party was in a distinct minority, and they were defecting from the rest of the party's agenda. As Figure 7.3 indicates, the first rise of moderates within the Democratic Party was among those in the North who came into office in the elections of 1912–1916. Then the party lost many of these northern seats during the 1920s, and there were fewer to dissent.

The election of 1930 changed the political source of moderates within the party. The party was struggling with what direction to take, and there was

the Political Center in American Politics, Rockefeller Center for Public Policy and the Social Sciences, Dartmouth College, June 19–21, 2008; and Jon R. Bond, Richard Fleisher, and Jeffrey M. Stonecash, "The Rise and Fall of Moderates in Congress." Presented at the Conference on Bicameralism, Duke University March 26–29, 2009. Typically, the term "moderate" refers to a member whose ideological voting record falls between the bases of each political party. In this case a moderate is defined as a Member with a DW-NOMINATE score between .2 and −.2, plus those who are on the other side of the majority of their party (Republicans below −.2 and Democrats above .2). The scores are taken from Keith Poole's Web page at: http://voteview.com/. These scores might also be conceived as reflections of party loyalty or unity, because there is a high correlation between the percentage of times a member votes with the majority of the party and that individual's DW-NOMINATE score.

[4] In contemporary theoretical terms, this was a case in which internal diversity increased and the condition of internal homogeneity declined, making it harder for the party to control the agenda and vote together. Instead, agreement within the conservative coalition increased. See Rohde, *Parties and Leaders in the Postreform House;* and Rohde and Aldrich, "Consequences of Electoral and Institutional Change."

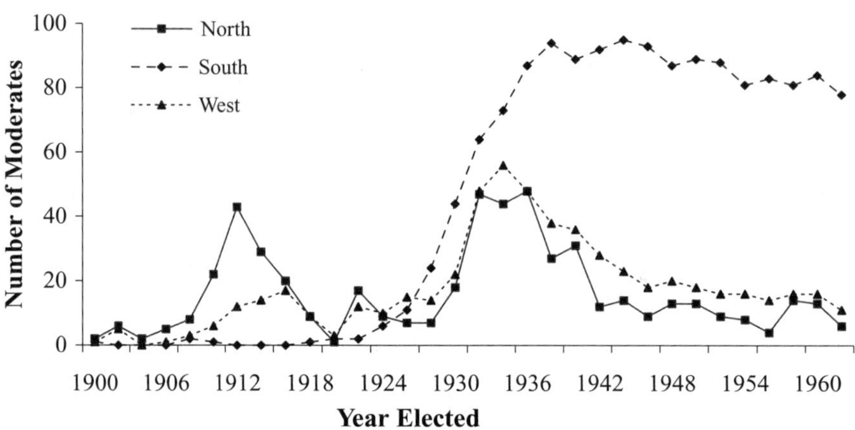

FIGURE 7.3. Moderates in the Democratic Party, 1900–1962

uncertainty about how liberal their agenda should be. As the Democratic Party moved in a more liberal direction and became influenced more by the non-southern components, the southern wing became the primary source of moderates.[5]

However, they were moderates only in the sense that they were unwilling to go along with the remainder of the party. They were not moderates because they were elected in districts where their presidential candidate received weak-to-modest support. Moderates are often seen in contemporary politics as House members trying to compile a middle-of-the-road record to cope with a district that contains a significant base of support for the opposing party, as indicated by the presidential vote. In the 1930s and 1940s most moderates within the Democratic Party came from districts in which Democratic presidential candidates won more than 60 percent of the vote, as Figure 7.4 indicates. These were primarily in southern districts where their presidential candidate did well, but they disliked where the party was going. They became the base within the party for the Conservative Coalition that dominated the Congress for the next several decades.[6] As the base of the party evolved in later decades, the alignment of moderates with presidential voting patterns came to fit the pattern

---

[5] There was also a corresponding shift in party unity scores during this time. In the early 1900s southern Democrats had the highest average party unity scores – percentage of times they voted with the party. By the late 1930s they had the lowest averages.

[6] There might have been realignment, but it did not occur. The alternative was the cross-party Conservative Coalition. James T. Patterson, "The Failure of Party Realignment in the South, 1937–1939," *Journal of Politics*, Vol. 27, No. 3 (August 1965), 602–617; James T. Patterson, *Congressional Conservatism and the New Deal: The Growth of the Conservative Coalition in Congress, 1933–1939* (Lexington: University of Kentucky Press, 1967); and Mack C. Shelley II, *The Permanent Majority: The Conservative Coalition in the United States Congress* (Tuscaloosa: University of Alabama Press, 1983).

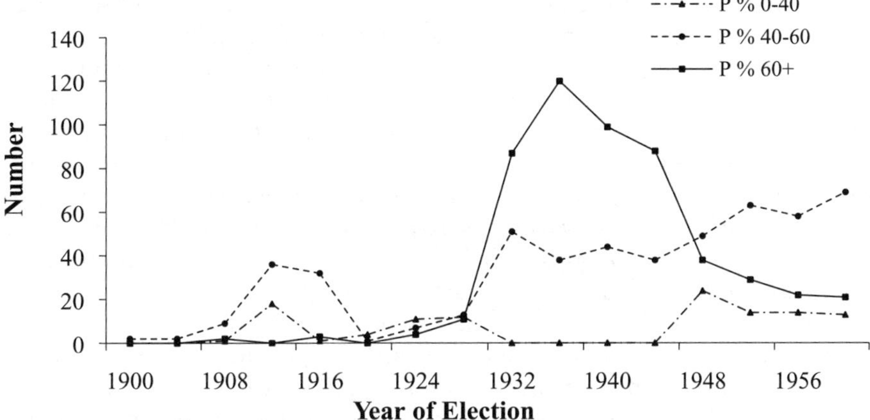

FIGURE 7.4. Number of Moderates by Democratic Presidential Vote, 1900–1960

we generally expect.[7] In 1948 and after, most moderates were from districts where the partisan vote for the president of the opposing party is more evenly divided.

The uneasy relationship between the southern wing of the party and the non-southern wing persisted from the 1930s through much of the 1950s. The South needed the North to retain a majority. The 1946 and 1952 elections confirmed this. In those years the party suffered losses in the North and lost the majority. This uneasy coalition was soon to be disrupted by the rise of liberalism and the civil rights movement within the Democratic Party. The northern Democratic base was moving to be more liberal on civil rights, creating a conflict with the southern wing and with northern Republicans.[8] The result was erosion of Democratic strength in the South. At the same time there was a rise of the conservative movement in the Republican Party. Together these changes disrupted the relationship between presidential and House results.

The rise of liberalism and the civil rights movement had a major impact on the Democratic Party. Together these two created an altered sense of the role government could and should play in society. The ideas of liberalism had been evolving, and during the 1950s and the early 1960s there were pronounced changes.[9] There was an increasing sense that individuals were not

---

[7] Robert S. Erikson and Gerald C. Wright, "Voters, Candidates, and Issues in Congressional Elections," in Lawrence C. Dodd and Bruce I Oppenheimer, Editors, *Congress Reconsidered*, Ninth Edition (Washington, DC: CQ Press, 2009), 86–87.

[8] Eric Shickler, "New Deal Liberalism and Racial Liberalism in the Mass Public, 1937–1952." Presented at the 2010 American Political Science Association Meetings, Washington, DC, September 2010.

[9] Mark D. Brewer and Jeffrey M. Stonecash, "Individual vs. Societal Responsibility: The Root of Partisan and Ideological Conflict." Presented at the 2012 Southern Political Science Association Meetings, New Orleans, January.

completely in control of their destiny. Studies from psychology and sociology were increasingly stressing that we are affected by our family and immediate context, and that these affected our sense of efficacy and our opportunities.[10] There was greater awareness of poverty and how it limited the opportunities of individuals and their subsequent success in life.[11] If individuals were not entirely responsible for their fate, and social conditions played a role in this, then many thought it appropriate that government play a role in trying to offset these conditions with various programs. This logic provided a basis for enacting more social programs to help individuals who had less opportunity than others. During the 1950s and early 1960s the percentage of the public that defined itself as liberal steadily increased.[12]

At the same time that the logic of liberalism was being accepted by more people, the civil rights movement was becoming more active. There were more and more marches in the South that had the intent of presenting America with a blunt discrepancy between its ideals and the reality of life that most blacks faced.[13] The combination of increasing support for liberal views and the pressure from the civil rights movement was even more support for a liberal agenda.

The vehicle for expressing these concerns was increasingly the northern wing of the Democratic Party. Northern state Democratic parties were putting much more emphasis on civil rights concerns.[14] This was in turn affecting the positions that House members were taking in Congress.[15] By the mid-1940s non-southern Democrats in the House of Representatives were making efforts to get civil rights legislation considered by signing discharge petitions and making speeches on the floor.[16] In 1948 President Harry Truman had announced several executive orders to eliminate racial segregation in the federal agencies.[17] The 1948 national convention adopted a plank on this issue more liberal than ever before. The national Democratic Party platforms in the 1950s

[10] Petigny, *The Permissive Society.*

[11] As an example, Michael Harrington, *The Other America* (New York: Macmillan, 1960).

[12] James A. Stimson, *Tides of Consent: How Public Opinion Shapes American Politics* (New York: Cambridge University Press, 2005); and Christopher Ellis and James A. Stimson, "On Symbolic Conservatism in America." Presented at the 2007 Annual Meetings of the American Political Science Association, Chicago, August–September.

[13] Gene Roberts and Hank Klibanoff, *The Race Beat: The Press, the Civil Rights Struggle, and the Awakening of a Nation* (New York: Vintage, 2006).

[14] Brian D. Feinstein and Eric Schickler, "Platforms and Partners: The Civil Rights Realignment Reconsidered," *Studies in American Political Development*, Vol. 22 (Spring 2008), 115–116.

[15] Eric Schickler, Kathryn Pearson, and Brian Feinstein, "Congressional Parties and Civil Rights Politics from 1933 to 1972," *Journal of Politics*, Vol. 72, No. 3 (July 2010), 672–689.

[16] Schickler, Pearson, and Feinstein, "Congressional Parties and Civil Rights Politics from 1933 to 1972."

[17] Michael Gardner, *Harry Truman and Civil Rights: Moral Courage and Political Risks* (Carbondale: Southern Illinois University Press, 2003).

and 1960s gave much more expression to concerns about poverty and civil rights.[18]

The tensions between the northern and southern wings were becoming more evident. That conflict increased when Democrats won many seats in liberal districts in 1958 and held them in subsequent elections. These new members and other liberals wanted a more liberal agenda, and following the 1958 election they formed the Democratic Study Group in the House to push for more liberal legislation.[19] The split between the southern wing and the rest of the party shown in Figure 7.3 had endured for some time and was creating sustained conflicts.

The Presidential Wing: As these ideas and conflicts within the Democratic congressional party played out, political change was also affecting the calculations of presidential candidates. In many ways Democrats seemed to be in a dominant situation in presidential contests. From 1932 through 1960, Democrats won six of eight presidential elections. That dominance in winning, however, concealed an eroding overall situation for Democratic presidential candidates. The New Deal electoral base was not as stable as many presumed, and changes were affecting electoral strategies. The party was losing ground in the South and not gaining ground in the North.

The issue of how much to accommodate the South had been handled delicately by Franklin Roosevelt. He had utilized his strong electoral situation in 1936 to get Democrats to repeal the requirement that any candidate had to have two-thirds of the delegates to win the nomination. That rule had given the South, if it voted together, the means to prevent the nomination of a candidate who would threaten segregation in the South. Despite this reduction of Southern influence over the nomination, Roosevelt was careful about how much he responded to issues involving race.[20] As noted before, a Democratic candidate had to win some non-Southern states to win the presidency. The essential questions were whether the South could be retained, and whether trying to retain it would limit the gains the party could make elsewhere.

The demise of southern support began in 1947 when President Truman, troubled by incidents of violence toward blacks in the South, expressed concern about civil rights.[21] His advisors presumed that the South was so consistently supportive that the party would not lose many votes. In 1948 he promised to send civil rights legislation to Congress, but then vacillated as the southern opposition was stronger than expected. After intense maneuvering at the Democratic convention between the conservative southern and liberal urban

[18] John Gerring, *Party Ideologies in America, 1828–1996* (New York: Cambridge University Press, 1998), 232–256.
[19] Stevens, Miller, and Mann, "Mobilization of Liberal Strength in the House, 1955–1970."
[20] Kevin J. McMahon, *Reconsidering Roosevelt on Race: How the Presidency Paved the Road to Brown* (Chicago: University of Chicago Press, 2003).
[21] Gardner, *Harry Truman and Civil Rights.*

northern wings, a statement of mild support for civil rights was included in the 1948 party platform.[22] The platform prompted Democratic Senator Strom Thurmond of South Carolina to run for the presidency in 1948 on a third-party line, winning four states and taking large chunks of votes away from Truman in the South. Support for Democratic candidates never returned to pre-1948 levels, and by the early 1960s it was clear that the party could no longer count on that region. In 1952 Democratic presidential candidate, Adlai Stevenson, lost four southern states (and another four were close), and in 1956 he lost six (and another one was close).

The problem for Democrat presidential candidates was whether to pursue and rely on the South or seek to move beyond it. On one hand the South had been Democratic for a century, and abandoning a reliable base did not seem like a way to win the presidency. On the other hand the conflicts in the South were becoming more pronounced, and any move regarding the South could yield a loss. Embracing the South had its disadvantages.[23] Southern politicians were becoming increasingly intransigent in opposing integration, with most Southern Democratic senators signing a "Southern Manifesto" in 1956 opposing desegregation. The party had tried moderation about civil rights in the 1956 presidential election. The civil rights movement was accelerating, and as blacks pushed for rights, southern whites were proving so resistant that they might desert a Democratic presidential candidate.[24]

Further, others were arguing that seeking to accommodate the South and not push for black rights was not generating strong support in the South, while it was costing the party votes in the North among blacks and liberals.[25] The argument put forth by many was that the party had to increase its support outside the South.[26] The problem was that the Democratic vote percentages in the North and West were not growing. As Figure 7.5 indicates, the party experienced higher percentages in 1932–1940 in the North and West, but by 1952 and 1956, its percentages in those regions were not very different than those that prevailed in the 1910s. The 1960 election produced a modest increase, but those results also confirmed that the party had lost its southern advantage, and it had none outside the South. It was hovering around 50 percent in all three regions of the nation.

---

[22] Sitkoff, "Harry Truman and the Election of 1948."

[23] William E. Leuchtenburg, *The White House Looks South* (Baton Rouge: Louisiana State University Press, 2005).

[24] Richard M. Valelly, *The Two Reconstructions: The Struggle for Black Enfranchisement* (Chicago: University of Chicago Press, 2004), 184–186.

[25] Klinkner, *The Losing Parties*, 33–35. For a valuable and detailed review of the dilemma facing Democratic presidential candidates regarding race during the 1950s and how they sought to cope with the opposing wings of the party, see Gary W. Reichard, "Democrats, Civil Rights, and Electoral Strategies in the 1950s," *Congress and the Presidency*, Vol. 13, No. 1 (Spring 1986), 59–81.

[26] Ware, *The Democratic Party Heads North*, 1–15 and 274.

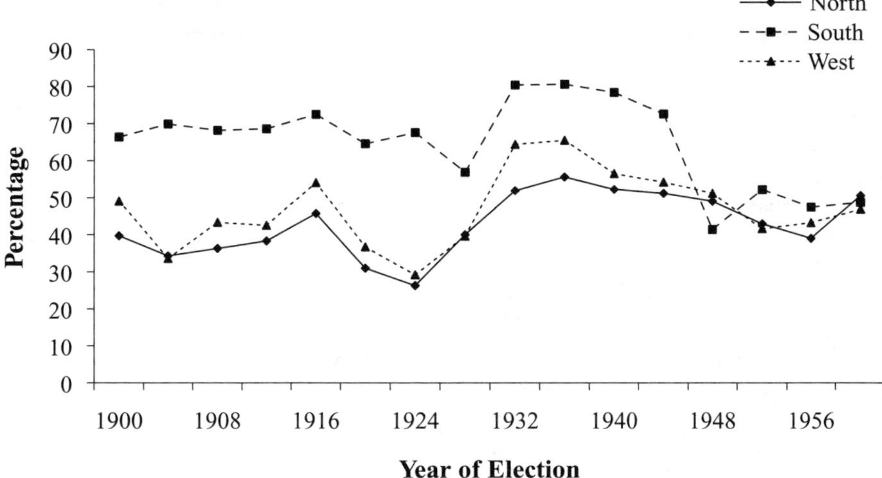

FIGURE 7.5. Average State Democratic Presidential Percentages, by Region, 1900–1960

Table 7.1 presents more detail on the situation of Democratic presidential candidates. Given the winner-take-all rule for awarding Electoral College votes within states, presidential candidates must assess their margins of victory state by state and consider where their prospects are best. The situation in the South was clearly precarious. The Solid South was a thing of the past: The party was winning only about half of the states in the region. Most disconcerting was the average vote percentage received from 1948 to 1960. The party was struggling to average 50 percent.

The situation in the North was also of concern. As of 1960, 48.6 percent of Electoral College votes were still in the North. Beginning in 1932, gaining votes outside the South had been the clue to creating a majority, and it was now even more important because of the erosion of support within the South. In the elections of 1948–1956 Democratic presidential candidates averaged between 39–49 percent of the vote in the North. Even in 1960 when John Kennedy won 76.2 percent of the Electoral College votes within the region, he averaged only 50.5 percent of the popular vote. The situation in the West was also troubling. After averaging 51.1 percent in 1948, Democratic presidential candidates had averaged less than 50 percent in subsequent years. The party had no region of great strength, a crucial weakness given the rules of the Electoral College.

At the same time, the prospects for gains in northern urban areas were uncertain. The party had been vacillating about civil rights, creating an unclear image to northern blacks and liberals. Then in 1957 President Eisenhower, however reluctantly, sent troops into Little Rock, Arkansas, to enforce integration orders, creating the impression that Republicans might be more supportive

TABLE 7.1. *The Democratic Presidential Electoral College Situation, 1948–1960*

	Year			
	1948	1952	1956	1960
North (18 states)				
Total electoral votes	265	261	261	261
% EC Democrats won	39.2	3.1	0	76.2
Number of states won	7	1	0	12
Number lost by < 10 %	9	5	2	3
Average popular vote %	49.0	42.9	39.0	50.5
South (11 states)				
Total electoral votes	129	130	130	130
% EC Democrats won	70.5	56.2	40.8	66.9
Number of states won	7	7	5	7
Number lost by < 10 %	0	2	2	4
Average popular vote %	41.3	53.4	48.7	49.8
West (no. of states)	19	19	19	21
Total electoral votes	137	140	140	146
% EC Democrats won	79.6	7.9	17.1	21.2
Number of states won	14	2	3	5
Number lost by < 10 %	5	3	1	9
Average popular vote %	51.1	40.9	42.5	46.2
D % EC votes from South	29.9	79.3	68.8	27.4
Party winning	D	R	R	D

of civil rights than Democrats.[27] Eisenhower had gained votes among blacks in 1956, creating more anxiety among Democrats.[28]

The history of John F. Kennedy illustrates the uncertainty and delicate balancing act a Democratic president faced.[29] During the 1950s he struggled with whether to cater to southern conservatism or appeal to the much more liberal sentiments of Massachusetts. As he pursued the presidency in the years prior to 1960, he began with the realization that the South had been Democratic but was slipping away. He had done well in Massachusetts, but the overall region still had a history of being heavily Republican. He chose Lyndon Johnson as his vice president to try to win Texas and some southern states. He struggled with how much to appear concerned with civil rights. A major concern during October 1960 was whether Kennedy should call Coretta Scott King after Martin Luther King, Jr., was arrested and jailed following a civil rights protest.[30] Some

[27] Reichard, "Democrats, Civil Rights, and Electoral Strategies in the 1950s," 65–69.

[28] Klinkner, *The Losing Parties*, 34.

[29] For an overview of his efforts to balance conflicting policy sentiments in the South and North, see Mark Stern, *Calculating Visions: Kennedy, Johnson, and Civil Rights* (New Brunswick, NJ: Rutgers University Press, 1992).

[30] Sean J. Savage, *JFK, LBJ, and the Democratic Party* (Albany: SUNY Press, 2004), 83–84.

thought he could win southern blacks and retain enough whites to win some states. Others thought he could win enough labor and black votes in northern states to win those states. His campaign was a sustained balancing act between the older Democratic base and the possibilities of doing better in the North.

The postmortems indicated the precariousness of a Democratic presidential candidate. Kennedy was able to win 27 of the 39 largest cities in 1960,[31] but his average margin of victory over Richard Nixon in northern states was only 1.3 percentage points. The party's success in the North was fragile, and after 1960 there was uncertainty about the prospects of relying on success in urban areas as a means of winning these states.[32] Despite all the gains of the 1930s the party was still not in good shape in the North after the 1960 elections.

The balancing act of trying to please southern and northern constituencies continued during the three years Kennedy was president. He had campaigned on a liberal platform, and poll results indicated that in northern states he had done well among Catholics, Jews, blacks, and union members. The prospects of appealing to urban areas had increased in recent decades because of a steady stream of blacks migrating from the South in search of northern urban jobs.[33] Blacks were gradually becoming a greater presence in northern cities, and were of sufficient size to provide the margin to secure a majority in many states.[34] Yet Congress was still dominated by the Conservative Coalition.[35] If Kennedy was to get any legislation through the Congress to make an appeal to voters in the northern urban areas, he had to find a way to maneuver around this coalition.

The pressures to deal with civil rights were steadily escalating. Activists were seeking to make the issue prominent. Democratic state party platforms outside the South were becoming much more supportive of civil rights policies than were Republicans.[36] By the mid-1940s non-southern Democrats in the House of Representatives were making efforts to get civil rights legislation considered by signing discharge petitions and making speeches on the floor.[37] The difficulty was that strong stands on civil rights would likely cost any Democratic candidate all southern states. However, because the South was sliding away from the party, it might be that a presidential candidate had to make such an appeal. The national party was continuing to try to compromise between the southern and non-southern wings on this issue.

[31] Degler, "American Political Parties and the Rise of the City," 58.
[32] Ware, *The Democratic Party Heads North*, 43.
[33] Lemann, *The Promised Land*; Savage, *JFK, LBJ, and the Democratic Party*, 101.
[34] Oscar Glantz, "The Negro Voter in Northern Industrial Cities," *Western Political Quarterly*, Vol. 13, No. 4 (December 1960), 999–1010.
[35] Savage, *JFK, LBJ, and the Democratic Party*, 87–89.
[36] Feinstein and Schickler, "Platforms and Partners."
[37] Schickler, Pearson, and Feinstein, "Congressional Parties and Civil Rights Politics from 1933 to 1972."

In the years 1961–1963 the pressures to deal with civil rights issues steadily grew.[38] Marches protesting the treatment of blacks in the South were increasing, and were being met with violent resistance. Nightly television shows presented America with a view of southern intransigence that was deeply troubling to many Americans. Blacks were seeking to enroll in southern universities and being met with strong official resistance and informal threats to their safety. In August 1963, Martin Luther King gave his "I Have a Dream" speech in Washington, increasing pressure for legislative action. The relentless issue for a Democratic president planning on running for reelection was how to handle the South at a time when public sentiment was building to give blacks more rights. The electoral base of the Democratic Party was precarious.[39]

Then in November 1963 President Kennedy was assassinated, and Lyndon Johnson assumed the presidency and had to decide what direction he should take. He faced the uncertainty about retaining the South and about how much support he could win outside it.[40] He quickly moved to support a strong civil rights bill and the other liberal programs of Medicare and federal aid to local education.[41] The civil rights issue presented one of the great moral dilemmas and most visible dramas of American politics. Blacks were peacefully petitioning for those rights, northern liberals were adamantly pushing for legislation to establish those rights, and Southern Democrats in the Senate were filibustering by reading telephone books aloud on the floor of the Senate as the South sought to preserve segregation. Johnson was pushing the legislation for moral

---

[38] Taylor Branch, *Parting the Waters: America in the King Years* (New York: Simon and Schuster, 1989).

[39] The advice that was being provided to Kennedy indicates just how much uncertainty there was about the future Democratic electoral base. In a memo of November 19, 1962, Lou Harris argued that in a comparison of 1962 election results with 1960, the party had lost ground with urban and ethnic voters and had to shore up its support among those groups. Given the geographical location of the bulk of these voters, that meant a focus on the North. Harris also argued that the Southern Democratic Party was becoming more moderate, leaving a void that conservative Republicans would likely exploit. The net implication was that the focus should be on the North, and that the South was precarious. See "Memorandum to the President from Louis Harris, Subject: Analysis of the 1962 Elections, November 19, 1962," Kennedy Papers, Part I, Reel 3. This was reinforced by a memo of April 29, 1963 from Matt Reese of the Democratic National Committee that reviewed the prospects for 1964 in the Electoral College. The memo provides a list of states of concern for 1964; seven of the top states of concern were in the North. See LBJ Library, DNC Collection, Box 83. In a September 3, 1963, memo Louis Harris argued that the South was changing rapidly, and the most important change was economic and not race. His suggestion was that a focus on economic development could help the party survive in the region. See "Memorandum to the President from Louis Harris, Subject: The South in 1964," September 3, 1963. Kennedy Papers, Part I, Reel 3. I am indebted to Daniel Galvin for providing those memos to me.

[40] Richard M. Valelly, *The Two Reconstructions*, 196.

[41] Sidney M. Milkis, "Lyndon Johnson, the Great Society, and the Modern Presidency," in Sidney M. Milkis and Jerome M. Mileur, Editors, *The Great Society and the High Tide of Liberalism* (Amherst: University of Massachusetts Press, 2006), 1–49.

and practical reasons. He apparently was not only convinced that the time had come for change, but that the future of the Democratic Party was with liberals outside of the South, including blacks.[42] In May 1964 he announced his vision of a Great Society program that would enhance opportunity through numerous federal government programs. The Democratic president was clearly staking out a position of sympathy to liberal interests in an effort to attract more votes outside the South.

In the 1964 presidential campaign he ran against Barry Goldwater and won in a landslide. That brought many more liberal non-southern Democrats to the party. He was able to use that expanded majority to enact a wide range of bills that implemented his vision of programs that would provide greater opportunity.[43] By 1965 and 1966, the Democratic Party had staked out an image of being a much more liberal party than it had been in prior years. The southern wing was still very significant, but the party had made a significant and marked transition away from dominance of the party by the South.

The Republican Party's Dilemma

While Democrats were struggling with who might comprise their electoral coalition, Republicans were confronting their own internal tensions. The party faced the problem that they were seen as the minority party in the nation. The record of presidential election results since 1932 was very troubling. Of the eight presidential elections held beginning with 1932, Republicans had lost six of them. Their only success came with Dwight Eisenhower, who some saw as more of a war hero than a committed Republican. Of the 15 House elections held from 1932 to 1960 Republicans had won a majority in two elections. The limits Republicans faced were also clear in party identification responses in surveys. When asked which party they identified with, surveys from the 1950s indicated that less than 30 percent of the public identified as being Republican.[44]

The result was a developing debate about whether the party should become more conservative and provide a clear alternative to the Democratic Party. The moderate wing of the party thought the party could develop an organization and philosophy to expand its appeal and remain moderate.[45] Eisenhower made extensive and persistent efforts to build the party to attract more moderates.[46] But Eisenhower could not overcome the emerging argument within the party to move in a conservative direction. The argument for change put forth by

---

[42] William E. Leuchtenburg, *The White House Looks South* (Baton Rouge: Louisiana State University Press, 2005).

[43] Brewer and Stonecash, *Dynamics of American Political Parties*, 81–103; Mackenzie and Weisbrot, *The Liberal Hour*.

[44] Brewer and Stonecash, *Dynamics of American Political Parties*, 83.

[45] Rae, *The Decline and Fall of Liberal Republicans*.

[46] Galvin, *Presidential Party Building*, 41–69.

TABLE 7.2. *Republican Presidential Fortunes, 1932–1960*

Averages for 1932–1960	North	South	Other
Percent Total EC votes in:	48.5	24.2	27.5
Percent popular votes won in:	50.0	30.8	47.1
Percent of EC votes won in:	43.2	18.1	31.8
Percent of EC votes from:	68.1	7.4	24.5

conservatives was multifaceted, but it began with electoral math. The party had relied for decades on the more moderate North as its base, but the region was not producing strong support for the party. The region still constituted almost one-half of all Electoral College votes, but as Table 7.2 indicates, states within the region were averaging only 50 percent for Republican presidential candidates.

Further, the region was gradually moving toward being more Democratic. Since the early 1900s Republicans' success in winning seats within the North had been gradually eroding. As Figure 7.6 indicates, the percentage of seats won within the region had gradually declined from 79.0 in 1900 to 55.1 in the House. The party still derived 70 percent of its seats in the House from the North, but this was only because it won so few seats outside the North. This reliance on the North was occurring at a time when the North was very gradually declining as a percentage of the national population because of growth in the West and South. The simple problem that the party faced was that it was the minority party and did not appear to have a base in the North that could produce a majority.

These electoral frustrations were matched by philosophical frustrations among conservatives. Ever since the 1930s there had been a wing of the party

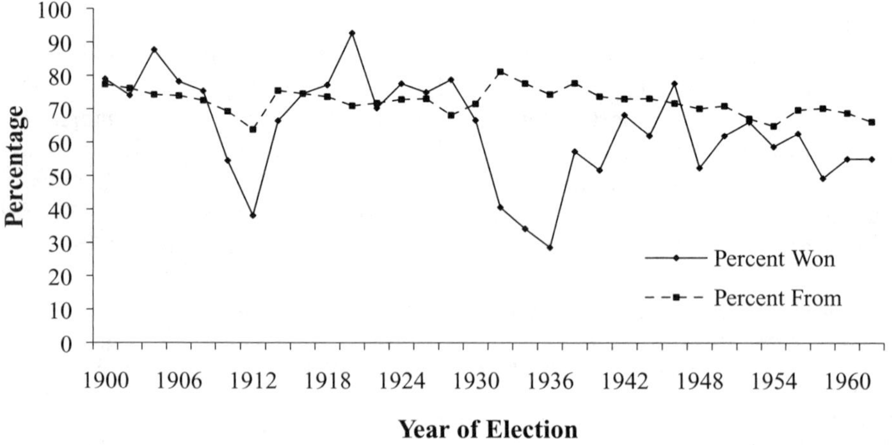

FIGURE 7.6. House Republican Success within and Reliance on the North, 1900–1962

that argued that they were not providing a clear alternative to the Democrats.[47] If Republicans accepted the programs and regulations of the New Deal, conservatives believed the party was accepting a growing government role in society. Drawing on conservative writers, they argued that free markets, capitalism, and individualism were essential to freedom and prosperity, and that the growth of government, with its regulations and redistribution, would ultimately squelch these virtues in America.[48] Others argued that the creeping liberalism of American society was leading to growing social disorder.[49]

The conservative vision was that individuals should be spurred on to do their best within a competitive capitalistic system, but individualism did not mean that people could behave as they pleased. The pursuits of individuals had to occur within traditional norms. These anxieties about the direction of America were prompting many formerly quiescent conservatives to become activists to counter the troubling liberal trends they saw. They wanted conservatives in power to support conservative values.[50]

The challenge for conservatives was where to seek voters who agreed with these views. The party had relied for decades on the North, and particularly the Northeast: areas that conservatives saw as insufficiently committed to their cause. Conservatives also thought that Republicans had suffered steady losses in the North and that the party was unlikely to regain votes and seats there.[51] Instead, they saw the future of the party as residing in the South. They saw evidence that the party could succeed in the South, whose voters would be more receptive to their appeals than Northeast voters. Democratic voters had deserted their party in 1948 when Strom Thurmond protested the party's civil rights plank.[52] In the 1952 and 1956 elections Eisenhower almost got 50 percent of the southern vote. There were indications that the South would respond positively to a Republican message of restraining the national government.

---

[47] The rise of the conservative movement in the 1950s and 1960s has received considerable attention in recent years. As examples see William A. Rusher, *The Rise of the Right* (New York: Morrow, 1984); Donald Critchlow, *The Conservative Ascendancy* (Cambridge, MA: Harvard University Press, 2007); George H. Nash, *The Conservative Intellectual Movement in America* (New York: Basic Books, 1976); Jerry Z. Muller, Editor, *Conservatism* (Princeton, NJ: Princeton University Press, 1997); John Micklethwait and Adrian Wooldridge, *The Right Nation: Conservative Power in America* (New York: Penguin Press, 2004); and Jerome Himmelstein, *To the Right: The Transformation of American Conservatism* (Berkeley: University of California Press, 1990).

[48] Friedrich A. Hayek, *The Road to Serfdom* (Chicago: University of Chicago Press, 1944); and Milton Friedman, *Capitalism and Freedom* (Chicago: University of Chicago Press, 1962).

[49] Russell Kirk, *The Conservative Mind from Burke to Santayana* (Chicago: Henry Regnery, 1953).

[50] McGirr, *Suburban Warriors*, 54–110. For a recent analysis of the rise of concern about traditional values, see Marc J. Hetherington and Jonathan Weiler, *Authoritarianism and Polarization in American Politics* (New York: Cambridge University Press, 2009).

[51] Reiter and Stonecash, *Counter Realignment*, 56–62.

[52] Sitkoff, "Harry Truman and the Election of 1948."

The party was making efforts to appeal to the South. Republican Party leaders were making visits to the South.[53] In 1957 the Republican National Committee (RNC) established Operation Dixie to try to build organizations in the region.[54] By 1961, the RNC was allocating more money to efforts in the South, and in 1962 the party began distributing a regular newsletter in the region.

The primary concern of conservatives, however, was with their ideological compatibility with the South. As Barry Goldwater, senator from Arizona, put it at a 1961 statement to southern Republican state party chairmen: "We're not going to get the Negro vote as a bloc in 1964 and 1968, so we ought to go hunting where the ducks are."[55] Brent Bozell, a conservative commentator, argued that

[A] successful appeal to the South is the *sine qua non* for beating John F. Kennedy in 1964 – indeed, that pursuit of such a strategy over the long term is the party's only realistic hope of escaping from the Hobson's choice of throwing itself on the mercy of an Eisenhower-type personality cult, or accepting national minority status.[56]

Conservatives had analyzed election results and had a plan about how to create a majority. William Rusher, publisher of *National Review*, made three arguments about the wisdom of pursuing the South.[57] First, he did not think the party needed to or was likely to win the large industrial states. Second, winning the South was feasible. The region was changing to a more of a modern economy, and was voting more Republican, as witnessed by Eisenhower's support in 1952 and 1956. The party was recruiting more House candidates in the South and winning more seats,[58] and the RNC was allocating more money to party efforts within the region.[59] Third, conservatives thought that tensions within the Democratic Party provided an opportunity for Republicans to exploit. The party was trying to please northern liberals and southern segregationists, an impossible task.[60]

Just as with the Democrats, Republicans considered the issue of whether the party could attract new voters and still retain enough of its older base to win. Rusher anticipated that pursuit of the South would lead to the charge that "any Republican concession to Southern sentiment is a venture in sheer racism, and

53 Joseph Lowndes, *From the New Deal to the New Right: Race and the Southern Origins of Modern Conservatism* (New Haven, CT: Yale University Press, 2008), 36.
54 Rae, *The Decline and Fall of Liberal Republicans*, 68–73; Klinkner, *The Losing Parties*, 50–69.
55 Klinkner, *The Losing Parties*, 58.
56 L. Brent Bozell, "Goldwater for President: Is It Feasible?," *National Review*, April 23, 1963, 313.
57 William A. Rusher, "Crossroads for the G.O.P.," *National Review*, February 12, 1963, 109–112.
58 Mark D. Brewer and Jeffrey M. Stonecash, *Dynamics of American Political Parties*, 110–113.
59 Klinkner, *The Losing Parties*, 56–57.
60 Rusher, "Crossroads for the G.O.P.," 111; and Frank S. Meyer, "Principles and Heresies: And Still... Goldwater Can Win," *National Review*, December 17, 1963, 528.

will lose the GOP crucial votes in the North and West."[61] He did not think this was a risk because the Democratic Party was too entangled in its own divisions about race to credibly make that charge against a Republican Party that had fewer segregationists in it. He also doubted that the North would be willing to embrace the Democratic Party:

Certainly there is not a shred of evidence that any large bloc of votes now sustaining Republican dominance in any northern or western state will bolt to the party of Kennedy (and Eastland and Ellender [segregationist Southern Senators]) because the GOP chooses to bid vigorously for the support of the new middle class of a changing south.[62]

Some thought the party could win enough states outside the Northeast to win the presidency.[63] Others were so frustrated by the continuing dominance of the eastern liberal wing that they wanted to pursue another direction just to reduce that wing's influence over the party.[64] Although there were variations in the logic underlying activism, the conservatives were organizing to secure the nomination for their desired candidate in the 1964 presidential race. They wanted Barry Goldwater because they thought he could redefine the party and win,[65] and they developed a plan to secure his nomination.[66] They were able to stop the candidacy of relatively liberal New York governor Nelson Rockefeller, and draw on heavy support within the South to win the nomination for Goldwater.[67]

The nomination of Goldwater came at the same time that the party was reconsidering its stance on civil rights. The national Republican Party had an image in the 1950s of being more supportive of civil rights than Democrats, but this was largely because the Democratic Party contained so many southerners opposed to change.[68] Within the Republican Party there were many who thought that a stance in favor of states' rights and opposition to federal desegregation efforts made ideological and political sense as a way to make

---

[61] Rusher, "Crossroads for the G.O.P.," 111.

[62] Rusher, "Crossroads for the G.O.P.," 112.

[63] Frank S. Meyer, "Principles and Heresies: A New Political Map," *National Review*, August 11, 1964, 687.

[64] Rae, *The Decline and Fall of Liberal Republicans*, 25–53; and McGirr, *Suburban Warriors*, 91–98.

[65] Frank S. Meyer, "Principles and Heresies: Why Goldwater Can Defeat Johnson," *National Review*, July 14, 1964, 581; and James J. Kilpatrick, "Goldwater Country," *National Review*, April 9, 1963, 281–282.

[66] Perlstein, *Before the Storm*, 158–190; Rae, *The Decline of Liberal Republicans*, 54–59.

[67] Klinkner, *The Losing Parties*, 69.

[68] Carmines and Stimson, *Issue Evolution*, 64–78, although Feinstein and Schickler document that in non-southern state party platforms Democrats were much more supportive than Republicans. Republican members of Congress were also less willing to advocate for civil rights. See Schickler, Pearson, and Feinstein, "Congressional Parties and Civil Rights Politics from 1933 to 1972." The significance is that although the Republican Party had an official voting record in Congress of being more supportive of civil rights than Democrats, the party was experiencing far less pressure than Democrats to support civil rights.

inroads in the South. It was also the case that within most non-southern states, Republican state party platforms were expressing considerably less support for civil rights legislation than Democrats.[69]

While the party was struggling with whether to continue supporting civil rights, Goldwater announced that he was voting against the 1964 Civil Rights bill. He argued that he was not in favor of segregation and the denial of rights, but that he was opposed to federal intrusion into state and local matters.[70] He sought to present his stance as one of principle, but was accused of pursuing a strategy of seeking votes in the South.[71] He was also portrayed as very conservative, and as opposed to social welfare legislation, civil rights, and an activist federal government; skeptical about Social Security; and willing to be much more aggressive in foreign affairs.

Goldwater presented an image to the electorate that conservatives wanted. He clearly expressed his conservative principles in *The Conscience of a Conservative*.[72] He supported the propriety of free markets and the fundamental importance of individual and states' rights to the preservation of freedom. He criticized high levels of federal taxing and spending, the New Deal welfare state, and federal involvement in education. He challenged the validity of continuing Social Security. He saw the Soviet Union as the ultimate threat to the United States. In his acceptance speech at the Republican national convention, he also issued his famous statement that "extremism in the defense of liberty is no vice, and moderation in the pursuit of justice is no virtue." The campaign of Barry Goldwater presented Americans with a clear statement of conservative principles. To his followers he was a crucial figure.[73]

The arguments of the conservative movement were not embraced by the more moderate northeastern wing of the party. The moderates still thought the party could improve its fortunes in northern urban areas by appealing to blacks.[74] After Nixon lost the 1960 election, analyses indicated that he lost several northern states (Delaware, New Jersey, and Pennsylvania) by small margins and New York by only five percentage points. Since the 1960 election had been so close, a moderate stance and modest gains in northern cities might swing the next presidential election to Republicans.[75]

---

[69] Feinstein and Schickler, "Platforms and Partners." For a discussion of the transition of views within the Republican Party, see Shamira M. Gelbman and Jesse H. Rhodes, "Why Didn't Republicans Adopt Racial Conservativism Earlier?" Presented at the 2010 Southern Political Science Association Meetings, Atlanta, Georgia, January, 2010.

[70] Perlstein, *Before the Storm*, 363–364.

[71] "Goldwater Solicits G.O.P. Votes from Southern Segregationists," *New York Times*, November 19, 1961, 70; Perlstein, *Before the Storm*, 266–267, 426–428, 507–510.

[72] Barry Goldwater, *The Conscience of a Conservative* (Shepherdsville, KY: Victor, 1960).

[73] McGirr, *Suburban Warriors*, 111–146.

[74] W. H. Lawrence, "G.O.P. Hopes for a Big Negro Vote," *New York Times*, October 6, 1957, 199; W. H. Lawrence, "G.O.P. to Cite Little Rock, Minimize 'Moon' in '58 Bid," *New York Times*, October 16, 1957, 1.

[75] Klinkner, *The Losing Parties*, 41–68.

Moderates perceived a societal consensus that government could address many major social problems. Goldwater was bucking that trend, arguing that government did too much, and should not address social problems, and that there would be negative effects from these efforts. Politicians in the Northeast, such as Senator Jacob Javits, argued that moving in the direction of Goldwater would polarize the parties along ideological lines and make the party less of a national party. His fear was that the Southern Strategy of states rights "could result most likely in the election-day loss of many of the great industrial and urban states of the North." "A candidacy based upon the 'Southern Strategy'... would do more than hazard the party's defeat in the 1964 contest; it could alienate millions of Americans – who could stay alienated for years."[76] The northeastern wing was strongly opposed to his candidacy.[77]

A Crucial Juncture: Interpreting Electoral Responses

The outcome of the 1964 election was clear, but the challenge in politics is to understand what the results mean. The battle over interpreting trends in American politics and acting on those interpretations were crucial for what happened in subsequent years. This juncture was crucial because those actions also altered the relationship between presidential and House election results for the next several decades.[78]

For Democrats, the results seemed clear. Lyndon Johnson had campaigned on a theme of creating a Great Society, and Goldwater had presented an alternative. Johnson received 61.1 percent of the national popular vote, and House Democratic candidates received 57.4 percent of the national vote. The party won 62.3 percent of seats outside the South, and the non-southern wing dominated the party 205 to 90.[79] Democrats won 26 of 33 Senate contests. Support for liberalism was on the rise.[80] The alternative of antigovernment conservatism, represented by Goldwater, seemed thoroughly rejected. Columnists asserted, "He has wrecked his party for a long time to come" or "The election has finished the Goldwater school of political reaction."[81] Given these interpretations, Democrats quickly enacted an extensive array of programs such as Medicaid, Medicare, and federal aid to local schools.

---

[76] Jacob K. Javits, "'To Preserve the Two-Party System'," *New York Times Magazine*, October 27, 1963, 15+.

[77] Rae, *The Decline and Fall of Liberal Republicans*, 61–64.

[78] It was not easy for anyone to see the emergence of the conservative movement while it was first forming. For example, academic analyses saw Goldwater as more of an oddity than anything. See Philip E. Converse, Aage R. Clausen, and Warren E. Miller, "Electoral Myth and Reality: The 1964 Election," *The American Political Science Review*, Vol. 59, No. 2 (June 1965), 321–336.

[79] Brewer and Stonecash, *Dynamics of American Political Parties*, 96.

[80] Ellis and Stimson, "On Symbolic Conservatism in America."

[81] Perlstein, *Before the Storm*, ix.

The debate within the Republican Party was reflective of the struggle that was to occur in subsequent years.[82] The moderates within the Republican Party argued that the Southern Strategy was of questionable morality and just would not work. The editors of the Ripon Society, founded in 1962 to advocate moderate positions, argued that appealing to southern opposition to the civil rights movement was "sad, shameful, and a collapse of courage."[83] They also argued that urban and black votes were increasing, and that the party could not win without these votes.[84] Further, some party leaders contended that the party had not benefited from any white urban backlash in northern cities,[85] and further appeals about "social disorder" might make the party appear to be racist.[86] To many moderates the Goldwater candidacy was an unfortunate venture that would hopefully fade away.

Conservatives, however, saw the results as a reason for optimism. William Rusher of *National Review* had argued that the party could succeed in the South, and Goldwater did win five Southern states – Alabama, Georgia, Louisiana, Mississippi, and South Carolina. The party increased its number of House seats in the South from 11 to 16. In 1950 the party had 35 candidates for the 114 seats in that region. Those 35 averaged 27.3 percent of the vote. In 1964 they had 81 candidates who averaged 38.6 percent. The party was making inroads, and many conservatives wanted to continue to pursue the South.

Presidential Aspirations and Electoral Strategies

As these debates about the direction the party continued, candidates for the 1968 presidential contest had to assess where they could win enough states to win a plurality or majority in the Electoral College. Richard Nixon was seeking to make a comeback following the losses of the presidential race in 1960 and the California governorship in 1962. His primary competition was Nelson Rockefeller, governor of New York. Nixon saw the South as very important to securing the presidential nomination. The South had 279 of the necessary 655 votes at the 1964 convention, and would have more in 1968 because convention votes were weighted according to recent success. Because

---

[82] Geoffrey Kabaservice, *Rule and Ruin: The Downfall of Moderation and the Destruction of the Republican Party from Eisenhower to the Tea Party* (New York: Oxford University Press, 2012), 123–160.

[83] [Editors] "The View from Here," *The Ripon Forum*, June 1965, Vol. 1, No. 4, 1.

[84] [Editors] "Republicans and the Negro Revolution–1965," *The Ripon Forum*, December, 1965, Vol. 1, No. 8, 1; [Editors] "Republicans and the South," *The Ripon Forum*, Vol. 1, No. 3 (May 1965), 2; and [Editors] "The State of the Democratic Coalition: The Maginot Line," *The Ripon Forum*, Vol. 11, No. 4 (June 1966), 5.

[85] Anthony Lewis, "White Backlash Doesn't Develop," *New York Times*, November 4, 1964, 1.

[86] John D. Morris, "Burch Asks G.O.P. to Reject Racism," *New York Times*, February 18, 1965, 18.

Goldwater had done so well in 1964 in the South, that region would have more votes in 1968.[87] But he also knew that northeastern states had a long history of voting Republican and could provide votes as long as he did not alienate voters there.[88]

During the two years leading up to 1968, Nixon sought to position himself as sympathetic to southern concerns but not so sympathetic that he would not enforce desegregation laws.[89] He had to be careful about not alienating northern states where support for desegregation was greater. He emulated Ronald Reagan by speaking about the "silent majority" and the need for social order.[90] This strategy was enormously complicated by the presence of George Wallace, the segregationist former governor of Alabama, who threatened to win many southern states and negate the logic of Nixon focusing on the South.

Following Nixon's very close victory in 1968, the crucial matter was again the interpretation of what the results meant and what direction Nixon should take in the future. Nixon won Florida, Kentucky, North Carolina, South Carolina, Tennessee, and Virginia, giving him 45 Electoral College votes in the South, more than Goldwater received, despite the presence of Wallace. Equally important, Nixon was able to win the presidency with only four states within the Northeast – Delaware, New Hampshire, New Jersey, and Vermont.

There were many interpretations offered about the 1960s and the 1968 election,[91] but perhaps the most prescient was that made by Kevin Phillips, who provided a conservative road map for where Nixon might want to take the party. He proved to be correct about the political trends of subsequent years.[92] Phillips argued that the "emerging Republican majority of the Nineteen-Seventies is centered in the South, the West, and in the 'Middle-American' urban-suburban districts." He saw the Republican Party as steadily increasing its "reliance [on the] South and West since the beginning of the New Deal cycle in 1932."[93] He argued that the "the 1964 election constituted a Rubicon for the

[87] Rick Perlstein, *Nixonland: The Rise of a President and the Fracturing of America* (New York: Scribner, 2007), 88.

[88] [Editors] "Republican Arithmetic," *The Ripon Forum*, Vol. 4, No. 8 (August 1968), 9–12. See also Klinkner, *The Losing Parties*.

[89] David S. Broder, "Nixon, in the South, Bids G.O.P. Drop Race Issue," *New York Times*, May 7, 1966, 14.

[90] Matthew D. Lassiter, *The Silent Majority: Suburban Politics in the Sunbelt South* (Princeton, NJ: Princeton University Press, 2007).

[91] For an overview, see Reiter and Stonecash, *Counter Realignment*, 81–100.

[92] Kevin Phillips, *The Emerging Republican Majority*, 21. Although Phillips asserted that the book "does *not* purport to set forth the past strategies or future intentions of Richard M. Nixon, his campaign organization or administration," it was difficult not to see it in that light.

[93] Phillips, *The Emerging Republican Majority*, 23 and 26. Although Phillips denied wanting to write off the Northeast, one reviewer summarized his argument as follows: "The Phillips doctrine thus amounts to institutionalizing Barry Goldwater's suggestion that the nation might be better off if its Northeastern corner were sawed off and allowed to drift out to sea." Warren Weaver, Jr., *New York Times*, September 21, 1969, BR3. The governor of Pennsylvania voiced

Republican Party; and its crossing marked off an era" (78). "The Republican Party shed the dominion of its Yankee and Northeast Establishment creators, while the Democrats, having linked themselves to the Negro socioeconomic revolution and to an increasingly liberal Northeastern Establishment shaped by the success of the New Deal, sank the foundations of their future into the Northeast" (33). The bold statement was that the clue to the future of the party was to focus on appealing to George Wallace's 1968 supporters and adding them to the Republican Party base:

> Some of Wallace's support came from aroused conservative Republicans, but most of it represented Democratic streams quitting their party (33). . . . [A] relatively conservative 1968–1972 Republican administration should [result in adding] as an important national bloc of popular votes a key Deep Southern group of electoral votes to the barebones Republican triumph of 1968 (35).

Over the next four years Nixon attempted to act on the logic that there was a conservative base he could attract.[94] His challenge was to appeal to a diverse coalition of conservatives, all the while not going so far in that direction that he would alienate too much of the traditional Republican base. The uncertainty of this pursuit cannot be underestimated. Just several years prior it appeared the nation was moving more liberal. The role of the national government had been expanded. There was considerable social turmoil, and it was difficult to be certain particular emphases would yield a new electoral base.

Nixon faced the task of preparing for another presidential campaign at a time when electoral bases were in transition. He had aspirations to alter the electoral base of the entire party, but he also faced the need to win in 1972. There was considerable ambiguity as to whether he could move former Democratic voters fast enough to replace the Republicans he might lose in the Northeast. He sought to present himself as a candidate of law and order at a time when social disorder seemed to be on the rise and commentators were discussing "backlash" against the Democrats for becoming too liberal.[95] Nixon commissioned numerous studies and polls to try to discern which voters might comprise a new majority that could change the status of the Republican Party.[96] Despite repeated analyses, it proved to be difficult to identify a conservative coalition, and in 1971 and 1972 he gave up on changing the congressional

---

similar concerns. [No author], "Governor Shafer Says He Fears G.O.P. Writes off Northeast," *New York Times*, December 7, 1969, 60.

[94] Perlstein, *Nixonland*, 459–525. Evidence about how issues were creating defections from the Democrats is presented in Richard W. Boyd, "Popular Control of Public Policy: A Normal Vote Analysis of the 1968 Election," *American Political Science Review*, Vol. 66, No. 2 (June 1972), 429–449.

[95] Perlstein provides a valuable summary of the chronology of events in *Nixonland*, 96–127 and 274–278; see also Edsall and Edsall, *Chain Reaction*. For evidence of shifting public opinion of liberals in the 1960s, see K. Elizabeth Coggins and James A. Stimson, "The Vanishing Liberal." Presented at the 2012 Southern Political Science Association Meetings, New Orleans, January.

[96] Mason, *Richard Nixon and the Quest for a New Majority*, 37–112.

party and focused on the short-term challenge of winning his reelection.[97] He appealed to southerners worried about federal government intrusions to require desegregation by stressing that he would do only what the law required. His campaign was helped when the Democrats nominated South Dakota Senator George McGovern, who was labeled as a liberal at a time when support for that position was declining.

The result was that Nixon was able to create a coalition comprised of much of the older Republican base and Wallace vote from the 1968 race. His electoral base was very different from that of Republican candidates from 1900 to 1940. It was also very different from his 1960 campaign.[98] These changes will be examined in detail in the next section. Nixon had succeeded in shifting the electoral base of the presidential wing of the party.

The permanence of this change was hard to see in the next several years as the consequences of the Watergate scandal unfolded. Nixon resigned in August 1974. The public's negative view of the matter had ensnared the entire Republican Party, and it suffered major losses in House elections in that year. Then in 1976 Democrats ran a southerner, Jimmy Carter, who was able to resurrect some, but not all, of the old Democratic coalition. Gerald Ford ran as more of a moderate Republican, creating less contrast in candidate positions. The political geography of the 1976 presidential election results had little association with prior results. It was not easy for politicians or analysts to see systematic and enduring change in the election results of the 1970s. Then in 1980 Ronald Reagan ran as the Republican candidate and sent a clear message to voters by opening his campaign in Philadelphia, Mississippi.[99] It was the site where several civil rights activists had been killed in the 1960s and a clear sign by Reagan that he was going to appeal to the South. His victories in 1980 and in 1984 were clear signs also of the emergence of conservatism in the Republican Party. During the 1980s party abortion stances also shifted, with Republicans moving in a pro-life direction and the Democrats becoming more pro-choice.[100]

The progression of change in subsequent years was not always clear as to where it was going. The choices made in the 1960s by each party's presidential candidates were not always accepted. Many Democratic candidates were pursuing minorities and northern urban constituencies. Liberals were on the rise within the party. But they were contested by moderates who argued that the party was becoming too liberal and needed to broaden its appeal. The debate within the party about how liberal to be has been sustained and

---

[97] Mason, *Richard Nixon and the Quest for a New* Majority, 128–131 and 161–162.

[98] The correlation of 1960 state-level Republican presidential results with 1972 is −.10.

[99] Joseph Crespino, *In Search of Another Country: Mississippi and the Conservative Counterrevolution* (Princeton, NJ: Princeton University Press, 2009).

[100] For detailed analyses of these shifts see Mellow, *The State of Disunion*; and Karol, *Party Position Change in American Politics*.

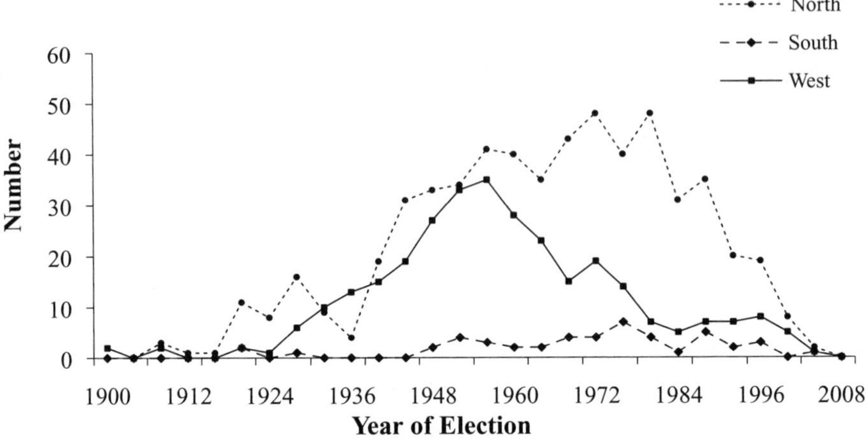

FIGURE 7.7. Number of Republican Moderates by Region, 1900–2008

intense since then.[101] Republicans have also struggled with what direction to take. There are those who argue that in the pursuit of the South, the party got caught up in devoting too much attention to social conservatives and not enough attention to fiscal conservativism. There are others who argue that both are relevant, and that America is more conservative than many want to recognize.[102] While these debates continued, the policy directions chosen in the 1960s persisted.[103] The Democratic Party moved somewhat more liberal and was less reliant on the South. The Republican Party moved somewhat more conservative and became less reliant on the Northeast.

Moderates and the Evolution of the Republican Party

Just as occurred with Democrats in the 1930s, the change in the policy focus of the Republican Party was not well received by everyone within the party. The change within the Republican Party came well after the shift within the Democratic Party, and the resistance also appeared later. The resistance, just as with the Democratic Party, came from the former base of the party. For decades the base of the Republican Party was the North. As Figure 7.7 indicates, that region was the source of a large number of moderates who were less inclined to vote with the majority of the party as it became more conservative. There were

---

[101] For overviews of that debate, see Stonecash, *Class and Party*; Kuhn, *The Neglected Voter*; and Brewer and Stonecash, *Dynamics of American Political Parties*, 147–165.

[102] These arguments are summarized in Reiter and Stonecash, *Counter Realignment*, 103–146; and Jeffrey M. Stonecash, "The 2010 Elections," *The Forum*, Byron Shafer, Editor, December, 2010.

[103] Polsby, *How Congress Evolves*; Baumer and Gold, *Parties, Polarization, and Democracy in the United States*.

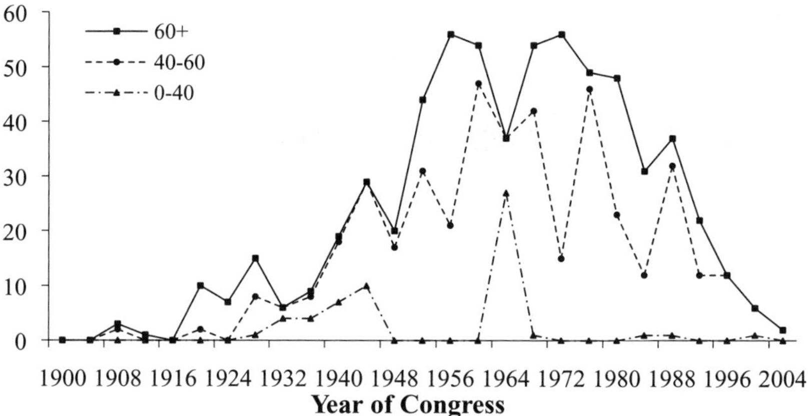

FIGURE 7.8. Number of Republican Moderates by Republican Presidential Voting in House Districts, 1900–2004

also a substantial number of moderates from the West during the 1940s and 1950s, but Republican members from that region were adopting conservative positions by the 1960s.

Just as with the Democrats, the emergence of moderates within the Republican Party was *not* a reflection of close presidential votes in their district. As Figure 7.8 indicates, the greatest number of moderates within the Republican Party came in districts that party presidential candidates won by large margins. The party was shifting its focus, and many of the northern districts, where presidential candidate still did well, were reluctant to go along with the altered party focus. There were many moderates in districts with a close presidential vote, but most were in districts where presidential candidates did well. The party was beginning to shift, and those from northern districts were reluctant to go along. Eventually, as realignment continued and many incumbents were replaced by conservatives, the presence of moderates declined.[104]

Each party had struggled for some time with how much to cater to its traditional base and with whether to continue with the positions that it had adopted. There was considerable debate within each party, and eventually a new direction began to emerge within each. The debates of subsequent years will be reviewed later. The important matter is what the decisions of the 1960s and later did to the presidential–House electoral connection.

[104] Richard Fleisher and Jon R. Bond, "The Shrinking Middle in the US Congress," *British Journal of Political Science*, Vol. 34, No. 3 (July 2004), 429–451; and Kabaservice, *Rule and Ruin*, 363–388.

8

The Consequences of Changing Electoral Bases

Presidential and congressional candidates were seeking to alter the geographical electoral bases of their parties. How successful were the parties in creating change? How did the process of change affect the relationship between presidential and House election results? To assess these questions, several analyses are relevant. Is there evidence of broad national changes in the geographical bases of support for the parties? Did the changes initiated in the 1960s persist? Did presidential and House elections change at the same rates, or did they proceed at different rates and create a separation of results? This chapter deals largely with national results. Changes within regions are dealt with in the next chapter.

Shifting Geographical Bases

The first issue is the extent of change in geographical electoral bases. Table 8.1 indicates the broad changes in presidential and House electoral bases by 1972. This repeats a table presented earlier as an introduction to the issue of national changes. The baseline is 1940 because it is after the initial surge in support for Democrats in 1932 and 1936 had subsided. The *relative* levels of partisan support for the parties within states in 1940 was similar to 1900 so the grouping of states provides a baseline for comparison with 1972, the year Richard Nixon sought to create a new coalition.

Several matters are important about the changes. How much change occurred by 1972 in relative levels of support across groups of states? By 1972 the relative levels of Republican support across states had shifted significantly. In states where presidential candidates got less than 45 percent in 1940, Nixon achieved the largest gains from 1940 to 1972. His gain in those states relative to 1940 was 42.3 percentage points. The worse the party did in 1940 in a state, the greater the gain and the higher the percentage in 1972. At the

TABLE 8.1. *Averages of State-Level Republican Presidential and House Results, 1940 and 1972*

% 1900	N	Presidential Results			House Results		
		1940	1972	Change	1940	1972	Change
0–44	13	25.6	67.9	42.3	17.5	42.4	23.1
45–51	9	42.2	65.8	23.6	41.2	50.7	9.5
52–55	10	46.5	59.4	12.9	50.1	49.0	−1.1
56+	13	49.6	56.9	7.3	53.6	51.6	−3.0
Region							
South	11	30.5	69.3	38.8	13.5	40.2	26.7
Remainder	17–22	47.3	62.7	15.4	43.1	49.6	6.5
North	18	57.4	58.6	1.4	50.2	49.9	−.3

Note: All percentages are averages of state percentages for states within the indicated group.

same time, Nixon did not lose the states where the party had done well in the past. Perceptions of a changed party focus and changes in partisan attachments are slow, and the states where Republicans had done well stayed with the party even as other states moved significantly to the Republican side.

The same pattern emerges if the states are grouped by regions. In 1940 the Republican presidential candidate received the least support in the South and the greatest support in the North. By 1972 Nixon received his highest level of support in the South (an increase of 38.8 percentage points) while there was almost no change in the North. He did not lose support in the North, but gained support within the South, and to a lesser degree within the remainder of the country.

These changes contrast with what happened with House results. For both groupings of states, the pattern is the same. In the states where Nixon made his largest gains, the increases in the Republican House results were also the greatest, but the changes lagged far behind the gains of Nixon. In the South the average Republican House percentage in 1972 was 29.1 points below that which Nixon received in 1972. Nixon altered the Republican presidential electoral base but changes in House results did not proceed at the same pace. The congressional party retained the areas where it had done well in 1940, and significantly improved its fortunes elsewhere. The change was just less than Nixon achieved.

Long-Term Changes

Although these changes appear to be significant, the results from the 1972 race could just reflect the one-year consequences of the Democrats running a candidate widely seen as very liberal. The issues are whether there was a fundamental and enduring shift in the Republican presidential base by 1972

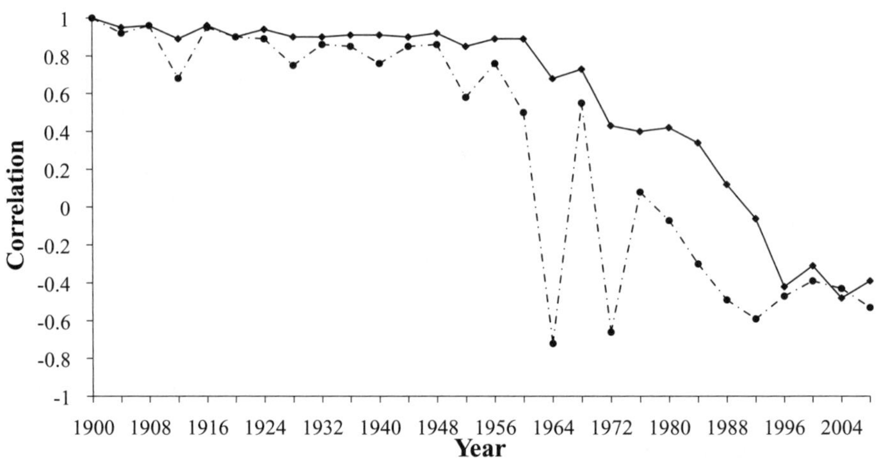

FIGURE 8.1. Correlation of State Republican Presidential and House Percentages for 1904–2008 with 1900

and after, and whether the congressional party base took longer to replicate what was happening in presidential elections. One way to assess this is to regard the 1900 vote as a base vote and then correlate subsequent state percentages with the 1900 percentages.[1] If the correlation is positive and high, it indicates that candidates are essentially replicating the *relative* levels of support found in 1900 across states in subsequent years. The absolute vote percentage within states might go up or down, but if the correlation is high, then the relative degree of support across states remains the same. If the correlation goes to 0, it indicates the relative variation across states for that year bears no relationship to the base year of 1900. A negative correlation indicates the relative position of states has reversed compared to 1900.

For presidential election results the state percentages can be used to assess the relationships of years after 1900 to the base of 1900. For House elections it is not possible to compare districts over time, because they are regularly reapportioned, but it is possible to aggregate the total votes by party to the state level and then use state-level percentages to see how House election patterns shift. This conceals within-state variations, but it allows comparisons across time. Figure 8.1 presents the correlation of presidential percentages with 1900 presidential percentages and the correlation of House percentages with 1900 House state percentages.

From 1904 through 1960, state presidential percentages largely repeated the relative levels of support that existed in 1900. The correlation of state percentages in 1948 with 1900 was .86. By 1960 it had dropped to .5. Then in 1964, Goldwater produced a fundamental shift. The correlation of his 1964

---

[1] Paulson, *Realignment and Party Revival*, 23–34.

state-level results with 1900 was highly negative at −.72. He had reversed the relative positions of states. In 1968 Richard Nixon sought to balance the old party electoral with the new as his campaign struggled to cope with the presence of George Wallace.[2] His results maintained the relative levels of Republican support across states that prevailed in 1900, and he barely won the presidency. In 1972, with Wallace out of the race, Nixon essentially replicated the reversal of relative success that Goldwater had achieved. When Democrats ran Jimmy Carter from Georgia in 1976, the correlation came back "up" to .08, but after 1976, Republican Party candidates began a much clearer move to pursue the South, and the association of the party's base with the 1900 situation was steadily negative. The relative success of Republican presidential candidates in the 1980s and beyond was essentially the reverse of what had prevailed from 1900 to 1960.

The results for House candidates also began to change in the 1960s, but the change was more gradual and took longer to match the changes in presidential results. Much of this delay is due to incumbents surviving as electoral change unfolded within their regions, but nonetheless changes in House results eventually followed changes in presidential results. It was not until 1992 – 28 years after the presidential correlation first turned negative in 1964 – that the state-level association of House results with 1900 turned negative. Finally in 1996, both presidential and House candidates had the same correlation of state results with 1900. By 1996 both wings of the party had essentially the same electoral base across the nation, and it was dramatically different from the 1900 situation.

The presidential wing of the Republican Party had changed its electoral base. To return to Phillip's analysis of political change in America, he argued that Nixon could succeed by combining the Nixon and Wallace votes of 1968, and that would be the future of the party.[3] Did votes in 1972 and after reflect this combination, and did the 1968 combined vote capture the break with the Republican base that prevailed prior to the 1960s? To assess this, Figure 8.2 presents the correlation of the combined Nixon-plus-Wallace state-level percentages from 1968 with the state Republican presidential and House vote in prior and subsequent years.[4] That is, the state-level presidential percentages (combined) for 1968 are correlated with 1900, 1904, and so forth. They are also correlated with 1972 and subsequent years.[5]

Three matters are important about the patterns. First, the combined presidential percentages from 1968 capture the break during the 1960s with the

---

[2] Perlstein, *Nixonland*.

[3] Phillips, *The Emerging Republican Majority*, 35.

[4] Mark D. Brewer and Jeffrey M. Stonecash, "Changing the Political Dialogue and Political Alignments: George Wallace and His 1968 Presidential Campaign." Presented at the 2009 Midwest Political Science Association Meetings, April, 2009.

[5] The year 1968 is omitted because the focus is on 1968 with years prior and after.

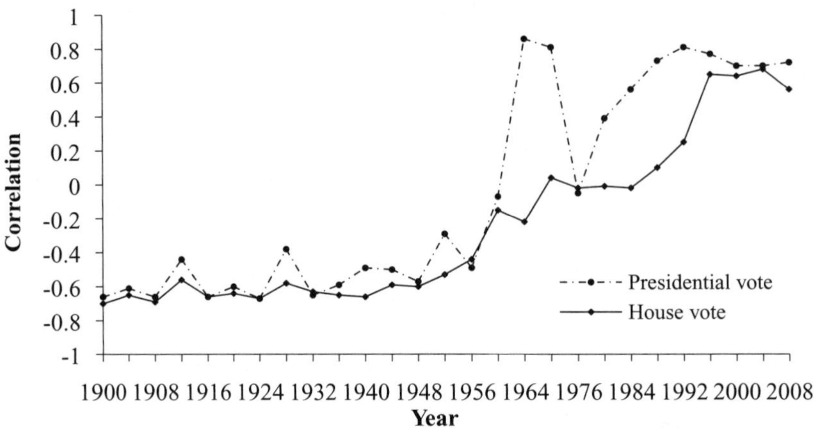

FIGURE 8.2. Correlation of State Republican Presidential and House Votes with Nixon+Wallace by Year, 1900–2008

past that also emerges in Figure 8.1. The combined 1968 results have a negative association with the results from 1900 to 1960 and a high positive correlation with 1964 and later years (with the exception of 1976). The electoral bases of presidential candidates were changing significantly and also fairly rapidly. Second, the combined 1968 vote largely predicts where Republican presidential candidates did well in the future and what states the party would lose as it moved in a more conservative direction.[6] The correlations of the combined 1968 percentages with the years 1972 and 1980 and after are high. The party went after a more conservative southern base, and attained it.[7] Third, the lagging correlation of House vote percentages (with vote totals aggregated to the state level) with the 1968 combined percentages also fits with Figure 8.1. Voting for Republican House candidates was moving away from the 1900 patterns, but at a slower rate than presidential results. Only in 1996 do House

---

[6] For how this affected the Northeast, see Reiter and Stonecash, *Counter Realignment*.

[7] Although the focus here is on district-level voting patterns, the individual-level results also indicate the Republican Party steadily attracted more conservatives from the 1970s and afterward. See: Alan I. Abramowitz and Kyle L. Saunders, "Ideological Realignments in the U.S. Electorate," *Journal of Politics*, Vol. 60, No. 3 (August 1998), 634–652; Alan I. Abramowitz and Kyle L. Saunders, "Exploring the Bases of Partisanship in the American Electorate: Social Identity vs. Ideology," *Political Research Quarterly*, Vol. 59, No. 2 (June 2006), 175–187; Alan I. Abramowitz, *The Disappearing Center: Engaged Citizens, Polarization, and American Democracy* (New Haven, CT: Yale University Press, 2010). There is also evidence from individual-level surveys that conflict between partisans gradually encompassed more issues – called issue extension – over time. Geoffrey C. Layman and Thomas M. Carsey, "Party Polarization and 'Conflict Extension' in the American Electorate," *American Journal of Political Science*, Vol. 46, No. 4 (October 2002), 786–802; and Mark D. Brewer, "The Rise of Partisanship and the Expansion of Partisan Conflict within the American Electorate," *Political Research Quarterly*, Vol. 58, No. 2 (June 2005), 219–229.

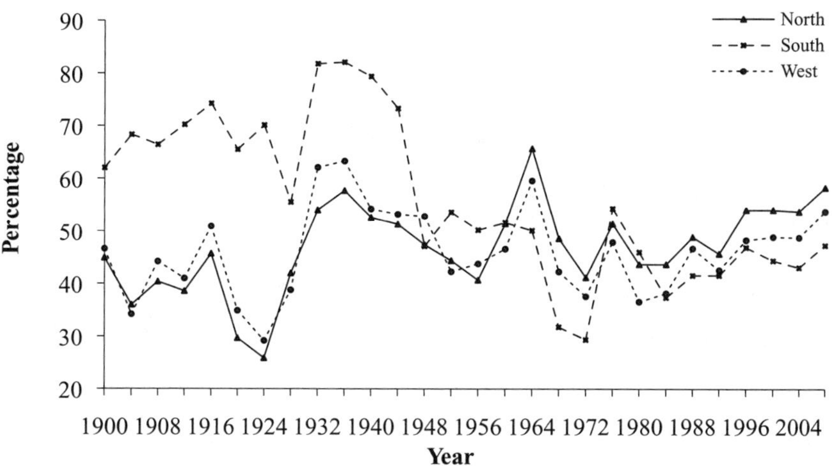

FIGURE 8.3. Average Democratic Presidential Vote by Region, 1900–2008

state-level results correlate highly with the 1968 presidential percentages and catch up with presidential changes. Party electoral bases were changing, but at different rates.

The changes in party bases were altering the correlations among results. While relative levels of partisan support across regions were reversing, were absolute levels also reversing? To assess whether the absolute partisan vote percentages were also reversing, the Democratic percentages by regions are shown in Figures 8.3 and 8.4. If we take presidential voting patterns first, in the early 1900s the South was consistently voting heavily Democratic. By 2008 its level of support for a Democratic candidate was lower than for any other region. In

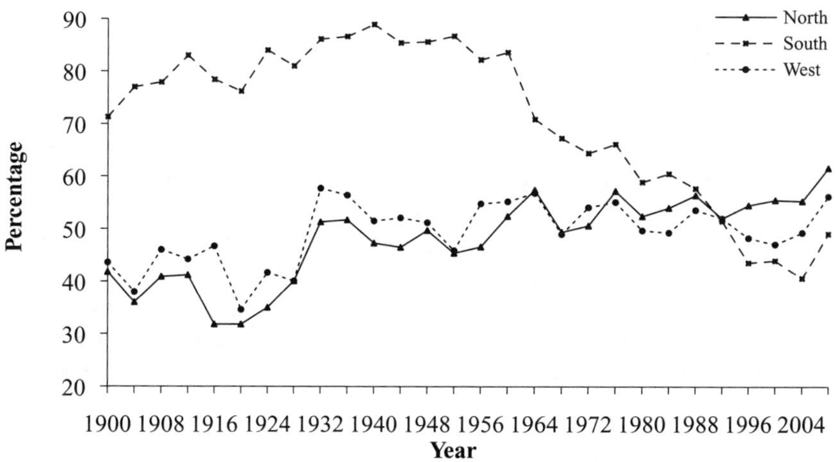

FIGURE 8.4. Average Democratic House Vote, by Region, 1900–1928

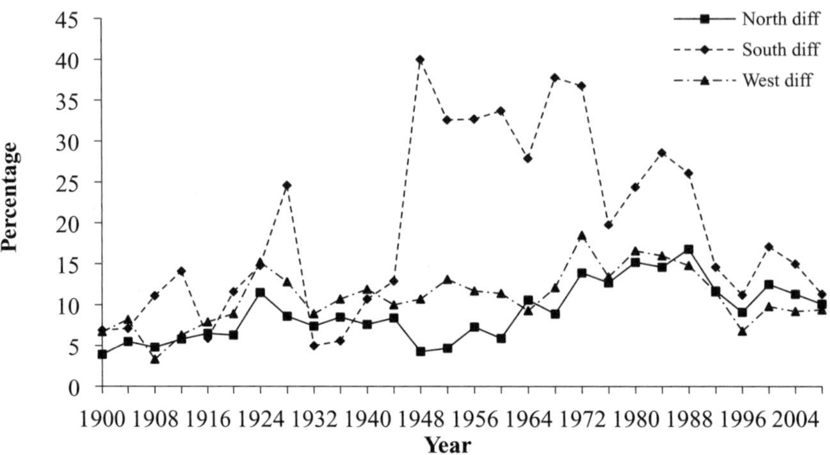

FIGURE 8.5. Differences between House–President Democratic Percentages, by Region, 1900–2008

the early 1900s the North had the lowest level of support for Democrats, but by 2008 it had the highest. The difference between the two regions was less than in 1900, but change had altered the absolute and relative levels of support by region. The West began the last century less supportive of Democrats, and has erratically and gradually become somewhat more Democratic.[8]

As presidential partisan voting has shifted, House results eventually followed these partisan trends. As Figure 8.4 indicates, the average Democratic vote in the South was very high from 1900 through 1964. Since then it has moved to a position of providing the lowest level of support for Democrats. The North began with the lowest average level of Democratic support and now has the highest. The West has to some extent followed the same pattern as the North, and by 2008 the average Democratic vote percentage was between the other two regions.

There has been remarkable change in the levels of partisan support within regions of the nation, but the timing of change has differed for the two offices. These differential rates of change have been most evident in the South, but they have occurred in all three regions of the nation. Figure 8.5 indicates by region the pattern of separation between presidential and House results that has occurred over time. In this case the measure is the average of the absolute deviations of the House vote from the presidential vote within a district. The goal is to capture the degree of separation so the signs of the deviations are removed. The average of positive and negative differences would not reflect

---

[8] David A. Hopkins, "The 2008 Election and the Political Geography of the New Democratic Majority," *Polity*, Vol. 41, No. 3 (July 2009), 368–387.

the dispersion of scores around the presidential results but only the net difference, so the mean of absolute deviations is used.

In the South the result of differential rates of change is that the average difference between presidential and House results increased markedly in 1948 and stayed at a high level from then until 1992. In the other two regions the differences came later and were not as great, but they still occurred. In the North differences increased in 1964 and declined somewhat beginning in 1992. In the West differences increased beginning in 1972 and remained higher until 1996. By 1992 the differences in the three regions were very similar, and in 2008 they were essentially the same. The regions differ in the timing and magnitude of separations but all experienced increases. It is these patterns of separation of results that are central to understanding the decline and return of the correlation between presidential and House voting percentages.[9]

The parties were experiencing changes in from where they drew support. These changes played out regionally. How those changes played out regionally, and how the fortunes of incumbents fared as change occurred will be taken up in those regional analyses. Before moving to those issues, however, there is an analytic implication of these changes: How do all these changes over time affect how we do analyses? Specifically, how do they affect the utility of cross-sectional analyses?

The Emergence of Candidate-Centered Campaigns

It was the differential progression of electoral change in the geographical bases of presidential and House election results that prompted so many candidates to try to develop their own organizations, resources, and campaigns. For many House candidates it was necessary to make the campaign centered on their positions and concern for local issues if they were to survive the partisan changes occurring. It was this situation that prompted so many students of politics to see politics as "candidate-centered."[10]

Although this term has become commonplace, it is important to clarify what candidate-centered politics means and does not mean. The notion of candidate-centered politics appears to involve four separate issues. The first is the extent to which candidates raise funds for, plan, organize, and conduct their campaigns.

---

[9] The focus here is on how rates of political change in presidential and House results affected the correlation of results. Another possible explanation is that the elimination of the one-party South altered the variances of the variables involved. The process of change may have reduced and then expanded variances and changed the correlations. That possibility is assessed in Appendix III.

[10] Barbara G. Salmore and Stephen A. Salmore, *Candidates, Parties, and Campaigns: Electoral Politics in America* (Washington, DC: CQ Press, 1989); Cain, Ferejohn, and Fiorina, *The Personal Vote*; Wattenberg, *The Rise of Candidate-Centered Politics*; and Menefee-Libey, *The Triumph of Candidate-Centered Politics*.

The second is whether the candidate or the party is the focus of attention as the campaign proceeds. The third is to what extent the national image of the party is homogeneous or diverse. The fourth is the extent to which the vote for the House candidate is separate from presidential voting in a district.

The actual organization of House campaigns, the first notion, has varied over time. By most accounts local party leaders and their organizations did manage most campaigns through much of the early part of the 1900s. These efforts declined somewhere in the middle of the last century. As this decline occurred, more resources were becoming available for candidates to manage their own campaigns.[11] This allowed candidates to make themselves the focus of campaigns. This second aspect of candidate-centered politics became more important as the changes in electoral patterns just reviewed unfolded. As political change occurred during the 1960s–1980s, the images of the parties became more diverse (the third aspect). This in turn created the separation of presidential–House election results (the fourth aspect). The presidential and House wings of the parties had different images and election results, supporting the notion that politics was candidate-centered.

But the presence of these four aspects of candidate-centered politics was a temporary phenomenon, a reaction to House results changing more slowly than presidential results did. As replacements in the House occurred gradually over time, and each House party won seats where its presidential candidate was winning, the image of the party became more homogeneous across the nation. More and more House members are voting strongly with their party and presenting the party position to voters. They may still raise considerable funds on their own and set up their own organization. Candidates do manage their own campaigns. They do present themselves as individuals to voters. But as a national party image becomes more homogeneous[12] and clear to voters, and the candidate largely agrees with party stances, the act of organizing a campaign and presenting herself as an individual does not result in separating election results. The tendency has been to treat the first two matters – organization and presentation of candidate images – as if they invariably are associated with a diverse party image and separation of presidential–House results. The first two can and do occur, whereas the clarity of party image and association of election results vary.

The Limits of Cross-Sectional Data

The separation and then rejoining of presidential–House results occurred over a lengthy period. Change proceeds slowly and is evident if a longtime perspective is employed. To return to an earlier theme, this process of change is very difficult to see when analyses employ repeated cross-sections and focus on relatively

---

[11] For a review of these changes, see Aldrich, *Why Parties? A Second Look*, 255–292.
[12] Rohde, *Parties and Leaders in the Postreform House*; Polsby, *How Congress Evolves*.

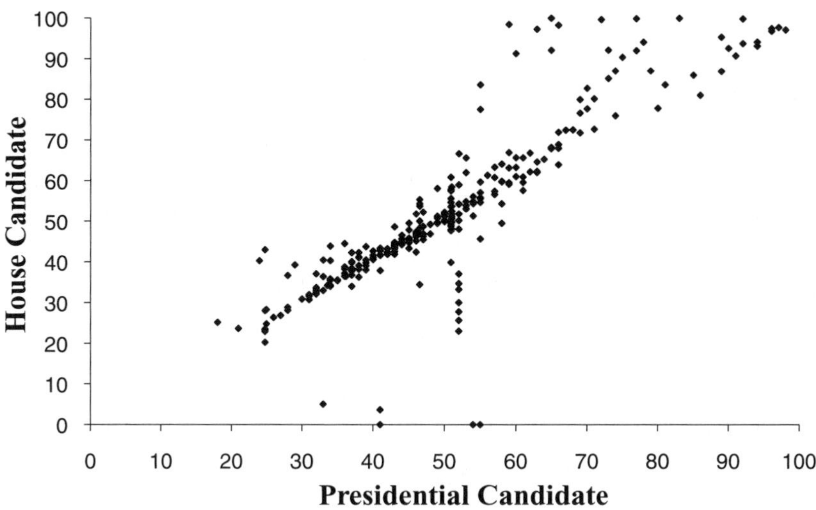

FIGURE 8.6. Democratic Presidential and House Vote Percentages, 1900

short-term relationships. A repeated focus on cross-sectional analyses conceals change. Figures 8.6 and 8.7 provide an indication of this. In 1900 there was a strong association between presidential and House results. In 2008 there is a very similar association. If a regression analysis is run on the two years the results would be very similar, but the location of specific state delegations would be very different in 2008 than in 1900. In 1900 southern delegations were in the upper right corner of the scatter-plot. By 2008 they were in the

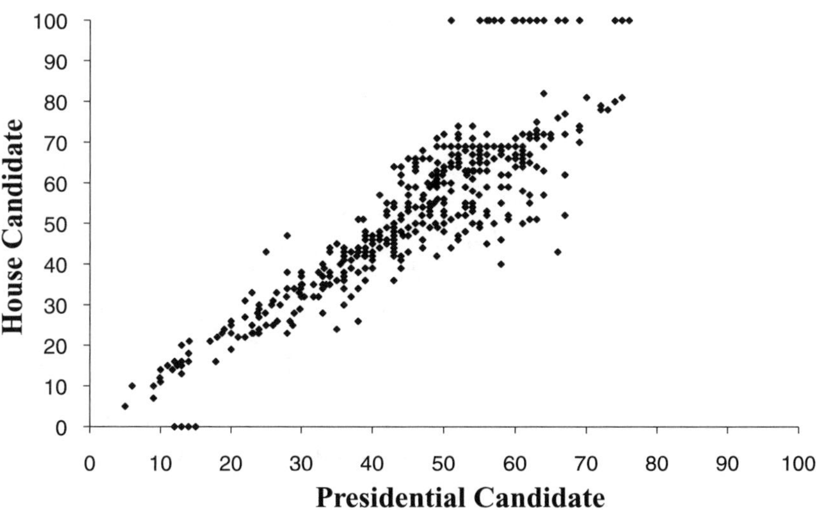

FIGURE 8.7. Democratic Presidential and House Vote Percentages, 2008

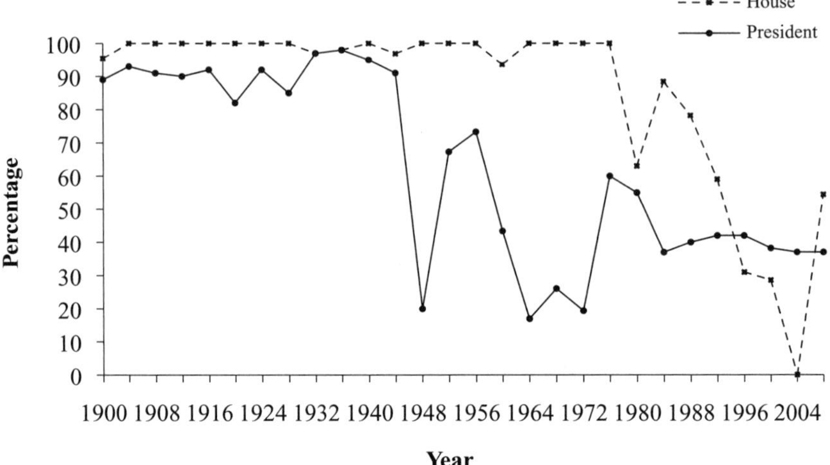

FIGURE 8.8. Democratic Vote for President and House, Mississippi 1, 1900–2008

lower left corner. The difficulty is that separate cross-sections in 1900 and 2008 suggest that things are essentially the same because a regression analysis yields the same relationship. In reality, however, the two scatter-plots represent the beginning and end of a lengthy process of change.

The process of change involved districts moving through time to different positions. Figures 8.8 and 8.9 indicate the paths over time of two illustrative districts, Mississippi One and Connecticut One. As the districts gradually shifted positions, they essentially passed each other in terms of relative positioning in scatter-plots for successive years.

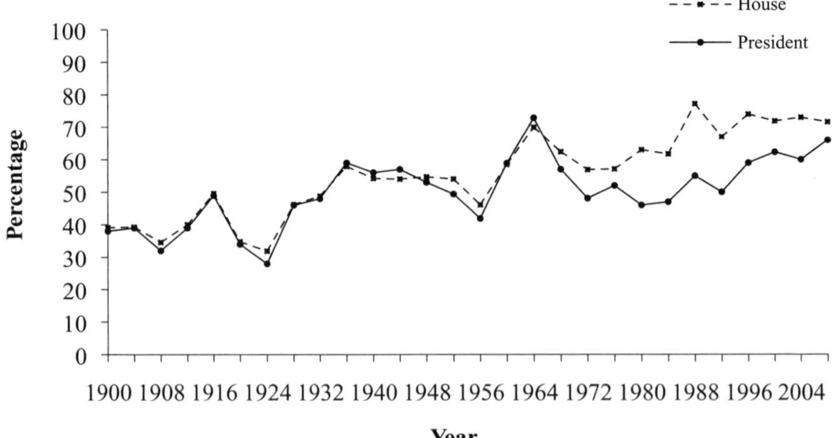

FIGURE 8.9. Democratic Vote for President and House, Connecticut 1, 1900–2008

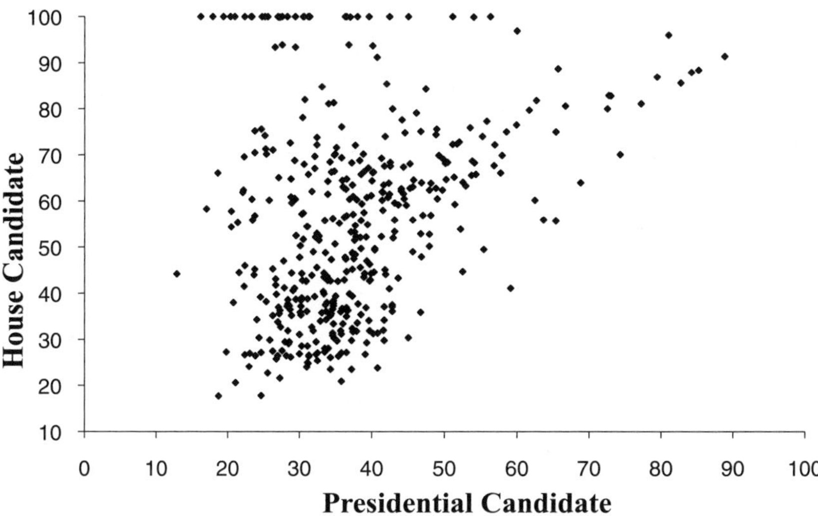

FIGURE 8.10. Democratic Presidential and House Vote Percentages, 1972

In 1900 Mississippi One would have been in the upper right quadrant of a scatter-plot. By 2008 it would be in the lower left quadrant. Connecticut One would have gone in the opposite direction, moving from the lower left to upper right quadrant. These transitions are not evident in a single cross-section. As these long-term transitions were in process, they resulted in the scatter-plot for 1972 shown in Figure 8.10. This scatter-plot suggested that the relationship between presidential and House results was essentially coming apart. In reality House districts were following different paths of change. If analyses had been able to incorporate time and the paths of change for results for the two offices, then 1972 would have been seen as a situation of transition, and not dealignment or the demise of the presidential–House relationship. The challenge is to incorporate changes over time in trying to understand how this relationship declined and then returned.

9

Regional Patterns of Change

The significant changes in presidential–House election results have occurred within regions. The implications have been national in scope, but it is within regions that there were differential rates of change within House districts for presidential and House election results. The following examines these changes by region.

In tracking change within regions, it is important to note that as the changes of the 1960s began to unfold, regions began with different situations. The South witnessed the greatest change because it began as the most distinct region within the nation. In 1950 it was a region in which the minority party within the region had a very poor image. The Republican Party had little in the way of state organizations for recruiting and supporting candidates.[1] The party had such a poor image that when the Republican national party organization made efforts to attract support within the region, it used names that did not identify the efforts as being associated with the party.[2] In the remainder of the nation the Democrats were generally seen as being in the minority when change started, but their disadvantage was not as bad as that faced by Republicans in the South.

The differences in the regional situations of each party in the late 1950s are presented in Figures 9.1 and 9.2. Figure 9.1 indicates the percentage of House seats that were uncontested by Republicans in the South and by Democrats in the other two regions. As an indicator of the weakness of their situation, the focus is on what percentage of seats the minority party did not contest. Another indicator Figure 9.2 tracks the percentage of seats won by Republicans in the South and by Democrats in the other two regions.

---

[1] Klinkner, *The Losing Parties*, 41–70.

[2] Daniel J. Galvin, "Presidential Partisanship Reconsidered: Eisenhower, Nixon, Ford, and the Rise of Polarized Politics," *Political Research Quarterly*, Vol. 65, No. 1 (January 2012), 1–15.

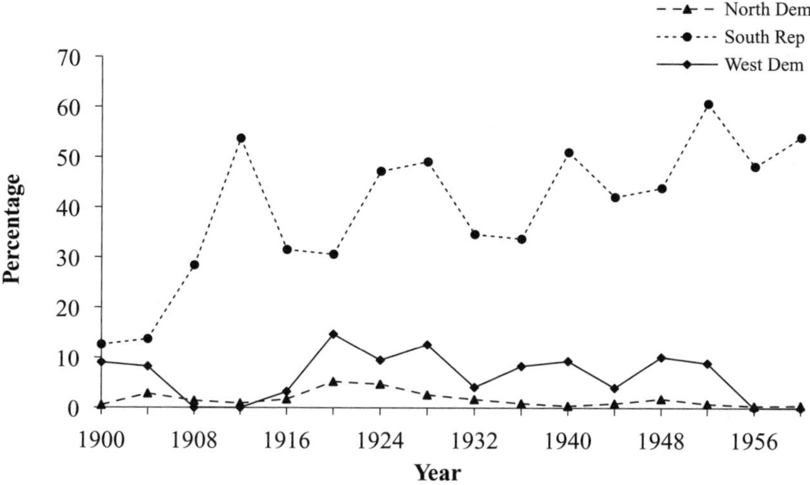

FIGURE 9.1. Percentage of House Seats Uncontested by Minority Party by Region, 1900–1960

From 1900 to 1960 the Republican Party was so weak in the South that it often did not contest 50 percent of House elections, and consequently won few seats. The party faced a serious challenge to persuade candidates that they should run as Republicans. In the other two regions Democrats were in much better shape. The party was able to recruit candidates, contest almost all seats, and win a substantial percentage of seats in some years. The elections of the 1930s significantly increased the party's success in winning seats in both

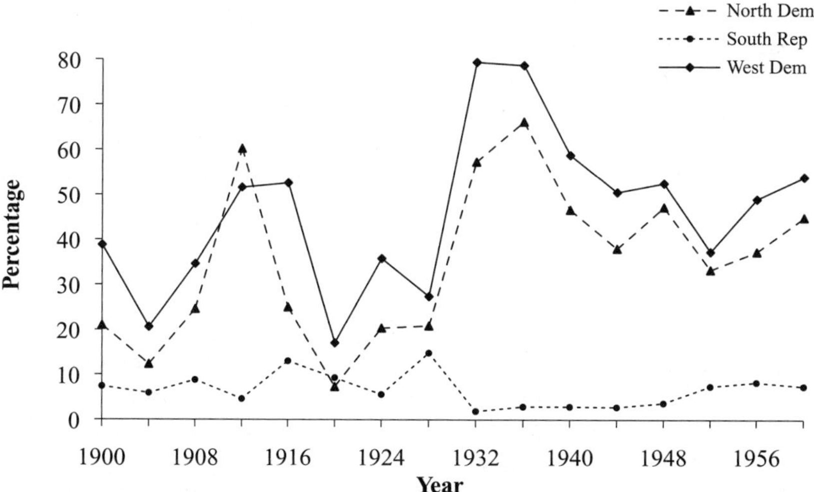

FIGURE 9.2. Percent of Seats Won by Minority Party by Region, 1900–1960

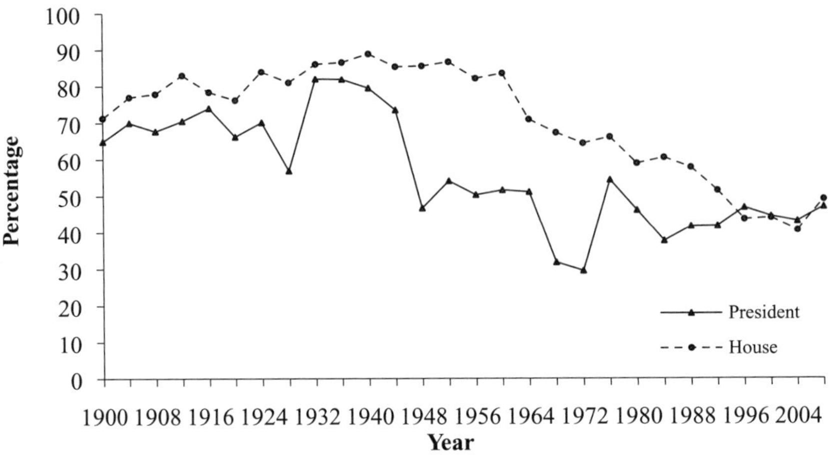

FIGURE 9.3. Southern Democratic Vote Percentages, 1900–2008

regions. Although Democrats were not in a weak situation outside the South, the gains they made in the 1930s eroded in the 1940s and 1950s, and only in the West was the party winning a majority of seats by 1960. The important matter is that the Republican Party began in a weak situation in the South, whereas Democrats began with a fairly good base of support outside the South.

To assess the process of change, four matters will be discussed here. First, at the aggregate level, how did partisan presidential and House vote percentages evolve? To what extent did they move together or separately? Second, if they proceeded separately, was there a timing to the pattern that accords with what we know was going on regarding the efforts of parties? Third, is there a pattern of separation and rejoining that coincides with the national pattern of a decrease and then increase in the correlation of presidential and House results? Fourth, what happened to incumbent vote percentages during these transitions? The common assertion is that they have been increasing. If partisan shifts were occurring within regions, the more likely matter is that the fortunes of candidates of one party were increasing and that of the other were declining. Is there evidence of such patterns?

The South

The South is the most obvious case of how change separated presidential and House results. In the early 1900s the region voted solidly Democratic for presidential and House candidates. The 1948 rupture over civil rights abruptly lowered support for Democratic presidential candidates, and it largely stayed at around 50 percent or lower for the next 60 years (Figure 9.3). In House races the region continued to vote strongly Democratic (at 60 percent or more) through 1984. It was not until 1996 that the average Democratic vote for presidential and House candidates came together. The lag in House voting patterns created a situation in which many Democratic House incumbents were running well ahead of their presidential candidate, resulting in a significant separation of votes between the two offices within the region.

These trends might also be presented in terms of how Republican candidates were faring, because the changes involved the rise of the Republican Party in the South (Figure 9.4). Republican presidential candidates were receiving higher levels of support faster than House candidates until 1992.[3]

The prevalence of cases in which Republican presidential candidates ran well ahead of or behind their party's House candidates is shown in Figure 9.5. This situation is defined as a difference of 10 percentage points between the presidential candidate (ahead or behind) and the House candidate. From 1900 through 1948 Republican presidential candidates were 10 percentage points or more ahead of their House candidates in less than 40 percent of districts (with the exceptions of 1928 and 1940). From 1952 through 1988 the percentage varied from 40 to 80. By 1992 Republican House candidates were doing much better in the region, and for the next four presidential elections there were roughly even percentages of districts where the presidential candidate ran ahead of or behind the House candidate. These changes within the South played a signifi- cant role in the declining national correlation between presidential and House results in the 1960s–1980s. During those years there was a growing and large separation between the percentages received for the two offices in the South.

The central issue is the lag in House results as presidential results changed. Figure 9.6 presents three relevant indicators of the progression of change. The first matter is how many House districts Republican presidential candidates won. As electoral change occurred, Republican presidential candidates began to win more House districts.[4] In 1952 this percent jumped to 39.3 and stayed at roughly that level until 1972 when the percentage increased dramatically. Beginning in 1980 the lowest percentage of House districts won by Republican presidential candidates was 55.9 in 1996.

Although results for House Democrats might have moved with presidential results, they did not. House Democrats continued to get elected in districts that Republican presidential candidates were winning (labeled as "Dem in RP Win" for Republican President Win). The percentage of House Democrats in districts won by Republican presidential candidates increased in 1952 and remained high through 1988. Only in 1992 did the percentage decline of Demo- cratic wins in districts won by Republican presidential candidates. For *36 years* a substantial percentage of Democratic winners were in districts their presiden- tial candidate *lost*. The result was that the average difference between the Democratic presidential and House vote increased significantly and generally fluctuated between 30 and 50 percentage points from 1948 through 1988. The

[3] Black and Black, *Politics and Society in the South*; and Joseph Aistrup, *The Southern Strategy Revisited* (Lexington: University of Kentucky Press, 1996).

[4] Winning is defined as the Republican presidential candidate percentage being higher than the Democratic presidential candidate's percentage.

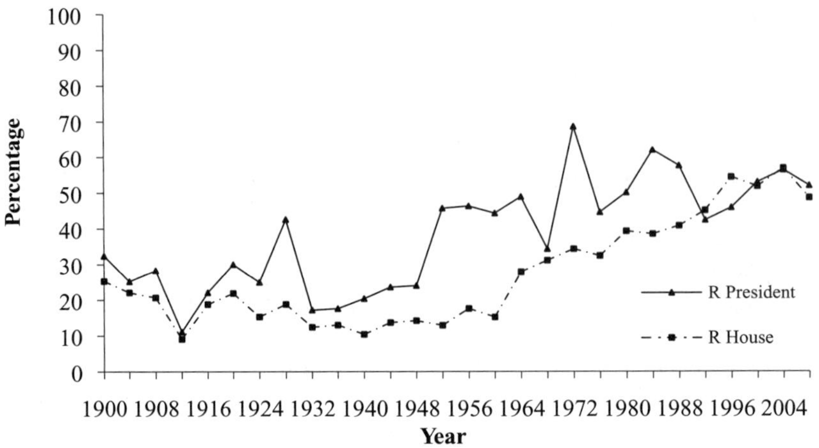

FIGURE 9.4. Republican Presidential and House Percentages in the South, 1900–2008

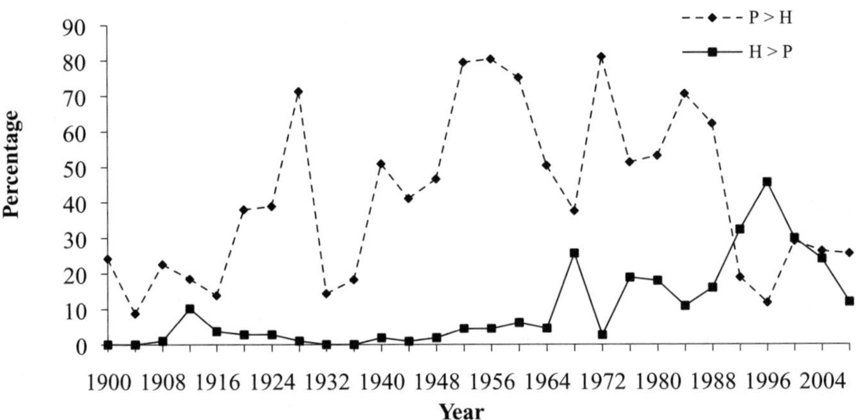

FIGURE 9.5. Percentage of Southern House Districts with Republican Presidential Candidate Running 10 Points ahead or behind the House Candidate, 1900–2008

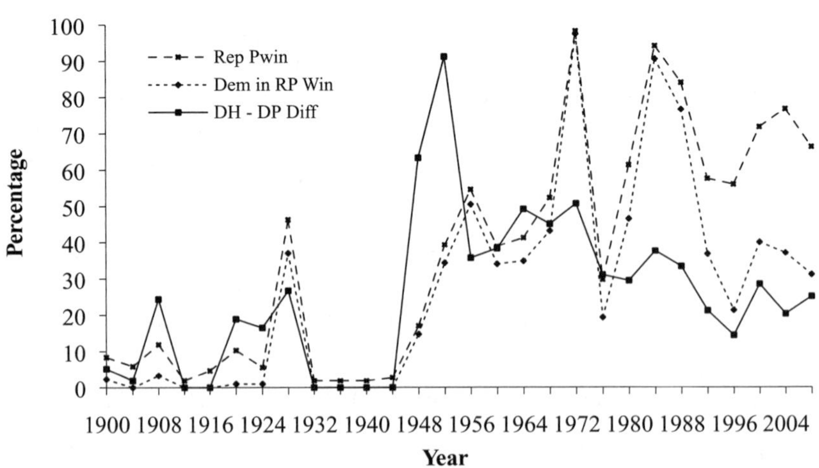

FIGURE 9.6. Electoral Patterns in the South, 1900–2008

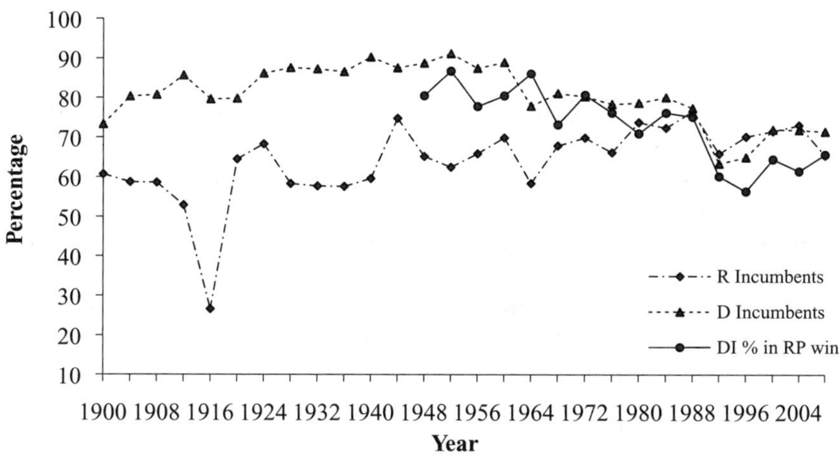

FIGURE 9.7. Southern Incumbent Vote Percentages, by Party, 1900–2008

separation of results, which diminished their correlation, reflected a lengthy lag before House outcomes matched presidential results. For almost 40 years many House Democratic Members were able to hold off the electoral tide sweeping the South. The number of Democrats steadily declined, but those who did survive were able to create a significant separation of their results from presidential results.

To return to the original issue of the fortunes of incumbents, did incumbent House Democrats create this separation by increasing their vote percentage? Or, is the mark of a successful incumbent the ability to hold off the effect of the broad partisan shifts occurring? Or, did the fortunes of Democratic and Republican incumbents gradually move in the direction of the partisan shift occurring? Did Democratic incumbent vote percentages decline, and Republican vote percentages increase over time? The South was moving away from Democrats and toward Republicans. As Figure 9.7 indicates, in 1964 the fortunes of Democratic incumbents began to decline. Their average declined from 89.0 in 1960 to the upper 70s from 1964 through 1988, and then to around 70 after that. In contrast the number of incumbent Republicans was increasing and their average vote percentages were very gradually increasing.

What happened to Democratic incumbents as partisan sentiment moved more Republican within their districts? Figure 9.7 also presents the trend for Democratic incumbents running in districts won by Republican presidential candidates. Their percentages gradually declined from the low 80s in 1948 to 75 in 1992 and then into the mid-60s. There was a gradual decline in the number of Democratic incumbents running in this category of districts, from at least 30 from 1948 through 1992, and then to about 20 after that. Democratic incumbents did not maintain their numbers or percentages as Republican presidential candidates did better.

This declining situation for Democratic members is evident in what happened to those exiting the House in different time periods. In this case the exit might be through retirement or via a loss. Many found that they were leaving office with a vote percentage less than they began with. Of all southern Democrats exiting the House during 1900–1949, 38.7 left with a lower percentage than their initial percentage. Among those exiting from 1950 to 2008, 53.6 percent had a lower percentage. Among Republicans the pattern is reversed. Among those exiting during 1900–1949, 79.6 percent left with a lower percentage, whereas among those exiting from 1950–2008 only 39.9 percent left with a lower percentage. The shifting partisan fortunes within the region were affecting the ability of a member to improve his or her vote percentage.

The South underwent a significant transition from 1952 to 1992. Republican presidential candidates made significant inroads into the region, winning an increasing number of House districts. Republican House candidates lagged in their success, and many Democratic incumbents were able to survive with declining vote percentages. This created a significant discrepancy between presidential and House results during the 40-year span. The discrepancy was not because House incumbents were able to increase or even maintain their vote percentages. As change unfolded, Democratic incumbents found themselves with declining vote percentages. However, the decline was not as fast as the changes occurring in presidential results, resulting in a reduced correlation within the South between presidential and House results from the 1950s through the 1980s.

Northern Changes

Change does not necessarily proceed in the same way across regions. Political conditions differ by region. The South had a very strong commitment to the Democratic Party when change commenced in the 1950s. The conservativism of Southern House members as Republican presidents made inroads into the region allowed many to survive for years and created a significant separation between presidential and House results. It was the compatibility of Southern House Democrats with shifting partisan sentiments that was important.

The North and the remainder of the nation began with more support for Democrats, and the extent of separation of presidential and House results was not as great. Although of lesser magnitude, there was still a pattern of much greater separation of results occurring for a sustained time period. Then the separation declined. The following first tracks the pattern of separation within the North and then the remainder of the nation. Then a possible explanation of the source and timing of the separation is offered.

The North as a region was never as committed to the Republican Party as the South was to the Democratic Party. The consequence is that as the major changes of the last 60 years began to unfold, northern House Republicans did not begin with strong backing from voters and high electoral support that

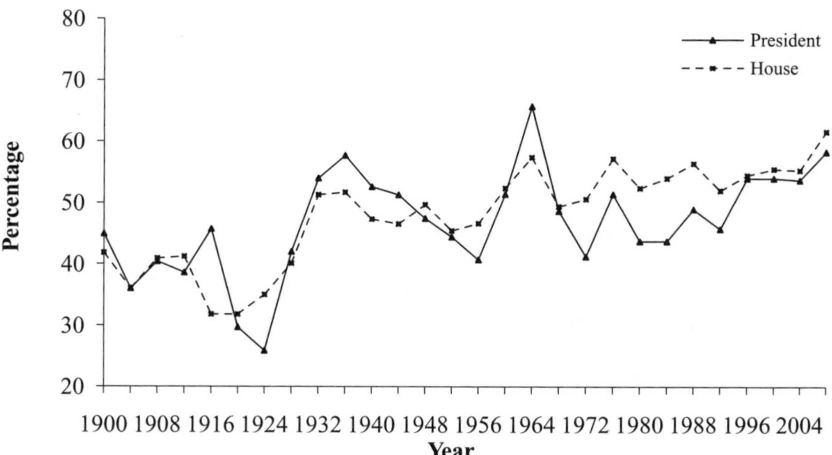

FIGURE 9.8. Average Democratic Presidential and House Vote, North, All Districts, 1900–2008

allowed them to survive and create a significant separation from presidential voting.[5] Whatever advantage Republicans had was largely eliminated by the elections of the 1930s. As the 1950s began Democrats were not far below 50 percent within the region, which created a competitive political situation across much of the North.

Despite these circumstances, presidential and House results still separated as political change began to unfold around the 1950s. As Figure 9.8 indicates, the North was gradually drifting more Democratic. Beginning in the 1960s, the Republican Party pursued a more conservative policy direction, which many voters in the region did not like, and support for the Democratic Party gradually increased.[6]

Although there was a general increase in Democratic support, the important matter is the sequence of that increase for the two offices. It is this difference within districts that played a role in creating some separation between voting results. Until 1932 many House Democrats ran ahead of their presidential candidates. In the 1930s Franklin Roosevelt was able to run ahead of more House candidates. Figure 9.9 indicates the percentage of northern House races in which the Democratic presidential candidate ran 10 points ahead of a Democratic House candidate, and the percentage of races in which the House candidate ran 10 points ahead of the presidential candidate. Presidential candidates can help a party by making voting for a party acceptable and encouraging candidates to run for House seats. During the 1930s and 1940s Roosevelt

[5] Stonecash, *Reassessing the Incumbency Effect*, 74–80.
[6] Reiter and Stonecash, *Counter Realignment*, 101–146.

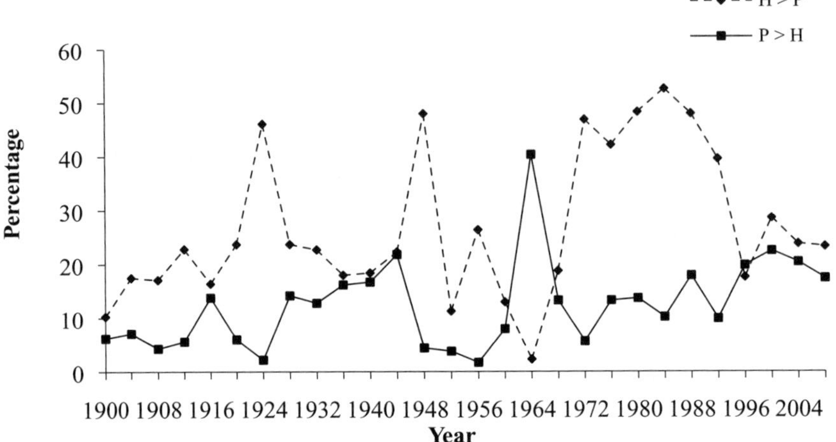

FIGURE 9.9. Percentage of Northern House Districts with President or House Results 10 Points ahead of the Other, 1900–2008

contributed to that in the North. As higher levels of voting for Democrats became more stable, there were more districts in which a Democratic House candidate could presumably build on that base and run well ahead of Democratic presidential candidates.

The distinct change (Figures 9.9 and 9.10) over time within the North is the separation between presidential and House candidates that occurred in 1972–1992, followed by a significant decline in that separation after 1992. That change will be discussed later.

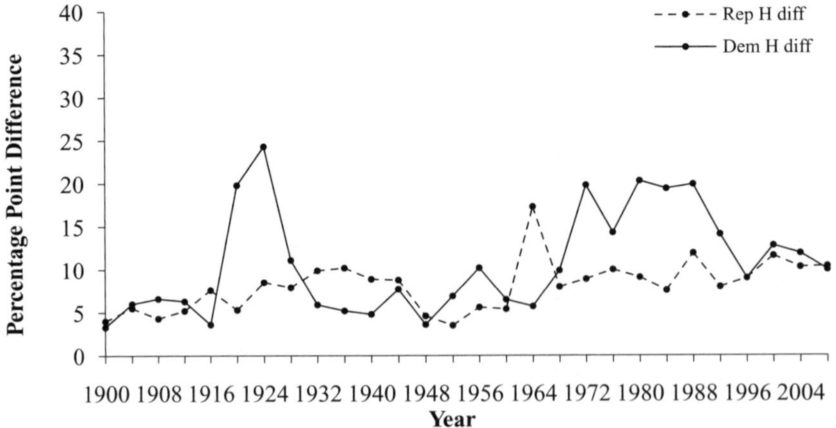

FIGURE 9.10. Average Percentage Point Separation between Democratic and Republican House Winners and Presidential Votes, North, 1900–2008

FIGURE 9.11. Republican Northern House Members, 1900–2008

As with the South, the interesting issue is what happened to Republicans, and particularly Republican incumbents. As support for the Republican Party was eroding, how did this decline affect incumbents? The long-term decline of the Republican situation in the North was severe. As Figure 9.11 indicates, the number of seats won by Republicans in the North over the last century has declined steadily, from a high of 215 in 1920 to below 50 in the late 2000s.[7] There were fewer and fewer districts in which a Republican incumbent was even available to run for reelection.

How did the erosion of the fortunes of the Republican Party affect incumbents? Were they able to ward off the changing partisanship of the region? Figure 9.12 indicates the average vote percentage for Republican incumbents and contrasts their situation with open-seat winners. There were fewer incumbents surviving as the party lost ground, but those who did survive from 1968 to 1988 did better than open-seat winners. But as the party continued its decline after 1988, both incumbents and open-seat winners experienced declining percentages.

Just as with the South, the ability of incumbents in the region to improve their vote percentages was contingent on the trend in partisan support. The contrast between the trends for Democratic and Republican incumbents is telling. The trend in partisanship within the region was toward Democrats. As this trend continued, Democratic House incumbents increased their vote

---

[7] The party's declining fortunes are also evident in how House members exited the House. From 1900 to 1949 the percentage of House Republicans exiting via a loss was 44.9 for Republicans and 56.0 for Democrats. From 1950 to 2008 the parties reversed the incidence of exiting via a loss with 39.1 percent of Republicans exiting via a loss and 33.9 of Democrats ending with a loss. For an earlier assessment of the frequency of exiting via a loss see Robert S. Erikson, "Is There Anything Such as a Safe Seat?," *Polity*, Vol. 8, No. 4 (Summer 1976), 623–632.

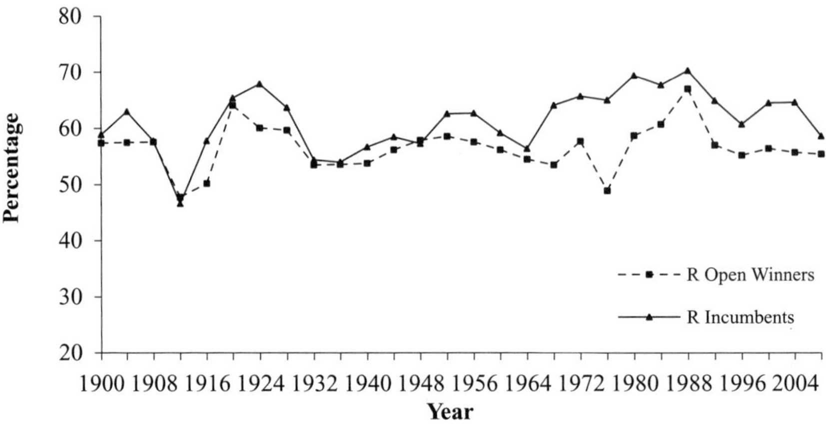

FIGURE 9.12. Vote Percentages of Northern Republican House Members, 1900–2008

percentages over time (Figure 9.13). As the number of Republican incumbents dwindled, these incumbents were increasingly in districts favorable to the party, and they were able to improve their fortunes from the 1950s through the 1980s. But after 1988 even these remaining Republican incumbents have not fared well. Incumbency alone does not yield higher vote percentages for House members. It is the partisan trend within the region that affects whether an incumbent's vote percentage increases or decreases.

The Remainder of the Nation

The most prominent political trends in the nation have involved the regions of the South and the North. The remainder of the nation has not had a clear

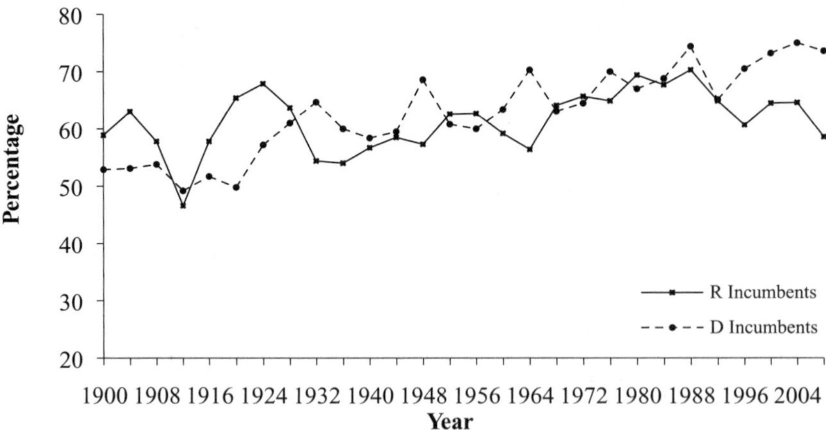

FIGURE 9.13. Northern Incumbent Vote Percentages, by Party, 1900–1928

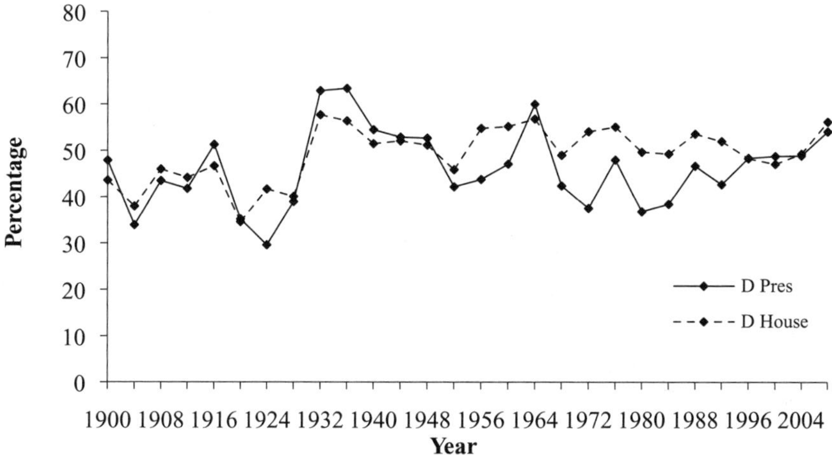

FIGURE 9.14. Vote Percentages for President and House, Remainder of Nation, 1900–2008

regional identity, and is generally not seen as reflecting an obvious pattern of change. Have the districts within this region experienced a separation of presidential and House results anything like the other two regions? The South was moving Republican, and the North was moving Democratic. The sequence of success for presidential and House candidates varied within each region, creating separation of results for several decades. Did that also occur in the remainder of the nation?

The remainder of the nation shows no clear partisan drift (Figure 9.14). The region was more Republican than Democratic until the elections of 1932–1948 brought the average percentage for Democrats to around 50 percent. Since then House Democratic candidates have fluctuated around 50 percent, and presidential candidates received a lower level of support from 1952 through 1992. The important matter is that there is no clear partisan trend such that we might expect presidential or House results to lead the other.

Although there is no partisan trend, essentially the same pattern of a separation of presidential and House results has played out in this region (Figure 9.15). The correlation of results before the 1950s was relatively high, but it then dipped beginning in the 1950s. After 1972 the correlation increased, reaching an average of .8 in 1996 and after. The percentage of districts with a split-outcome rose steadily from the 1920s until 1984 and then declined significantly. The absolute difference between presidential and House results also increased during this time, and has declined in recent years. The pattern is very similar to that in the other two regions.

House candidates for the Democratic Party were able to do better than the Democratic presidential candidates. The result (Figure 9.16) was that from

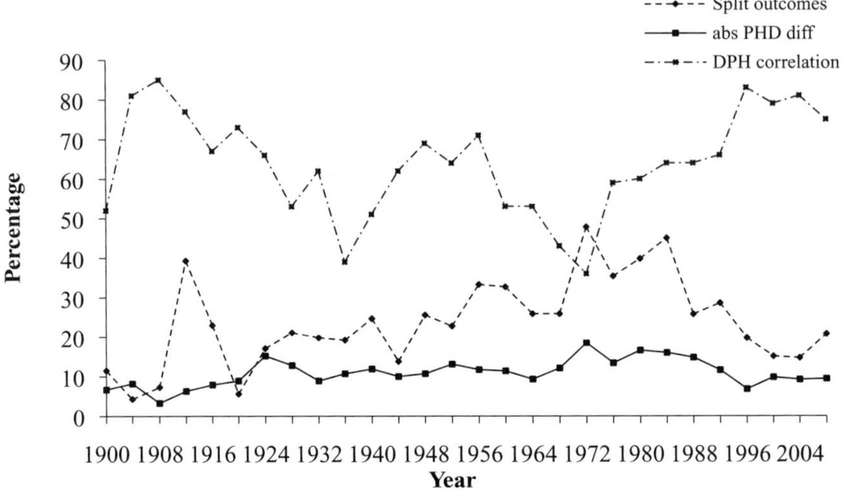

FIGURE 9.15. Presidential–House Trends in Remainder of Nation, 1900–2008

1948 through 1992 almost half of House districts had a situation where the Democratic House candidate was running 10 points or more ahead of the Democratic presidential candidate. Then in 1996 and after presidential and House candidate percentages came closer together.

The lack of a clear partisan trend in the district also appears to have resulted in neither Democratic nor Republican incumbent vote percentages changing much over time. As Figure 9.17 indicates, there is no clear pattern for incumbent

FIGURE 9.16. Percentage of Districts in Remainder of Nation with Democratic President or House Results 10 Points ahead of the Other, 1900–2008

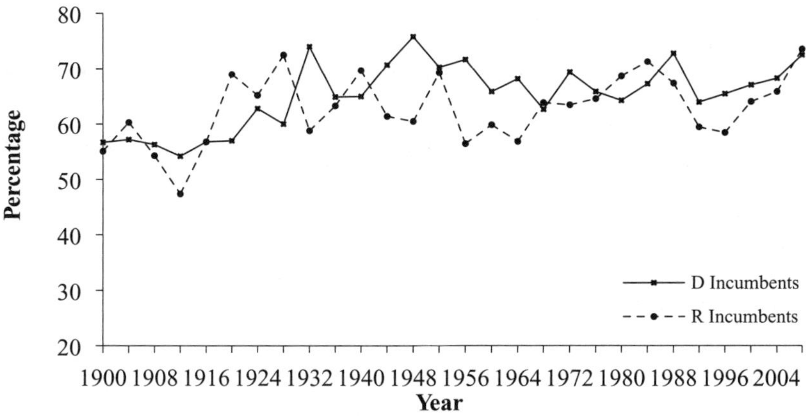

FIGURE 9.17. Remainder Incumbent Vote Percentages, by Party, 1900–2008

vote percentages in recent decades. For the most part percentages fluctuated in the 65–70 percent range.

Sources and Timing of Separation

In all three regions a separation of presidential and House results developed in or after the 1950s, reducing the correlation of results. The presence of this pattern in the South fits with our sense of how the Republican Southern Strategy played out in that region. Republican presidential candidates pursued conservatives and achieved success before the party's House candidates did. Eventually success in House elections caught up.

The far less-studied issue is why a separation occurred elsewhere in the nation. Explaining that will require detailed studies of what happened in those regions, but a speculative and tentative answer involves the problems of Democratic presidential candidates during this time. If there is an issue that has caused problems for the Democratic Party, and particularly presidential candidates, it is race.[8] The party made a decision in the 1960s to align itself with civil rights.[9] That issue created an identity that some have argued drove away many white voters.[10] It prompted some in the party to argue for less attention to race and more to economic issues. By some accounts Bill Clinton sought to distance himself and the party somewhat from identification with nonwhites.[11]

---

[8] Rogers M. Smith and Desmond S. King, "Racial Orders in American Political Development," *American Political Science Review*, Vol. 99, No. 1 (February 2005), 75–92.

[9] Carmines and Stimson, *Issue Evolution*.

[10] Edsall and Edsall, *Chain Reaction*; Kuhn, *The Neglected Voter*.

[11] Jon F. Hale, "The Making of the New Democrats," *Political Science Quarterly*, Vol. 110. No. 2 (Summer 1995), 207–232.

TABLE 9.1. *Differences in Presidential–House Success by Percent Nonwhite in District, North, 1952–2008*

	Years		
	1952–1968	1972–1988	1992–2008
Nonwhite 10%	N = 856	N = 718	N = 432
House percentage	46.7	48.7	46.5
President percentage	47.1	41.6	45.0
Percent split	24.5	33.3	25.7
Average absolute difference	7.8	14.7	12.2
Nonwhite 10–19%	N = 134	N = 166	N = 236
House percentage	57.0	57.2	54.7
President percentage	56.0	45.8	52.5
Percent split	14.2	42.2	22.7
Average absolute difference	6.6	16.5	11.7
Nonwhite 20–29%	N = 43	N = 62	N = 79
House percentage	61.1	67.8	62.7
President percentage	59.3	55.3	58.0
Percent split	11.6	21.0	12.7
Average absolute difference	4.6	16.3	11.0
Nonwhite 30% +	N = 75	N = 79	N = 143
House percentage	72.9	86.2	81.3
President percentage	70.0	78.5	76.8
Percent split	5.3	1.3	2.1
Average absolute difference	5.8	8.9	6.0

This political positioning problem suggests that examining districts and election results by their racial makeup may help explain what happened to the congruence of presidential–House results in the non-South. Table 9.1 presents a simplified summary of election results in the North for 1952–2008, the years for which we have data on the presence of nonwhites by district. The results are organized into three periods. During 1952–1968 there was less separation of presidential–House results. For 1972–1988 the separation increased, and then for 1992–2008 the separation declined. The years 1972–1988 are particularly interesting because this was when Democratic presidential candidates were seriously struggling with how to position themselves regarding race.

The interesting changes involve districts that were largely white (0–9 and 10–19 percent nonwhite). The vote for Democratic House candidates for each grouping of nonwhites was fairly stable across the three sets of years. What did occur in 1972–1988 was that Democratic presidential percentages declined in districts with more whites. These districts experienced a marked increase in the percentage of split-outcome districts and in the average absolute difference between presidential and House results. House candidates presumably

TABLE 9.2. *Differences in Presidential–House Success by Percent Nonwhite in District, Remainder of the Nation, 1952–2008*

	Years		
	1952–1968	1972–1988	1992–2008
Nonwhite<10%	N = 424	N = 351	N = 170
House percentage	48.0	48.3	42.4
President percentage	45.2	39.3	40.0
Percent split	30.7	39.0	26.0
Average absolute difference	9.6	14.5	10.7
Nonwhite 10–19%	N = 46	N = 120	N = 168
House percentage	67.8	51.9	45.1
President percentage	51.0	39.4	44.0
Percent split	32.6	40.0	21.4
Average absolute difference	18.1	18.6	9.3
Nonwhite<20–29%	N = 21	N = 52	N = 119
House percentage	74.3	62.3	46.0
President percentage	59.9	47.1	46.4
Percent split	4.8	42.3	29.4
Average absolute difference	17.1	17.0	10.8
Nonwhite 30% +	N = 33	N = 56	N = 181
House percentage	72.8	69.6	66.4
President percentage	58.7	54.8	62.1
Percent split	3.0	30.3	6.1
Average absolute difference	22.1	17.3	6.9

can create some differentiation of their image and preserve their vote percentage as presidential percentages fluctuate. In 1992–2008 in districts with less than 20 percent nonwhites, Democratic presidential results returned to roughly the levels of 1952–1968, reducing the presence of split-outcomes and absolute differences between presidential and House results. The suggestion is that Democratic presidential candidates struggled with the issue of race. Their identification with nonwhites cost them votes in largely white districts, whereas House candidates were affected less, creating a greater separation for the years 1972–1988.

There is not as clear of a pattern in the remainder of the nation (Table 9.2). One analytic difficulty is that the separation of results had already developed by 1952, the first year with data for the presence of nonwhites. Why that separation had already developed by the 1950s is not clear. Two matters are clear, however. First, Democrats experienced their largest separations in districts with fewer nonwhites. The party was struggling in 1952–1988 to build support for its presidential candidates in districts with higher percentages of whites.

Second, in 1992 and after, just as in the North, the results for the two offices came closer together, with the average House percentage falling and the presidential percentage rising. There is much to explore about why this evolved as it did, but it does appear that the party's struggles with its image affected its success in largely white districts. In recent years the results have come together, producing a greater association between the two.[12]

[12] Interpreting change in what many would characterize as the West is made more difficult because of the remarkable recent changes in the racial composition of districts occurring in that region. In the 1960s, 11 percent of House districts in that region had 20 percent or more nonwhites. The 2000 census indicated that 58 percent of House districts had 20 percent or more nonwhites. The 2010 census and reapportionment will likely indicate an even greater presence of nonwhites within the region. This change has been relatively recent and abrupt. How that will affect politics in this region in the future is unknown.

10

Realignment and Converging Results

By the 1980s presidential and House results were beginning to come together. The correlation between results was low during the 1960s and 1970s, but in 1980 the association began to increase, and by 2008 it was close to the level that prevailed in the early 1900s. Why and how did that happen? If results were converging, what was happening to incumbents?

The simple answer as to why the presidential–House correlation increased is that the number of split-district outcomes declined. A split district is one in which the presidential and House winners differ. The difference that creates this split could be small. It is possible that a presidential candidate might lose a district with 49 percent and the House candidate could win the district with 51 percent of the vote, creating a difference of two percentage points.

Although the difference might be small, over the last century split-outcome districts have averaged much larger deviations of House results from presidential results than for non-split districts. Figure 10.1 indicates the average absolute value deviation of House results from presidential results for split and non-split districts. From 1900 through 1916 the differences between the two types of districts were minimal. Beginning in 1920 and continuing through 1988 the average deviation increased significantly, rising from somewhat over 10 to the high 20s. Then in 1992 it declined, and has fluctuated between 15 and 20 since then. For non-split districts the deviations of House results from presidential results has been relatively constant and much lower.

Given this difference in results for split districts, the simplest explanation of the convergence of presidential and House results is that the percentage of districts with a split-outcome decreased. As Figure 10.2 indicates the percentage of districts with a split-outcome generally fluctuated between 15 and 20 percent from 1900 through 1952. Then in 1956 the percentage jumped to 29.7, and then erratically rose to a peak of 46 percent in 1984. It then declined, and

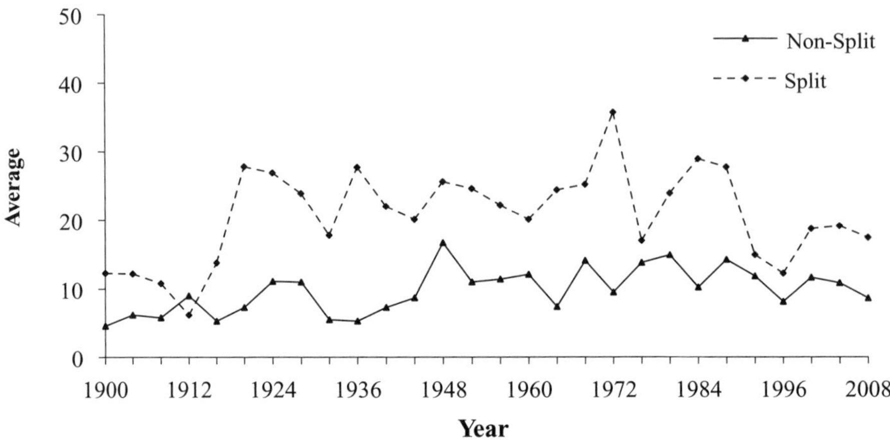

FIGURE 10.1. Absolute Average Difference House–Presidential Percentages, Non-Split and Split Outcomes, 1900–2008

in 2008 was 19.1 percent. That decrease brought presidential–House results closer.

The rise and decline of split-outcomes may explain why the correlation declined and then increased, but this only describes the pattern. What happened that led to the results converging after several decades of a reduced association? The primary reason was how realignment was playing out. From 1900 through the 1940s there was a rough correspondence between the aggregate success of Republican presidential and House candidates. As Figure 10.3 indicates, fluctuations in the success rate of House candidates followed the fluctuations of presidential candidate fortunes. Then from 1952 to 1988 the fortunes of

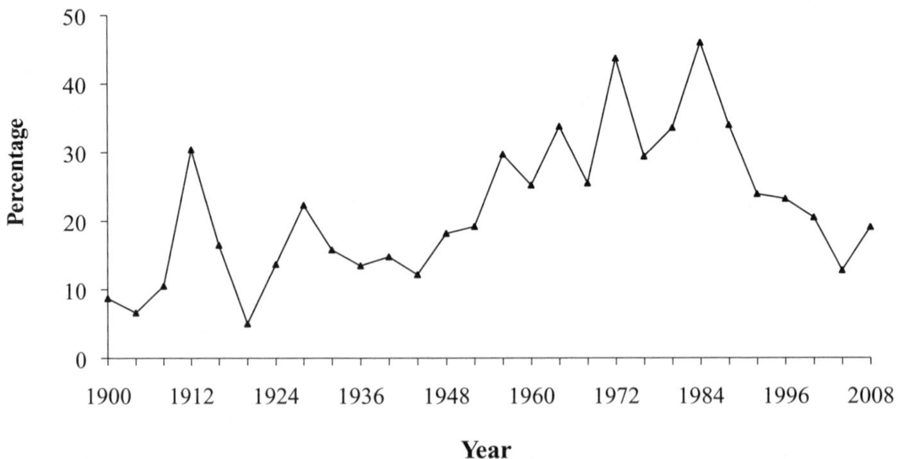

FIGURE 10.2. Percentage of House Districts with Split Outcomes, 1900–2008

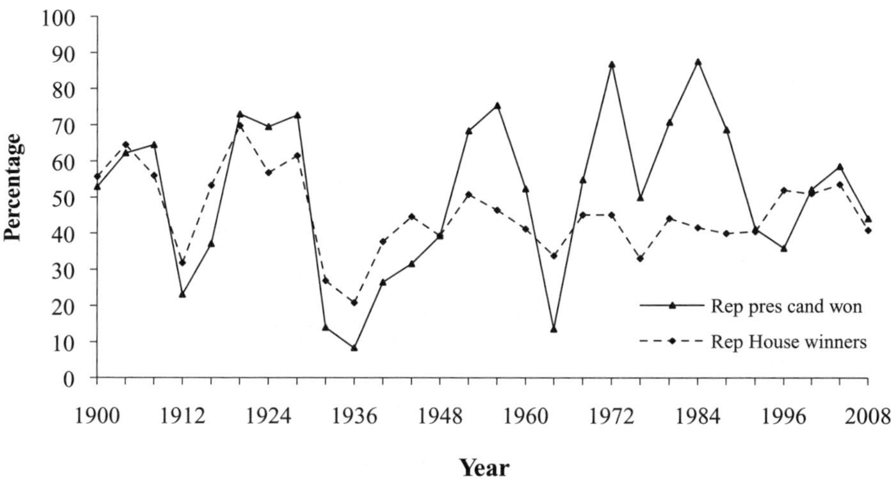

FIGURE 10.3. Percentage of House Districts Won by Republican Presidential and House Candidates, 1900–2008

Republican presidential candidates became disconnected from the success rates of House candidates.

The problem for the Republican Party was its yield rate for House candidates in districts won by its presidential candidates. After the difficult decades of the 1930s and the 1940s, the party began to recover in the 1950s in presidential elections, but it could not bring House winners along with it as well. As shown in Figure 10.4, the party was not able to win a high percentage of House seats in districts that Republican presidential candidates were winning. From

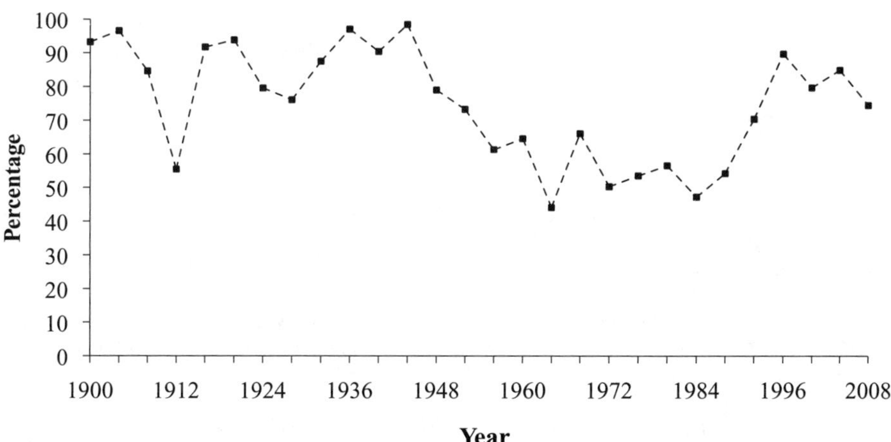

FIGURE 10.4. Success Rate of Republican House Candidates in Districts Won by Republican Presidential Candidates, 1900–2008

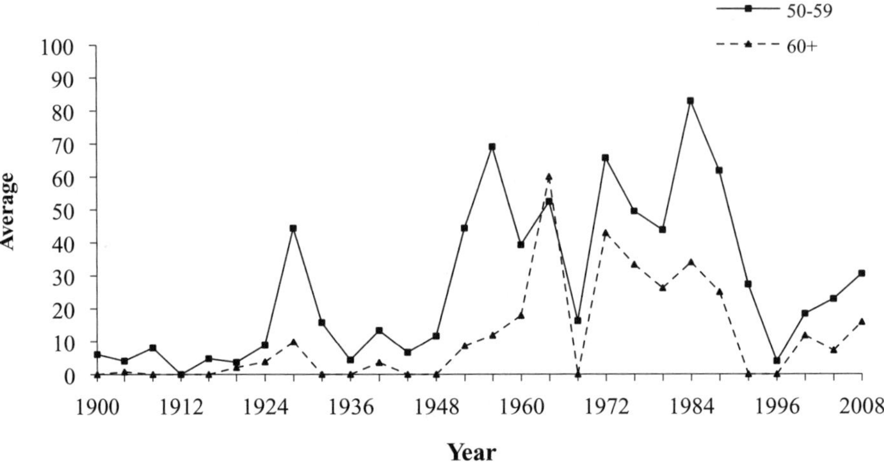

FIGURE 10.5. Percentage of Seats Won by House Democratic Candidates by Percentage for Republican Presidential Candidates, 1900–2008

1948 through 1992 this success rate was relatively low.[1] Indeed, for several decades House candidates were winning only about 50 percent of the districts their presidential candidate won. Then in the 1990s and 2000s they increased their success rate to roughly 80 percent. Republican presidential candidates were attracting a different base, and it took a long time for House candidates to catch up in terms of victories. Even the much-discussed success of Ronald Reagan in altering the party base did not generate victories.[2]

The problem for Republicans was that many Democrats continued to win in districts Republican presidential candidates were winning. Figure 10.5 presents Democratic success for districts in which Republican presidential candidates won 50–59 or 60 or more percent of the vote. As late as 1988, House Democratic candidates won the majority of districts in which a Republican presidential candidate won 50–59 percent of the vote.

---

[1] This may be because Republican House members were likely to retire sooner out of frustration with their minority status, or because it was harder to recruit new candidates. On the former, see Ansolabehere and Gerber, "Incumbency Advantage and the Persistence of Legislative Majorities," and John B. Gilmour and Paul Rothstein, "Early Republican Retirement: A Cause of Democratic Dominance in the House of Representatives," *Legislative Studies Quarterly*, Vol. 18, No. 3 (August 1993), 345–365. On candidate recruitment see Earl Black and Merle Black, *The Rise of Southern Republicans* (Cambridge, MA: Harvard University Press, 2002).

[2] For an analysis of how Ronald Reagan's political context and approach differed from that of George Bush, see Sidney M. Milkis and Jesse H. Rhodes, "George W. Bush, the Republican Party, and the 'New' American Party System," *Perspectives on Politics*, Vol. 5, No. 3 (September 2007), 461–488.

TABLE 10.1. *Number of Seats Won by Democrats by Republican Presidential Vote Percentages*

Republican Presidential%	N	Reagan in 1984			N	Using Election Results from: Bush in 1988	
		1984		1986		1988	1990
		Rep	Dem	Dem		Dem	Dem
<40	28	1	27	27	48	47	47
40–49	26	0	26	25	90	77	77
50–59	146	26	120	120	165	100	106
60+	235	155	80	86	132	34	38
Total Dems	435	182	253	258	435	258	268

Change in electoral alignments proceeds slowly,[3] and the 1980s are a striking indication of the ability of a party and its incumbents to survive while the partisan sentiment expressed in presidential election was shifting. In 1984 Reagan did very well, winning 381 of 435 (87.6 percent) House districts. While he was doing well, Democrats continued to win elections where he won the district. Table 10.1 presents the success of House Democrats by the percentage of the vote received in districts by Republican presidential candidates from 1984 to 1990. There was a remarkable lack of connection between presidential and House outcomes in those years. In 1984 the Democratic Party won 253 seats, but 200 of their seats were in districts that Reagan won. In districts where Reagan received 60 percent or more of the vote, Democrats won 80 of the 235 seats. In the 1986 elections Democrats maintained their 1984 pattern of successes.

In 1988 George H. W. Bush won fewer districts than Reagan did in 1984,[4] but he still won 299 of 435 (68.7 percent). Although Bush was making inroads into fewer districts, it was still the case that many House Democrats were in districts won by a Republican presidential candidate. In 1988, 134 of the 258 Democrats who won came from districts George Bush won. That continued in 1990 with 144 Democrats winning in districts that Bush had won in 1988. Democratic candidates were demonstrating remarkable staying power in inhospitable districts.

[3] Edward G. Carmines and Michael Wagner, "Political Issues and Party Alignments: Assessing the Issue Evolution Perspective," *Annual Review of Political Science*, Vol. 9 (2006), 67–81.

[4] The continuity of relative success from 1984 to 1988 is high, however, as the correlation of 1984 with 1988 is .93. George Bush's percentages in 1988 were lower than Reagan's by four to seven points for each category, but his relative pattern of support was essentially the same as Reagan's.

TABLE 10.2. *Republican House Candidates in Districts Where Republican Presidential Candidates Did Well, 1982–1990*

Republican Presidential%	Presidential Candidate Results				
	Reagan			Bush	
	82	84	86	88	90
Number Uncontested by Republicans					
50–59	19	24	22	31	26
60+	16	17	16	10	13
Average House Republican Vote Percentage[5]					
50–59	34.4	34.5	31.9	29.7	33.0
60+	50.4	56.2	54.1	56.7	53.7

Much of this was achieved by maintaining the same set of incumbent candidates over time. Of the 80 House Democrats who won in districts where Reagan received 60 percent or more in 1984, 54 were still running and winning office in the 1990 elections. Of the 120 House Democrats who won in districts where Reagan received 50–59 percent in 1984, 94 were still running and winning office by the 1990 elections. Incumbents were providing a strong buffer against partisan trends. It should be noted that these Democrats were not just from the South. In 1984 there were 200 Democrats in split-outcome districts. This was not just a southern phenomenon. Sixty-seven of these Democrats were in the South, and 133 were outside the South.

The stability of Democratic strength in districts voting Republican for president can also be seen in the pattern of voting percentages. Table 10.2 indicates the number of House seats uncontested by Republicans, grouped by the vote percentages of Republican presidential candidates. It also indicates the average Republican vote percentage for House candidates in those districts. Republicans consistently did not contest about 40 of the districts where Republican presidential candidates received 50 percent or more. In these districts Republican House candidates were only able to achieve a percentage in the low 30s. Although Republican presidents Reagan and to a lesser extent Bush had a significant impact of political discussion and on perceptions of where a Republican presidential candidate could win, House results did not change much during the time they held office.

The crucial transition came in the years from 1990 through 1996. Table 10.3 indicates just how much change occurred. The results are organized by the percentages of the vote that Republican presidential candidates won. For

---

[5] This includes all districts in each category, regardless of whether the district is contested or uncontested. The concern is overall Republican support, not just that for districts where their support may be higher, which may prompt a Republican candidate to run.

TABLE 10.3. *Party Success in House Elections by Republican Presidential Success, 1990–1996*

Republican Pres.%	Year of Election							
	1990		1992		1994		1996	
	Rep	Dem	Rep	Dem	Rep	Dem	Rep	Dem
Number of Seats Won by Each Party								
<40	1	47	6	95	6	95	5	119
40–49	13	77	44	110	68	86	84	70
50–59	58	106	89	48	118	19	105	15
60+	94	38	37	5	38	4	34	2
TOTAL	166	268	176	257	230	204	228	206
Average Percentage of Vote Won								
<40	20.6	76.5	26.7	68.0	29.8	67.9	26.7	69.9
40–49	32.3	65.0	41.9	55.0	48.3	49.7	44.1	53.0
50–59	42.9	54.9	54.0	42.2	64.8	33.5	60.1	37.6
60+	58.4	38.5	64.2	32.8	76.9	20.6	71.5	25.1

1990 the percentages are those George Bush won in his first election. For 1992–1996 the calculation is based on the total vote for the two major parties because H. Ross Perot ran as a third-party candidate in 1992 and 1996. For 1992 and 1994 it is the percentage of the two-party vote won by Bush in his reelection bid. For 1996 it is the percentage of the two-party vote won by Robert Dole in his campaign against Bill Clinton. The varying success of Bush and Dole in winning House districts makes comparisons across time difficult, but the change that occurred is still evident.

In 1990 Democrats won 144 seats in districts that George Bush won in 1988. Following the 1992 elections there were only 53 Democrats in that situation, a remarkable decline. Two factors contributed to this situation. First, some of this took place because George Bush won fewer House districts (41.2 percent compared to 68.7 four years earlier). In 1984 and 1988 Republican presidential candidates won many districts held by Democrats, but in 1992 that did not happen. Much of this was because real change occurred in the relationship between presidential and House results. This change was due to a combination of an exceptionally high number of retirements[6] and the steady rise in the presence of Republican candidates in the South.[7] The next significant change involved the 1994 elections. Republicans were able to win a substantial number of seats, particularly in districts in which Bush won more than 50 percent of

[6] Herrnson, *Congressional Elections*, 39.
[7] Byron E. Shafer and Richard Johnston, "The Transformation of Southern Politics Revisited: The House of Representatives as a Window," *British Journal of Political Science*, Vol. 31, No. 4 (September 2001), 619–624.

the vote. In 1996 Republican success increased even more in districts won by their presidential candidate.

From 1990 to 1996 the percentage of seats won by Republican House candidates in districts won by their presidential candidates increased from *51.4 to 70.4 to 87.2 to 89.1*. The set of districts involved in this calculation is affected by the fact that Republican presidential candidates were winning fewer House districts – reducing their success to more reliably Republican districts – but nonetheless the party's success in winning seats won by their presidential candidates was increasing. Presidential and House results were more closely associated with each other by 1994 and 1996.

The change in House Republican percentages in districts won by Republican presidential candidates was not marginal. The bottom half of Table 10.3 indicates the average Republican House vote percentage. In districts where Republican presidential candidates won between 50 and 59 percent, the Republican House percentage increased from 42.9 in 1990 to 54.0 in 1992, then to 64.8 in 1994 before slipping down slightly to 60.1 in 1996. It was a level of success that persisted and brought the presidential–House relationship to a higher level.

The transition in Republican success from 1990 to 1996 was the product of the exodus of many Democratic incumbents in 1992 and the defeat of many Democratic incumbents in 1994. In 1990 the Democrats had 268 seats, and in 1992 they had 257. In that year Democrats had 209 incumbents running and 92.3 percent won. Republicans also maintained their situation with 138 incumbents running and 92.0 percent winning. The 1992 elections maintained the dominance of House Democrats even though many of their members retired. In 1992, 87 incumbents retired, a relatively high number, and 59 of the retirees were Democrats.

The 1994 elections represent a case in which the congressional wing of a party took the initiative to try to reshape the party's electoral base. There are diverse interpretations of what issues motivated voters in that election,[8] but it is clear that the party made a major effort to recruit candidates and use issues to try to change the outcomes in House districts.[9] Democrats again

---

[8] For a review of the varying arguments about what electoral divisions were important in elections leading up to and including 1994, see Everett Carll Ladd, "The 1994 Congressional Elections: The Postindustrial Realignment Continues," *Political Science Quarterly*, Vol. 110, No. 1 (Spring 1995), 1–23; and Jeffrey M. Stonecash and Mack D. Mariani, "Republican Gains in the House in the 1994 Elections: Class Polarization in American Politics," *Political Science Quarterly*, Vol. 115, No. 1 (Spring 2000), 93–114.

[9] For analyses of the role of short-term conditions and party strategies for the 1994 elections, see Gary C. Jacobson, "The 1994 House Election in Perspective," *Political Science Quarterly*, Vol. 111, No. 2 (Summer, 1996), 203–223; Paul Frymer et al., "Party Elites, Ideological Voters and Divided Party Government," *Legislative Studies Quarterly*, Vol. 22, No. 2 (May 1997), 195–216; Elizabeth Drew, *Showdown: The Struggle between the Gingrich Congress and the Clinton White House* (New York: Touchstone Books, 1997); Dan Balz and Ronald Brownstein, *Storming the Gates: Protest Politics and the Republican Revival* (Boston: Little Brown,

TABLE 10.4. *The 1992–1994 Transition in Republican Success*

						1994 Results					
								Dem			
Rep	1992 Results				Open Seats			Incumbents		Overall Results	
Pres.%	R	D	% R	#	R won	% R	#	% R	R	D	% R
<40	6	95	5.9	7	0	0	90	2.2	6	95	5.9
40–49	44	110	28.6	19	13	68.4	96	16.7	68	86	44.2
50–59	89	48	65.0	17	17	100	37	48.6	118	19	86.1
60+	37	5	88.1	3	3	100	4	0	38	4	90.5
TOTAL	176	258	40.5	46	33	71.7	227		230	204	52.9

had more incumbents retire (31) than did Republicans (16). Over the course of two elections, 90 Democratic incumbents chose to retire, whereas only 44 Republicans retired.

The 1994 elections produced considerable success for Republicans (Table 10.4). Of the 160 Republican incumbents who ran for reelection, not a single one lost. There were 46 open seats, and Republicans won 33. Of the 227 Democratic incumbents who ran 191 won. The important matter was how House district results varied with presidential results from 1992. This pattern of relative success created the basis for the increased correlation between presidential–House results that was evident in 1996. Republican success in 1994 was strongly associated with how the Republican presidential candidate in 1992 had done. In the open-seat races Republican House candidates won all 20 seats that George Bush had won in 1992. Among those districts that he lost, the party won 13 of 26 districts. The crucial change was in 58 House districts that Democrats held in 1992 but Republican House candidates won in 1994. In 1992 George Bush averaged 50.2 percent of the two-party vote in those districts, but Republican House candidates averaged only 40.9 percent. In 1994 Republican House candidates averaged 54.4. In races against Democratic incumbents Republican challengers did much better in 1994 in districts Bush had won. There were 41 Democratic incumbents in districts Bush won, and Republican candidates won 43.9 percent of those races.

The overall result was a shift in the association between presidential and House results.[10] As Table 10.5 indicates, the altered relationship that emerged

1996); Philip A. Klinkner, Editor, *Midterm: The Elections in 1994 in Context* (Boulder, CO: Westview Press, 1996); and Polsky, "The 1996 Elections and the Logic of Regime Politics."

[10] This approach to analyzing election results provides a contrast with the assumptions of analysis that had developed by the 1990s. As noted by Newman and Ostrom, "Elections in the 1990s surprised analysts and politicians alike" (385) because it was assumed that "national and district-level races have become detached" (388). There was no reason to examine districts

TABLE 10.5. *Republican Presidential–House Success in House Districts*

Republican Pres. %	1996		2000		2004		2008	
	#	% Rep	#	% Rep	#	% Rep	#	% Rep
<40	181	17.1	115	6.1	92	0	141	2.1
40–49	167	66.5	116	38.8	88	19.3	107	32.7
50–59	75	96.0	136	80.9	131	77.1	118	69.5
60+	12	100.0	68	88.2	124	92.7	69	84.1
TOTAL	435	52.0	435	51.0	435	53.6	435	40.9

in 1994 persisted in 1996. Comparing the election years in the period 1992 and 1996 has some limitations because the number of districts that Republican presidential candidates won varied from 1992 to 1996, but Republican House candidates were increasingly winning districts that their presidential candidate won. If the focus is on only those districts that the Republican presidential candidate won, in 1992 George Bush won 179 districts, and House candidates won 70.4 percent of those districts. In 1994 Republican House candidates won 156 of 179, or 87.2 percent. In 1996 Bob Dole won only 156 seats, and Republican House candidates won 89.1 percent of those seats. In 1998 House Republicans won 87.1 percent of districts Dole won. In 2000 George W. Bush won more districts, 204, and Republican House candidates won 170, or 83.3 percent. In 1990 Republican House candidates won 152 of 296 districts (51.4 percent) won by their presidential candidate in 1988. By 1994 they were winning 87.2 percent of districts won by their presidential candidate in the prior election.

The important matter is that the change that occurred in 1994 persisted in subsequent years. In 1996 the correlation between presidential and House results increased to .78, and it has remained at around .80 in subsequent elections. The percentage of split-outcome districts declined in the 1990s along with the average absolute difference between presidential and House results (see Figure 3.3). The long process of change that began in the 1950s appears to have evolved into a more stable situation in the sense that partisan presidential and House results had a higher association within each year, even as presidential results fluctuated.

This persistence of party success in House elections did not just happen. Parties conducted studies, recruited candidates, raised money, and distributed it

in terms of the extent of a split between presidential–House results and the efforts of parties to target them. The assumption was that election outcome shifts were a product of national aggregate factors such as presidential job approval, income changes, and number of seats each party had at risk, so examining district-level political conditions were not seen as relevant to explaining changes within the decade. See Brian Newman and Charles Ostrom, Jr., "Explaining Seat Changes in the U.S. House of Representatives, 1950–1998," *Legislative Studies Quarterly*, Vol. 27, No. 3 (August 2002), 383–405.

TABLE 10.6. *Changing Electoral Support for Republican House Candidates, 1992–2000*

R pres.% Vote[11]	N	Election Year					Δ 92–00
		1992	1994	1996	1998	2000	
House Republican Average Percentage of Vote							
<40	125	29.0	31.4	27.5	23.4	20.3	−8.8
40–49	131	45.1	52.7	47.9	48.5	46.5	1.5
50–59	134	52.9	64.1	59.9	64.0	61.7	8.9
60+	45	59.0	70.2	67.5	73.6	71.9	12.8
Times Republican House Candidates Held Seat during 1992–2000 and Average Republican House Candidates Percentages							
0	166	28.7	32.8	28.8	23.8	22.3	−6.4
1	24	40.8	44.1	39.4	32.5	36.8	−4.0
2	23	46.4	51.1	46.5	45.0	40.3	−6.0
3	29	40.0	46.3	54.6	63.2	61.8	21.8
4	39	41.5	56.3	57.3	63.6	62.1	20.6
5	152	63.3	74.1	66.3	72.7	68.3	5.1

strategically. This increased congruence between presidential and House results affected the electoral security of House candidates and surely contributed to the party polarization that was becoming widely noted.[12] More members of Congress were winning in districts their presidential candidate won, and more of them were winning by larger margins. This occurred in two ways. If Republican presidential percentages are averaged for 1992, 1996, and 2000, the result indicates the degree of support for presidential candidates of the party. Table 10.6 presents the average percentage for Republican House candidates by these averaged Republican presidential percentages.

From 1992 through 2000 the percentages won by Republican House candidates decreased in districts where Republican presidential candidates received less than 40 percent. In districts where presidential candidates received greater than 50 percent, the House candidates improved their percentages. The result was that Democrats were more secure in the 125 districts where Republican presidential candidates did poorly, and Republicans were more secure in the 179 districts in which Republican presidential candidates averaged over 50 percent.

[11] This is calculated by averaging Republican presidential percentages across the three elections of 1992, 1996, and 2000. For 1992 and 1996 the percentage of the two-party vote is used to avoid using an artificially low and perhaps unrepresentative percentage.

[12] As examples, see Jon R. Bond and Richard Fleisher, *Polarized Politics* (Washington, DC: CQ Press, 2000); Pietro S. Nivola and David W. Brady, Editors, *Red and Blue Nation: Characteristics and Causes of America's Polarized Politics* (Washington, DC: Brookings Institution, 2006); Alan I. Abramowitz, *The Disappearing Center: Engaged Citizens, Polarization, and American Democracy* (New Haven, CT: Yale University Press, 2010).

The polarization of results is also evident if districts are grouped by how many times each party held the district from 1992 to 2000. In districts that Republicans won 0, 1, or 2 of 5 elections, Republican House percentages declined from 1992 to 2000. In districts in which Republicans held the seat 3, 4, or 5 of 5 elections, their average vote percentages increased from 1992 to 2000. The shift in Republican success that resulted in a higher correlation between presidential and House percentages also resulted in greater electoral security for House candidates, with that security closely tied to presidential success. A House Republican in a district where the Republican presidential candidate did well had greater confidence she was representing a solidly Republican district. A House Democrat in a district where the Democratic presidential candidate did well had greater confidence he was representing a solidly Democratic district. Although the concern here is not polarization, these changes surely have contributed to the current polarization in Congress.

A Caution: A Party Role but Persisting Vote Divergences

Since the 1980s there has been a significant increase in the relationship between presidential and House votes. The correlation has increased, and there have been declines in the percentage of House districts with split-outcomes and the average deviation of House votes from the presidential vote within a district. The trend is for the two votes to be tied together more than in the 1960s–1980s. The efforts of the wings of the parties to make inroads into new constituencies and areas proceeded at different paces, but gradually brought the results together.

These changes have occurred because parties have formulated plans with accompanying policy stands and focused their efforts on particular districts they feel they have a chance to win. That does not mean there is complete consensus within each party about what policies to pursue. There is an ongoing debate within each party: Democrats continue to argue about how much to focus on issues of class, minority concerns, and the cultural wars; Republicans struggle with whether to emphasize fiscal versus social conservativism. These debates are likely to persist.[13] This continuing diversity of views is seen within the House. Members of Congress disagree with their party and stake out varying positions.

This affects the presidential–House relationship. Although the association of presidential–House results is increasing, it should not be overstated. Members are still largely responsible for organizing, funding, and running their own campaigns. There are still some members trying to differentiate their personal image from that of the party. The issue is how many are doing that, how much does their district constrain their efforts, and to what extent can their efforts create some separation between presidential and House results. The

---

[13] For an overview of these debates, see Brewer and Stonecash, *Dynamics of American Political Parties*, 145–199.

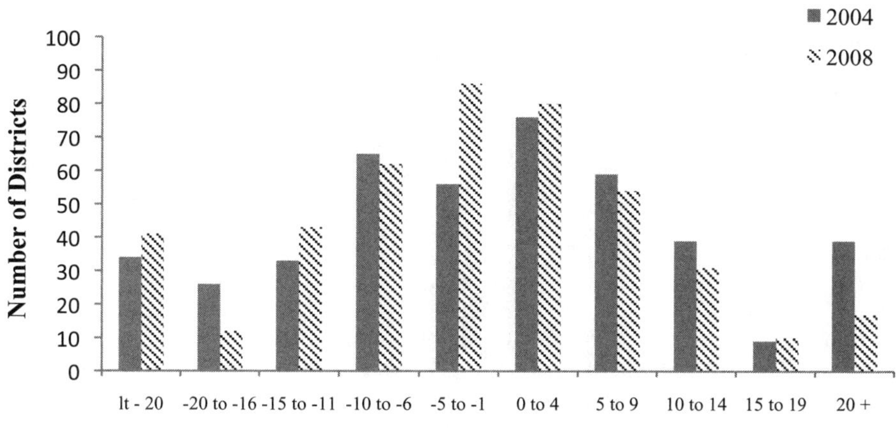

FIGURE 10.6. Distribution of House Differences from Republican Presidential Vote, 2004 and 2008

candidate-centered view of elections has a significant problem in that it conveys a sense that results became disconnected and that most House candidates are operating independently of the composition of their district, the dominant partisan sentiment, and presidential results in their district.[14] The presidential–House connection declined, then returned in recent decades. But there are still separations between presidential and House vote percentages. Some of this is due to the efforts of incumbents. Some is also because the district is heavily Democratic or Republican, and weak challengers emerge because the prospects of winning are limited. The presumption has been that separation is because of incumbency, but it may be due to partisanship. The difference needs to be sorted out and not just attributed to incumbency effects.

The point is that there is still considerable divergence of House election results from presidential results, and the covariation of changes from one presidential election to another is by no means high. Although the correlation between the results was .81 in 2004 and .76 in 2008, the average absolute deviation of House percentages from presidential percentages was 11.8 in 2004 and 10.3 in 2008, a level lower than in the 1960s–1980s, but still not close to zero.

That average conceals the diversity of differences that existed in 2004 and 2008. That diversity is shown in Figure 10.6, which indicates the distribution of

---

[14] At one time districts traits were central to analyses. See Shannon, *Party, Constituency, and Congressional* Voting, 115–131; and Turner and Schneier, *Party and* Constituency, 107–164. Within the last decade it appears analyses are returning to incorporating matters such as the nature of the district, political views in the district, and the extent of loyalty to the party by members. For examples, see Canes-Wrone, Brady, and Cogan, "Out of Step, Out of Office: Electoral Accountability and House Members' Voting;" and Jamie L. Carson, Gregory Koger, Matthew J. Lebo, and Everett Young, "The Electoral Costs of Party Loyalty in Congress," *American Journal of Political Science*, Vol. 54, No. 3 (July 2010), 598–616.

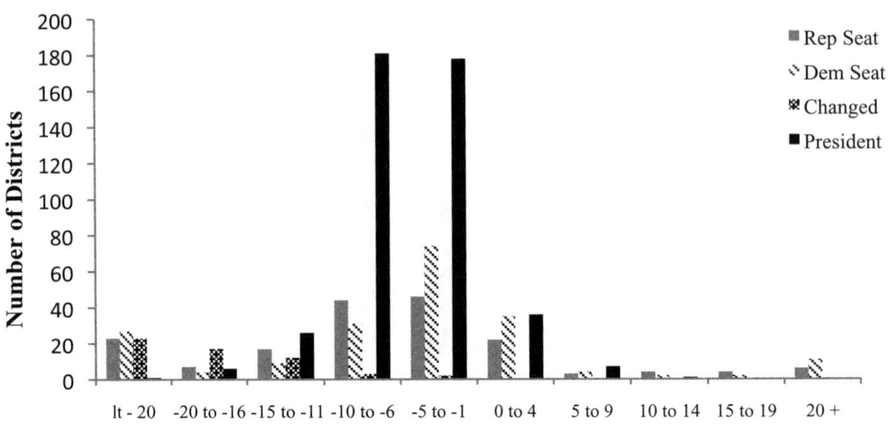

FIGURE 10.7. Distribution of Changes in Presidential and House Republican Percentages from 2004 to 2008

differences of Republican House candidates from the Republican presidential vote in their district. In 2004, 39.2 percent of House districts had a deviation of more than 10 percentage points, and in 2008, 35.3 had deviations greater than 10. The efforts of House candidates to create a vote percentage greater than that of their presidential candidate do matter. Some are able to obtain a vote considerably divergent from the presidential vote, even in an era of strong national partisanship.

Not only is there diversity in how much House percentages differ from presidential votes, but there is also considerable diversity in how much the vote percentages of House members change from one presidential election to another. Figure 10.7 indicates the distribution of changes scores for seats remaining Republican or Democrat over four years, and for those districts in which party control changed. From 2004 to 2008 the fortunes of Republicans generally declined, so the percentages for most cases are distributed on the left or negative side. Although the average shift is negative, there is considerable diversity of changes over the four years. In contrast the diversity of presidential changes is much more limited. Almost all (81.8 percent) fall within the range of 0 to −9. Changes in House elections are much more diverse than those occurring for presidential candidates. There are clearly long-term trends in election patterns, but short-term factors also matter a great deal.

Party Pursuits and American Democracy

Over the last several decades an interpretation of American elections has dominated that suggests they do not result in a coherent expression of the differing views of voters in both presidential and House elections. To briefly repeat matters reviewed earlier, a series of changes were seen as altering elections. Voters were less attached to parties. House candidates were presumed to be able to present themselves separately from their party, allowing them to boost their vote percentages and buffer their vote swings from presidential fluctuations. The result of greater incumbent autonomy from partisan swings was that voters could reject the policies of one party, but that swing may well not produce changes in who holds seats and which party controls government. There would be less likelihood of unified control of government, resulting in more stalemates and less responsiveness to shifts in public opinion.

These conclusions are all derived from the candidate-centered interpretation of American elections that emerged in the 1970s. That framework has become an assertion without any specific predictions that might allow us to refute it. Without any specific expectations to compare to actual events it becomes asserted again and again, and there is little consideration of alternative interpretations.

It survives even as polarization increases, as partisan voters increasingly vote for candidates of their party, as party members in Congress increasingly line up in unified opposition to each other, and as the correlation between presidential and House vote percentages increases. To return to the initial quote, the development of political polarization in a candidate-centered world is odd and confusing. Although some seek to explain it as just the result of independent candidate and voter sorting, there is something very odd and contradictory with a framework that is built around the idea of candidate independence while party unity increases.

What has been lost in the adherence to this framework is a focus on party plans and how those plans work out over long periods of time. Parties are faced with an endless struggle to balance the demands of an existing base versus the concerns of a different constituency that a faction within the party seeks to attract to expand the party or change its ideological positioning. Some want to preserve that which exists, and some want change. Some want to focus on what will win, and some are more concerned with ideological positioning. These struggles over direction result in endless debates within parties about what it should present to voters.

These struggles are complicated by the fact that politicians do have considerable autonomy. The argument made here that greater uniformity of voting results has emerged over the past two decades does not mean that there is not some autonomy. House members can disagree with the direction of the party and seek to relentlessly present themselves to their district as somewhat different from the remainder of the party. For many years southern Democrats made it clear that they were not like the rest of the party. Northeast Republicans sought to distance themselves from the party as it drifted more conservative. The bulk of a party may be changing its position, but individual House members may hold out as they seek to preserve their seat in a district less sympathetic to the new direction. There are just fewer members doing that now.

Despite these complications the evidence is clear that the Democratic and Republican parties have gradually changed who they represent and what kinds of districts they represent. In some cases presidential candidates led and in other cases they lagged change. Elections have gradually become more nationalized in that they have more uniform policy images and more uniform voting responses for presidential and House candidates. There is still considerable diversity, but much less than several decades ago.

Some will continue to argue that this is a result of independent candidate self-selection. Candidates sort themselves out between parties, and voters do the same. Although this preserves the candidate-centered framework, it ignores the connection between political concerns and activism in American politics. In recent decades we have seen the development of fundamental divisions revolving around ideology, race, religious attachment, personal responsibility, and class. These divisions are animating citizens, activists, interest groups, and party leaders to organize to make their case about the direction our society should take. These efforts are resulting in donations, party recruitment of candidates,[1] and efforts to shape who is and who is not nominated as candidates for the party. It is those efforts that over a long period of time brought us the greater association between presidential and House results.

---

[1] Cherie D. Maestas, L. Sandy Maisel, and Walter J. Stone, "National Party Efforts to Recruit State Legislators to Run for the U.S. House," *Legislative Studies Quarterly*, Vol. 30, No. 2 (May 2005), 277–300.

Although it may be intriguing to conceive of a process in which a multitude of independent actions and decisions gradually yields a situation of more uniformity of partisan voting outcomes, that ignores the vast organized efforts that have played a role in creating these changes. Political parties have played a central role in this change, both as instigators of change and as vehicles for those seeking change.[2] The notion of party involved is, to be sure, slippery. It is more than just formal party organizations, and more than party leaders. It is a network of actors, often with differing arguments about what actions should be pursued.[3]

This network nature makes it difficult to track, but efforts to understand these connections are now emerging.[4] We can gather information on who holds formal party positions, on who constitutes convention delegates, on who contributes to parties and candidates, and on how much party organizations raise and to whom they allocate funds. But gathering information on the informal communications and the recruitment process is very demanding, and has largely eluded us because of how difficult it is. But those activities exist, and the sum of these activities has gradually shifted the composition of the parties.

The preceding analysis does not by any means provide enough evidence about the role of parties in creating this greater uniformity. The presumption of this analysis is that there are party goals and actions, and those should create an increase in the separation of results followed at some point by a rejoining of results. Divergences remain, but the essential argument is that it is

---

[2] J. P. Monroe, *The Political Party Matrix: The Persistence of Organization*. Albany: State University of New York Press, 2001); Paul S. Herrnson, "The Roles of Party Organization, Party-Connected Committees, and Party Allies in Elections," *Journal of Politics*, Vol. 71, No. 4 (October 2009), 1207–1224; Seth E. Masket, *No Middle Ground: How Informal Party Organizations Control Nominations and Polarize Legislatures*, (Ann Arbor: University of Michigan Press, 2009). For the party efforts that were crucial in recruiting House members who would stand for fiscal conservativism see Brady Dennis, Alec MacGillis, and Lori Montgomery, "Origins of the Debt Showdown," *The Washington Post*, August 6, 2011. Accessed at: http://www.washingtonpost.com/business/economy/origins-of-the-debt-showdown/2011/08/03/gIQA9uqIzI_story.html.

[3] For an interesting argument about who in this network is most important see: Kathleen Bawn, Marty Cohen, David Karol, Seth Masket, Hans Noel, and John Zaller, *A Theory of Political Parties*, 2011. Unpublished. http://www9.georgetown.edu/faculty/hcn4/Downloads/ToP%20October%205.pdf.

[4] See, for example, Matt Grossman and Casey B. K. Dominguez, "Party Coalitions and Interest Group Networks," *American Politics Research*, Vol. 37, No. 5 (September 2009), 767–800; Gregory Koger, Seth Masket, and Hans Noel, "Cooperative Party Factions in American Politics," *American Politics Research*, Vol. 38, No. 1 (January 2010), 33–53; Gregory Koger, Seth E. Masket, and Hans Noel, "Partisan Webs: Information Exchange and Party Networks," *British Journal of Political Science*, Vol. 39, No. 3 (July 2009), 633–653; Casey B. K. Dominguez, "Does the Party Matter? Endorsements in Congressional Primaries," *Political Research Quarterly*, Vol. 64, No. 3 (September 2011), 534–544; and Richard M. Skinner, Seth E. Masket, and David A. Dulio, "527 Committees and the Political Party Network," *American Politics Research*, Vol. 40, No. 1 (January 2012), 60–84.

party activity that brought these results back together. The evidence supports that and indicates why we now have such unified opposition in Washington. The candidate-centered framework has removed parties as central actors and resulted in diminished attention to the goals, analyses, plans, and efforts of parties to create electoral coalitions and change where they win votes and seats.

This analysis also has implications for our interpretations of the role of parties as vehicles to create responsiveness to the American public. Although we have been presented with many arguments that House incumbents were buffering themselves from responsiveness, which was reducing responsiveness, that conclusion may have been shortsighted and premature. Parties have been seeking to respond to social change and build homogeneous electoral bases to respond, but it took a lengthy period of time in a decentralized political system for them to achieve what they wanted. It has taken some time to bring presidential and House electoral bases together, but as we watch American politics it now appears they have achieved considerable success in doing so.

Appendix I

Presidential–House Elections by House Districts

The creation of a reasonably correct data set for both House and presidential election results was fairly involved. First, the creation of the House data set will be discussed, and then the presidential data set will be discussed.

House election results: The primary source of data for House results is Michael J. Dubin, *United States Congressional Elections, 1788–1997*. This contains considerable detail. For the years 2000–2008 results from the official results from the House of Representatives Clerk are used.

Presidential election results: The presidential election results were based largely on two sources. Results from 1952 through 2000 were taken from various Congressional Quarterly (CQ) reference books or reports or other sources such as the *Almanac of American Politics* for various years. In some years CQ reported the results in March of the year following the presidential election. In other cases CQ published the results in *Congressional Districts in the 1980s* or *Congressional Districts in the 1990s*. For a few years the results were available only in editions of *Almanac of American Politics*. The 2000 results were obtained directly from CQ.

The results for 1900–1948 come from a project conducted by Peter Nardulli at the University of Illinois. He compiled data on presidential results by county, and using information from Kenneth C. Martis, *The Historical Atlas of United States Congressional Districts, 1789–1983* (New York: The Free Press, 1982) on which counties comprise each House district, it was possible for him to aggregate county presidential results to the congressional district level and have presidential results by congressional district. A complete explanation of how these data were compiled are available at his Web page, http://www.pol.uiuc. edu/nardulliresearch.html, under "Appendix I: Local Electorates: Data Sources and Methodological Procedures." I greatly appreciate his willingness to share these data. This procedure of grouping counties by congressional district also makes it possible to aggregate population and land area for House districts, and then calculate the density per House district. Using this procedure it was possible to aggregate raw presidential vote totals for House districts comprised of multiple counties and then calculate the partisan presidential percentages within those districts.

The remaining difficulty is assigning presidential vote percentages for those cases in which the district includes part of a county or a county includes multiple districts. As an example of these are the highly populated urban counties (Suffolk County [Boston], Massachusetts; New York City; Baltimore, Maryland, etc.). The result is that presidential results are not available for these counties. To address these missing cases, the following rules were used.

If a House district was wholly contained within a county, but there were multiple districts within the county, then the partisan vote presidential percentage for that county was used for any district wholly contained within the county. Given that the historical records indicate that House districts varied in the partisan vote in such counties, this reduces the variation in voting in this set of districts, which is likely to reduce the correlation. This does allow the inclusion of cases in more urban counties that might otherwise be excluded.

If a district includes more than one county, but one of the counties is not completely included, then the overall results for a district are calculated by averaging the results for the counties involved.[1]

These procedures are by no means perfect, but they will have to suffice until someone reconstructs presidential results by districts for the above cases of missing data.

[1] The county results were taken from Robinson, *They Voted for Roosevelt and* Robinson, *The Presidential Vote.*

Appendix II

The Presidential–House Relationship and Uncontested Races

This provides a comparison of the correlation between presidential–House results using all districts, and then only those with House races contested by a major party candidate.

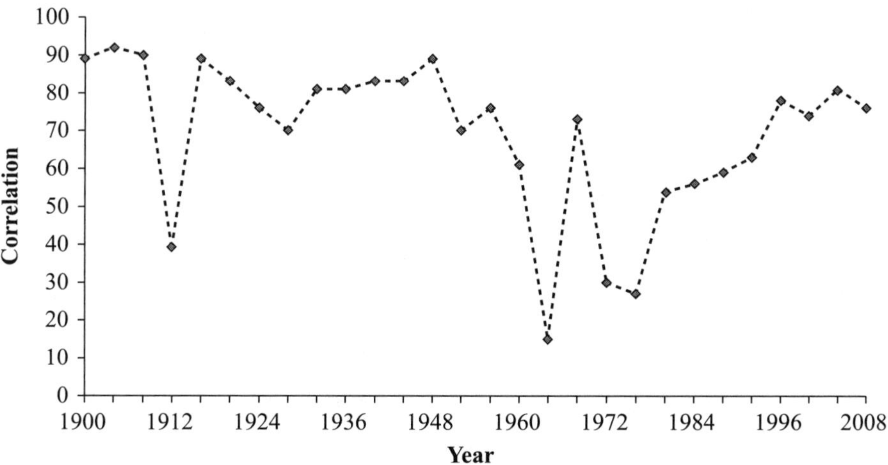

Correlation of All Republican Presidential–House Election Results, 1900–2008

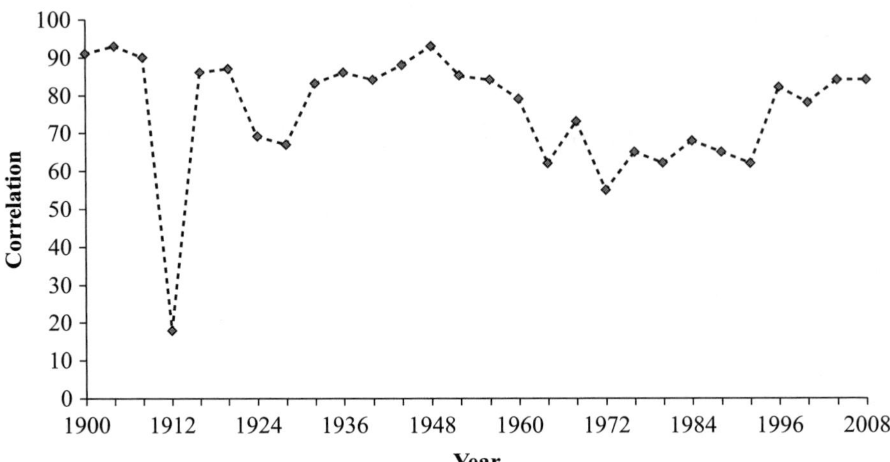

Correlation of Democratic Presidential–House Election Results, 1900–2008, Contested Seats Only, 1900–2008

Appendix III

Alternative Explanations of Change

As with any long-term change, there are several possible explanations of why the correlation between presidential and House results declined and then returned to a higher level. There is another possible alternative that is statistical in nature. A plausible statistical explanation is that the changes shown in Figures 8.3 and 8.4 may have changed the dispersion of presidential and House votes such that the resulting correlation declined. That is, the decline may just reflect trends in variable variance.

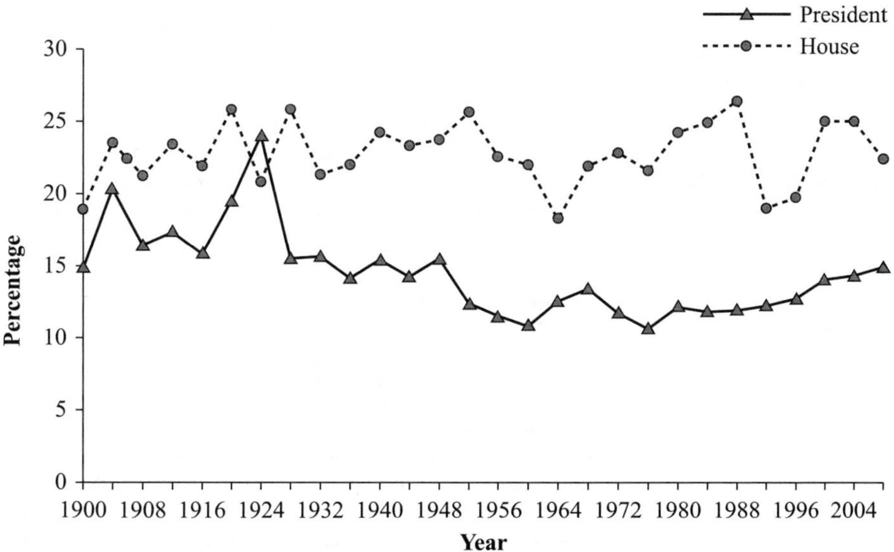

Standard Deviation of Democratic Presidential and House Percentages, 1900–2008

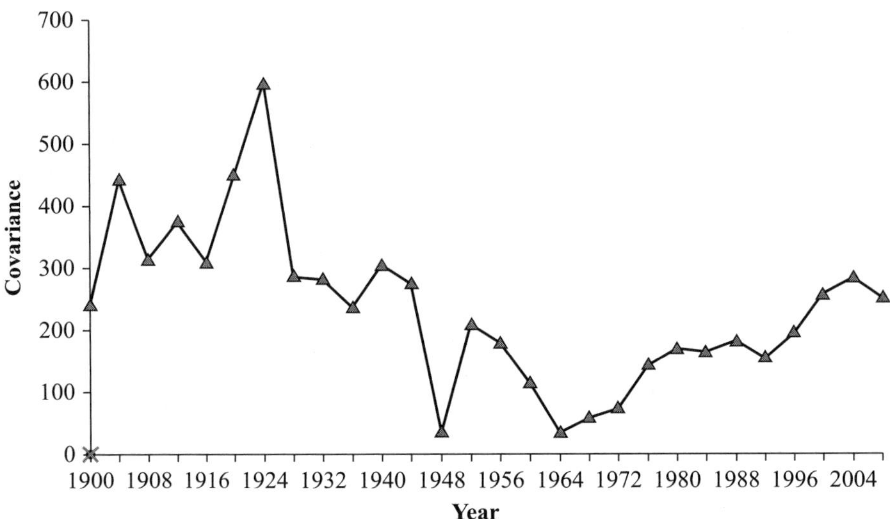

Covariance of Democratic Presidential and House Percentages, 1900–2008

The technical explanation involves the consequences of change. For the first half of the last century, the differences in partisan support between regions were very large. The Democrat's dominance of the South and the high vote percentages for Democrats created considerable variance in presidential and House votes. A correlation is a calculation of the covariance of two variables with the variance of each variable affecting the results. The greater the covariance and the greater the variance of the variables involved, the greater the correlation.[1] It is possible that the variance of one or both variables also might decline as partisan changes occur. As regional differences declined from the 1950s through the 1980s, the results for one or both offices might cluster more in the 40–60 percent range, resulting in reduced national variance for scores for the office. This decline in the standard deviation of presidential results up until 1980[2] (Figure 8.5) occurred, whereas the House standard deviation has not changed.

---

[1] Specifically, a correlation is (covariance xy / (standard deviation x) (standard deviation y). If the standard deviation of x or y were to decline, even while covariance of x and y remained constant, then the correlation would decline.

[2] Since then the dispersion has begun to increase. One of the oddly unexamined issues in the study of elections has been how the distribution of presidential results across districts has changed over time. There is evidence that the distribution is changing. See Bill Bishop, *The Big Sort: Why Clustering of Like-Minded American Is Tearing Us Apart* (New York: Houghton Mifflin, 2008). There has been recognition of the importance of distributions but not much study of it. See John K. Wildgen and Richard L. Engstrom, "Spatial Distribution of Partisan Support and the Seats / Votes Relationship," *Legislative Studies Quarterly*, Vol. 5, No. 3 (August 1980), 423–435. For a succinct presentation of the implications of the geographical sorting issue, see Theriault, *Party Polarization in Congress*, 59–61 and 91–94.

This decline in the dispersion of presidential votes, although modest, has some relevance in explaining the declining correlation. The lowest standard deviation was from 1952 through 1996, a period according roughly with when the large regional differences in presidential voting declined. During this time there were a higher percentage of presidential vote percentages within the range of 40–60 percent.[3]

Although this declining variance may have had some effect, the major change is in the covariance of presidential and House results. As noted in the footnote, a correlation value is a joint product of covariance in the numerator and variance in the denominator. The significant change over time was in the extent of covariance between the two percentages (Figure 8.6). Beginning in 1948 this covariance declined and did not return to the levels of 1900–1944 until 2000. The point is to affirm that the matter to be explained is the declining association between these percentages and not just the variation in the variables (election results) over time.

[3] From 1900 to 1948 the average percentage of House districts with a Democratic presidential percentage between 40–60 percent was 44. From 1952 to 1984, the period when the correlation between results was at its lowest and split-outcomes were at the highest, the average percentage was 53.0.

Bibliography

Abramowitz, Alan I. 1975. "Name Familiarity, Reputation and the Incumbency Effect in a Congressional Election." *Western Political Quarterly.* Vol. 28, No. 4 (December). 668–84.

———. 1980. "A Comparison of Voting for U.S. Senator and Representative in 1978." *American Political Science Review.* Vol. 74, No. 3 (September). 633–640.

———. 1983. "Partisan Redistricting and the 1982 Congressional Elections." *Journal of Politics.* Vol. 45, No. 3 (August). 767–770.

———. 1985. "Economic Conditions, Presidential Popularity, and Voting Behavior in Midterm Congressional Elections." *Journal of Politics.* Vol. 47, No. 1 (February). 31–43.

———. 1989. "Campaign Spending in U.S. Senate Elections." *Legislative Studies Quarterly.* Vol. 14, No. 4 (November). 487–507.

———. 1991. "Incumbency, Campaign Spending, and the Decline of Competition in U.S. House Elections." *Journal of Politics.* Vol. 53, No. 1 (February). 34–56.

———. 2010a. "Ideological Realignment among Voters." In Jeffrey M. Stonecash, Editor, *New Directions in American Political Parties.* New York: Routledge. 126–147.

———. 2010b. *The Disappearing Center: Engaged Citizens, Polarization, and American Democracy.* New Haven, CT: Yale University Press.

Abramowitz, Alan I., and Jeffrey A. Segal. 1986. "Determinants of the Outcomes of U.S. Senate Elections." *Journal of Politics.* Vol. 48, No. 2 (May). 433–439.

Abramowitz, Alan I., and Kyle L. Saunders. 1998. "Ideological Realignments in the U.S. Electorate." *Journal of Politics.* Vol. 60, No. 3 (August). 634–652.

———. 2006. "Exploring the Bases of Partisanship in the American Electorate: Social Identity vs. Ideology." *Political Research Quarterly.* Vol. 59, No. 2 (June). 175–187.

Abramson, Paul R. 1976. "Generational Change and the Decline of Party Identification in America: 1952–1974." *American Political Science Review.* Vol. 70, No. 2 (June). 469–478.

Abramson, Paul R., and Charles W. Ostrom, Jr. 1991. "Macropartisanship: An Empirical Assessment." *American Political Science Review*. Vol. 85, No. 1 (March). 181–192.

———. 1992. "Response." *American Political Science Review*. Vol. 86, No. 2 (June). 475–486.

Aistrup, Joseph. 1996. *The Southern Strategy Revisited*. Lexington: University of Kentucky Press.

Aldrich, John H. 1995. *Why Parties: The Origin and Transformation of Party Politics in America*. Chicago: University of Chicago Press.

———. 2011. *Why Parties? A Second Look*. Chicago: University of Chicago Press.

Aldrich, John H., and David W. Rohde. 2000. "The Consequences of Party Organization in the House: The Role of the Majority and Minority Parties in Conditional Party Government." In Jon Bond and Richard Fleisher, Editors, *Polarized Politics: Congress and the President in a Partisan Era*. Washington, DC: CQ Press. 31–72.

Alford, Robert R. 1963. *Party and Society: The Anglo-American Democracies*. Westport, CT: Greenwood Press.

Alford, John R., and John R. Hibbing. 1981. "Increased Incumbency Advantage in the House." *Journal of Politics*. Vol. 43, No. 4 (November). 1042–1061.

Alford, John R., and David W. Brady. 1989. "Personal and Partisan Advantage in U.S. Congressional Elections, 1846–1986." In Lawrence C. Dodd and Bruce I. Oppenheimer, Editors, *Congress Reconsidered*. Fourth Edition. Washington, DC: Congressional Quarterly. 153–169.

Alford, John R., and Kevin Arceneaux. 2000. "Isolating the Origins of the Incumbency Advantage: An Analysis of House Primaries, 1956–1998." Presented at the 2000 Southern Political Science Association Meetings, Atlanta, November.

American Political Science Association, Committee on Parties. 1950. "Toward a More Responsible Two-Party System." *American Political Science Review*. Vol. 44, No. 3, Part 2, Supplement (September). v–96.

Andersen, Kristi. 1979. *The Creation of a Democratic Majority*. Chicago: University of Chicago Press.

Ansolabehere, Stephen, David Brady, and Morris Fiorina. 1992. "The Vanishing Marginals and Electoral Responsiveness." *British Journal of Political Science*. Vol. 22, No. 1 (January). 21–38.

Ansolabehere, Stephen, and Alan Gerber. 1997. "Incumbency Advantage and the Persistence of Legislative Majorities." *Legislative Studies Quarterly*. Vol. 22, No. 2 (May). 161–178.

Ansolabehere, Stephen, James M. Snyder, Jr., and Charles Stewart III. 2000. "Old Voters, New Voters, and the Personal Vote: Using Redistricting to Measure the Incumbency Advantage." *American Journal of Political Science*. Vol. 44, No 1 (January). 17–34.

Ansolabehere, Stephen, John Mark Hansen, Shigeo Hirano, and James M. Snyder, Jr. 2007. "The Incumbency Advantage in U.S. Primary Elections." *Electoral Studies*. Vol. 26, No. 3 (September). 660–668.

Ansolabehere, Stephen, Shigeo Hirano, and James M. Snyder, Jr. 2007. "What Did the Direct Primary Do to Party Loyalty in Congress?" In David W. Brady and Mathews D. McCubbins, Editors, *Party, Process, and Political Change in Congress*, Volume 2. Palo Alto, CA: Stanford University Press. 21–36.

Balz, Dan, and Ronald Brownstein. 1996. *Storming the Gates: Protest Politics and the Republican Revival*. Boston: Little, Brown.

Bartels, Larry M. 1996. "Uninformed Votes: Information Effects in Presidential Elections." *American Journal of Political Science*. Vol. 40, No. 1 (February). 194–230.

———. 1998. "Electoral Continuity and Change, 1868–1996." *Electoral Studies*. Vol. 17, No. 3 (September). 275–300.

———. 2000. "Partisanship and Voting Behavior, 1952–1996." *American Journal of Political Science*. Vol. 44, No. 1 (January). 35–49.

———. 2008. *Unequal Democracy: The Political Economy of the Gilded Age*. Princeton, NJ: Princeton University Press.

Basinger, Scott, and Helmut Norpoth. 2007. "Incumbency and Realignment: Partisan Change in House Elections." Presented at the 2007 Midwest Political Science Association Meetings, Chicago, Illinois. April.

Baumer, Donald C., and Howard J. Gold. 2010. *Parties, Polarization, and Democracy in the United States*. Boulder, CO: Paradigm.

Bawn, Kathleen, Marty Cohen, David Karol, Seth Masket, Hans Noel, and John Zaller. 2011. *A Theory of Political Parties*. Unpublished. Available at: http://www9.georgetown.edu/faculty/hcn4/Downloads/ToP%20October%205.pdf.

Bean, Louis H. 1942. "Tides and Patterns in American Politics." *American Political Science Review*. Vol. 36, No. 4 (August). 637–655.

Bell, Daniel. 1962. *The End of Ideology*. New York: Collier Books.

Bensel, Richard F. 2000. *The Political Economy of American Industrialism, 1877–1900*. New York: Cambridge University Press.

Bibby, John F. 2002. "State Party Organizations: Strengthened and Adapting to Candidate-Centered Politics and Nationalization." In L. Sandy Maisel, Editor, *The Parties Respond: Changes in American Parties and Campaigns*. Boulder, CO: Westview Press. 19–46.

Bishop. Bill. 2008. *The Big Sort: Why Clustering of Like-Minded American Is Tearing Us Apart*. New York: Houghton Mifflin.

Black, Earl, and Merle Black. 1987. *Politics and Society in the South*. Cambridge, MA: Harvard University Press.

———. 2002. *The Rise of Southern Republicans*. Cambridge, MA: Harvard University Press.

Bond, Jon R. 1985. "Dimensions of District Attention over Time." *American Journal of Political Science*. Vol. 29, No. 2 (May). 330–347.

Bond, Jon R., Cary Covington, and Richard Fleisher. 1985. "Explaining Challenger Quality in Congressional Elections." *Journal of Politics*. Vol. 47, No. 2 (June). 510–529.

Bond, Jon R., and Richard Fleisher, Editors. 2000. *Polarized Politics*. Washington, DC: CQ Press.

Bond, Jon R., Richard Fleisher, and Jeffrey M. Stonecash. 2009. "The Rise and Fall of Moderates in Congress." Presented at the Conference on Bicameralism. Duke University. March 26–29.

———. 2008. "The Rise and Decline of Moderates in the House, 1876–2004." Presented at the Conference on Going to Extremes: The Fate of the Political Center in American Politics. Rockefeller Center for Public Policy and the Social Sciences. Dartmouth College. June 19–21.

Born, Richard. 1977. "House Incumbents and Inter-Election Vote Change." *Journal of Politics.* Vol. 39, No. 4 (November). 1008–1034.

———. 1979. "Generational Replacement and the Growth of Incumbent Reelection Margins in the U.S. House." *American Political Science Review.* Vol. 73, No. 3 (September). 811–817.

———. 1984. "Reassessing the Decline of Presidential Coattails: U.S. House Elections from 1952–1980." *Journal of Politics.* Vol. 46, No. 1 (February). 60–79.

———. 1985. "Partisan Intentions and Election Day Realities in the Congressional Redistricting Process." *American Political Science Review.* Vol. 79, No. 2 (June). 305–319.

———. 1990. "The Shared Fortunes of Congress and Congressmen: Members May Run from Congress, but They Can't Hide." *Journal of Politics.* Vol. 52, No. 4 (November). 1223–1241.

———. 1994. "Split-Ticket Voters, Divided Government, and Fiorina's Policy-Balancing Model." *Legislative Studies Quarterly.* Vol. 19, No. 1 (February). 95–115.

———. 2000. "Congressional Incumbency and the Rise of Split-Ticket Voting." *Legislative Studies Quarterly.* Vol. 25, No. 3 (August). 365–387.

———. 2008. "National Forces and the U.S. House Vote, 1980–2004: The Uncertain Progress of Nationalization." *Congress and the Presidency.* Vol. 35, No. 1 (Spring). 87–103.

Box-Steffensmeier, Janet, and Renee M. Smith. 1996. "The Dynamics of Aggregate Partisanship." *American Political Science Review.* Vol. 90, No. 3 (September). 567–580.

Box-Steffensmeier, Janet M., David C. Kimball, Scott R. Meinke, and Katherine Tate. 2003. "The Effects of Political Representation on the Electoral Advantages of House Incumbents." *Political Research Quarterly.* Vol. 56, No. 3 (September). 259–70.

Boyd, Richard W. 1969. "Presidential Elections: An Explanation of Voting Defection." *American Political Science Review.* Vol. 63, No. 2 (June). 498–514.

———. 1972. "Popular Control of Public Policy: A Normal Vote Analysis of the 1968 Election." *American Political Science Review.* Vol. 66, No. 2 (June). 429–449.

Brady, David W. 1973. "A Research Note on the Impact of Interparty Competition on Congressional Voting in a Competitive Era." *American Political Science Review.* Vol. 67, No. 1 (March). 153–156.

———. 1985. "A Reevaluation of Realignments in American Politics: Evidence from the House of Representatives." *American Political Science Review.* Vol. 79, No. 1 (March). 28–49.

Brady, David W., and Bernard Grofman. 1991. "Sectional Differences in Partisan Bias and Electoral Responsiveness in US House Elections, 1850–1980." *British Journal of Political Science.* Vol. 21, No. 2 (April). 247–256.

Brady, David W., Brandice Canes-Wrone, and John F. Cogan. 2000. "Differences in Legislative Voting Behavior between Winning and Losing House Incumbents." In David W. Brady, John F. Cogan, and Morris P. Fiorina, Editors, *Continuity and Change in House Elections.* Palo Alto, CA: Stanford University Press. 178–192.

Brady, David W., Robert D'Onofrio, and Morris P. Fiorina. 2000. "The Nationalization of Electoral Forces Revisited." In David W. Brady, John F. Cogan, and Morris P.

Fiorina, Editors, *Continuity and Change in House Elections*. Palo Alto, CA: Stanford University Press. 130–148.

Brady, David W., and Kara Z. Buckley. 2002. "Governing by Coalition: Policymaking in the U.S. Congress." In L. Sandy Maisel, Editor, *The Parties Respond: Changes in American Parties and Campaigns*. Fourth Edition. Boulder, CO: Westview. 231–266.

Brewer, Mark D. 2005. "The Rise of Partisanship and the Expansion of Partisan Conflict within the American Electorate." *Political Research Quarterly*. Vol. 58, No. 2 (June). 219–229.

Brewer, Mark D., and Jeffrey M. Stonecash. 2007. *Split: Class and Cultural Divides in American Politics*. Washington, DC: CQ Press.

———. 2009. "Changing the Political Dialogue and Political Alignments: George Wallace and His 1968 Presidential Campaign." Presented at the 2009 Midwest Political Science Association Meetings, April.

———. 2009. *The Dynamics of American Political Parties*. New York: Cambridge University Press.

———. 2012. "Individual vs. Societal Responsibility: The Root of Partisan and Ideological Conflict." Presented at the 2012 Southern Political Science Association Meetings, New Orleans, January.

Broockman, David E. 2009. "Do Congressional Candidates Have Reverse Coattails? Evidence from Regression Discontinuity Design." *Political Analysis*. Vol. 17, No. 4 (Autumn). 418–434.

Brown, Robert D., and James A. Woods. 1991. "Toward a Model of Congressional Elections." *Journal of Politics*. Vol. 53, No. 2 (May). 454–473.

Brownstein, Ronald. 2007. *The Second Civil War: How Extreme Partisanship Has Paralyzed Washington and Polarized America*. New York: Penguin Press.

Brunell, Thomas L., and Bernard Grofman. 1998. "Explaining Divided U.S. Senate Delegations, 1788–1996: A Realignment Approach." *American Political Science Review*. Vol. 92, No. 2 (June). 391–399.

Bullock, Charles S. 1972. "House Careerists: Changing Patterns of Longevity and Attrition." *American Political Science Review*. Vol. 66, No. 4 (December). 1295–1300.

———. 1975. "Redistricting and Congressional Stability, 1962–72." *Journal of Politics*. Vol. 37, No. 2 (May). 569–575.

Burden, Barry, and David C. Kimball. 2004. *Why Americans Split Their Tickets: Campaigns, Competition, and Divided Government*. Ann Arbor: University of Michigan Press.

Burnham, Walter Dean. 1965. "The Changing Shape of the American Political Universe." *American Political Science Review*. Vol. 59, No. 1 (March). 7–28.

———. 1968. "American Voting Behavior and the 1964 Election." *Midwest Journal of Political Science*. Vol. 12, No. 1 (February). 1–40.

———. 1970. *Critical Elections and the Mainsprings of American Politics*. New York: W. W. Norton.

———. 1975a. "Insulation and Responsiveness in Congressional Elections." *Political Science Quarterly*. Vol. 90, No. 3 (Fall). 411–435.

———. 1975b. "American Politics in the 1970's: Beyond Party?" In William Nisbet Chambers and Walter Dean Burnham, Editors, *The American Party Systems: Stages of Political Development*. Second Edition. New York: Oxford University Press. 277–307.

______. 1976. "Revitalization and Decay: Looking toward the Third Century of American Electoral Politics." *Journal of Politics.* Vol. 38, No. 3 (August). 146–172.

Burner, David. 1968. *The Politics of Provincialism: The Democratic Party in Transition.* New York: Alfred Knopf.

Cain, Bruce E., John A. Ferejohn, and Morris P. Fiorina. 1984. "The Constituency Basis of the Personal Vote for U.S. Representatives and British Members of Parliament." *American Political Science Review.* Vol. 78, No. 1 (March). 110–125.

______. 1990. *The Personal Vote: Constituency Service and Electoral Independence.* Cambridge, MA: Harvard University Press.

Cain, Sean A. 2012. "Political Consultants and Party-Centered Campaigning? Evidence from the 2010 U.S. House Primary Election Campaigns." Presented at the 2012 Southern Political Science Association Meetings, New Orleans, Louisiana, January.

Calvert, Randall L., and John A. Ferejohn. 1983. "Coattail Voting in Recent Presidential Elections." *American Political Science Review.* Vol. 77, No. 2 (June). 407–419.

Campbell, Angus, Philip E. Converse, Warren E. Miller, and Donald E. Stokes. 1960. *The American Voter.* New York: John Wiley.

Campbell, Angus. 1966. "Surge and Decline: A Study of Electoral Change." In Angus Campbell, Philip E. Converse, Warren E. Miller, and Donald E. Stokes, Editors, *Elections and the Political Order.* New York: John Wiley. 40–62.

Campbell, Angus. 1966. "A Classification of the Presidential Elections." In Angus Campbell, Philip E. Converse, Warren E. Miller, and Donald E. Stokes, Editors, *Elections and the Political Order.* New York: John Wiley. 63–77.

Campbell, James E. 1983. "The Return of the Incumbents: The Nature of the Incumbency Advantage." *Western Political Quarterly.* Vol. 36, No. 3 (September). 434–444.

______. 1985. "Explaining Presidential Losses in Midterm Congressional Elections." *Journal of Politics.* Vol. 47, No. 4 (November). 1140–1157.

______. 1986. "Presidential Coattails and Midterm Losses in State Legislative Elections." *American Political Science Review.* Vol. 80, No. 1 (March). 45–63.

______. 1986. "Predicting Seat Gains from Presidential Coattails." *American Journal of Political Science.* Vol. 30, No. 1 (February). 165–183.

______. 1987. "A Revised Theory of Surge and Decline." *American Journal of Political Science.* Vol. 31, No. 4 (November). 965–979.

______. 1991. "The Presidential Surge and Its Midterm Decline in Congressional Elections, 1868–1988." *Journal of Politics.* Vol. 53, No. 2 (May). 477–87.

______. 1997. "The Presidential Pulse and the 1994 Midterm Congressional Election." *Journal of Politics.* Vol. 59, No. 3 (August). 830–857.

______. 1997. *The Presidential Pulse of Congressional Elections.* Second Edition. Lexington: University Press of Kentucky.

______. 2006. "Party Systems and Realignments in the United States, 1868–2004." *Social Science History.* Vol. 30, No. 3 (Fall). 359–386.

______. 2010. "Explaining Politics, Not Polls: Reexamining Macropartisanship with Recalibrated NES Data." *Public Opinion Quarterly.* Vol. 74, No. 4 (Winter). 1–27.

Campbell, James E., and Joe E. Summers. 1990. "Presidential Coattails in Senate Elections." *American Political Science Review.* Vol. 84, No. 2 (June). 513–524.

Canes-Wrone, Brandice, David W. Brady and John F. Cogan. 2002. "Out of Step, Out of Office: Electoral Accountability and House Members' Voting." *American Political Science Review*. Vol. 96, No. 1 (March). 127–140.

Carmines, Edward G., Steven H. Renten, and James A. Stimson. 1984. "Events and Alignments: The Party Image Connection." In Richard Niemi and Herbert Weisberg, Editors, *Controversies in Voting Behavior*. Washington, DC: CQ Press.

Carmines, Edward G., John P. McIver, and James A. Stimson. 1987. "Unrealized Partisanship: A Theory of Dealignment." *Journal of Politics*. Vol. 49, No. 2 (May). 376–400.

Carmines, Edward G., and James A. Stimson. 1989. *Issue Evolution: Race and the Transformation of American Politics*. Princeton, NJ: Princeton University Press.

Carmines, Edward G., and Michael Wagner. 2006. "Political Issues and Party Alignments: Assessing the Issue Evolution Perspective." *Annual Review of Political Science*. Vol. 9. 67–81.

Carson, Jamie L., and Jeffrey A. Jenkins. 2011. "Examining the Electoral Connection across Time." *Annual Review of Political Science*. Vol. 14 (June), 25–46.

Carson, Jamie L., Erik J. Engstrom, and Jason M. Roberts. 2007. "Candidate Quality, the Personal Vote, and the Incumbency Advantage in Congress." *American Political Science Review*. Vol. 101, No. 2 (May). 289–302.

Carson, Jamie L., Gregory Koger, Matthew J. Lebo, and Everett Young. 2010. "The Electoral Costs of Party Loyalty in Congress." *American Journal of Political Science*. Vol. 54, No. 3 (July). 598–616.

Carson, Jamie L., and Carrie P. Eaves. 2011. "Congressional Elections: Why Some Incumbent Candidates Lose." In Stephen K. Medvic, Editor, *New Directions in Campaigns and Elections*. New York: Routledge. 183–199.

Claassen, Ryan. 2011. "Political Awareness and Partisan Realignment: Are the Unaware Unevolved?" *Political Research Quarterly*. Vol. 64, No. 4 (December). 818–830.

Clausen, Aage R. 1973. *How Congressmen Decide: A Policy Focus*. New York: St. Martin's Press.

Coggins, K. Elizabeth, and James A. Stimson. 2012. "The Vanishing Liberal." Presented at the 2012 Southern Political Science Association Meetings. New Orleans. January.

Cohen, Jeffrey E., Michael A. Krassa, and John A. Hamman. 1991. "The Impact of Presidential Campaigning on Midterm U.S. Senate Elections." *American Political Science Review*. Vol. 85, No. 1 (March). 165–178.

Cohen, Marty, David Karol, Hans Noel, and John Zaller. 2008a. "Political Parties in Rough Weather." *The Forum*. Vol. 5, Issue 4. http://www.bepress.com/forum/vol5/iss4/art3.

————. 2008b. *The Party Decides: Presidential Nominations before and after Reform*. Chicago: University of Chicago Press.

Coleman, John J., and Jeffrey M. Stonecash. 2004. "Political Parties versus Preferences: An Assessment." Revision of a paper originally presented at the 2004 Midwest Political Science Association Meetings, Chicago, Illinois, April 15–18.

Collie, Melissa P. 1981. "Incumbency, Electoral Safety, and Turnover in the House of Representatives, 1972–1976." *American Political Science Review*. Vol. 75, No. 1 (March). 119–131.

————. 1989. "Electoral Patterns and Voting Alignments in the U.S. House, 1886–1986." *Legislative Studies Quarterly*. Vol. 14, No. 1 (February). 107–127.

Congressional Quarterly. 1957. *Congressional Quarterly Almanac*. Washington, DC: Congressional Quarterly Press, 1957.

Congressional Quarterly. 2001. *Congressional Quarterly's Guide to U.S. Elections*. Fourth Edition. Washington, DC: Congressional Quarterly Press.

Converse, Philip E. 1966. "The Concept of a Normal Vote." In Angus Campbell, Philip E. Converse, Warren E. Miller, and Donald E. Stokes, Editors, *Elections and the Political Order*. New York: John Wiley. 6–39.

———. 1976. *The Dynamics of Party Support*. Beverly Hills, CA: Sage.

———. 1966. "On the Possibility of Major Political Realignment in the South." In Angus Campbell, Philip E. Converse, Warren E. Miller, and Donald E. Stokes, Editors, *Elections and the Political Order*. New York: John Wiley. 212–242.

Converse, Philip E., Aage R. Clausen, and Warren E. Miller. 1965. "Electoral Myth and Reality: The 1964 Election." *The American Political Science Review*. Vol. 59, No. 2 (June). 321–336.

Converse, Philip E., and Gregory Markus. 1979. "Plus ça Change... The New CPS Election Study Panel." *American Political Science Review*. Vol. 73, No. 1 (March). 32–49.

Cooper, Joseph, and David W. Brady. 1981. "Toward a Diachronic Analysis of Congress." *American Political Science Review*. Vol. 75, No. 4 (December). 988–1006.

Cover, Albert. 1977. "One Good Term Deserves Another: The Advantage of Incumbency in Congressional Elections." *American Journal of Political Science*. Vol. 21, No. 3 (August). 523–541.

———. 1985. "Surge and Decline in Congressional Elections." *Western Political Quarterly*. Vol. 38, No. 4 (December). 606–619.

———. 1986. "Presidential Evaluations and Voting for Congress." *American Journal of Political Science*. Vol. 30, No. 4 (November). 786–801.

Cover, Albert D., and David R. Mayhew. 1977. "Congressional Dynamics and the Decline of Competitive Congressional Elections." In Lawrence C. Dodd and Bruce I. Oppenheimer, Editors, *Congress Reconsidered* (Washington, DC: CQ Press). 62–82.

Cover, Albert D., and Bruce S. Brumberg. 1982. "Baby Books and Ballots: The Impact of Congressional Mail on Constituent Opinion." *American Political Science Review*. Vol. 76, No. 2 (June). 347–359.

Cox, Edward F. 1962. "Congressional District Party Strength and the 1960 Election." *Journal of Politics*. Vol. 24, No. 2 (May). 277–302.

Cox, Gary, and Jonathan Katz. 1996. "Why Did the Incumbency Advantage Grow?" *American Journal of Political Science*. Vol. 40, No. 2 (May). 478–497.

———. 1999. "The Reapportionment Revolution and Bias in U.S. Congressional Elections." *American Journal of Political Science*. Vol. 43, No. 3 (July). 812–841.

———. 2002. *Elbridge Gerry's Salamander: The Electoral Consequences of the Reapportionment Revolution*. New York: Cambridge University Press.

Craig, Douglas B. 1992. *After Wilson: The Struggle for the Democratic Party, 1920–1934*. Chapel Hill: University of North Carolina Press.

Crotty, William. 1984. *American Parties in Decline*. Second Edition. Boston: Little, Brown.

Cummings, Milton C., Jr. 1966. *Congressmen and the Electorate*. New York: Free Press.

Dark, Taylor E., III. 2011. "Liberals, Labor, and Party Government." *Polity*. Vol. 43, No. 3 (July). 358–387.

De Boef, Suzanna, and James A. Stimson. 1995. "The Dynamic Structure of Congressional Election." *Journal of Politics*. Vol. 57, No. 3 (August). 630–648.

Deckard, Barbara Sinclair. 1976. "Political Upheaval and Congressional Voting: The Effects of the 1960s on Voting Patterns in the House of Representatives." *Journal of Politics*. Vol. 38, No. 2 (May). 326–345.

Degler, Carl N. 1964. "American Political Parties and the Rise of the City: An Interpretation." *Journal of American History*. Vol. 51, No. 1 (June). 41–59.

Delli Carpini, Michael, and Scott Keeter. 1996. *What Americans Know about Politics and Why It Matters*. New Haven, CT: Yale University Press.

Dennis, Brady, Alec MacGillis, and Lori Montgomery, "Origins of the Debt Showdown." *The Washington Post*, August 6, 2011. http://www.washingtonpost.com/business/economy/origins-of-the-debt-showdown/2011/08/03/gIQA9uqIzI_story.html.

Desposato, Scott W., and John R. Petrocik. 2003. "The Variable Incumbency Advantage: New Voters, Redistricting, and the Personal Vote." *American Journal of Political Science*. Vol. 47, No. 1 (January). 18–32.

Dewan, Shaila. 2010. "Southern Schools Mark Two Majorities." *The New York Times*. January 7: A20.

Dionne, E. J., Jr. 1997. *They Only Look Dead*. New York: Touchstone.

Dominguez, Casey B. K. 2011. "Does the Party Matter? Endorsements in Congressional Primaries." *Political Research Quarterly*. Vol. 64, No. 3 (September). 534–544.

Drew, Elizabeth. 1997. *Showdown: The Struggle between the Gingrich Congress and the Clinton White House*. New York: Touchstone Books.

Dubin, Michael J. 1998. *United States Congressional Elections, 1788–1997*. Jefferson, NC: McFarland.

Dulio, David A. 2004. *For Better or Worse: How Political Consultants Are Changing Elections in the United States*. Albany: SUNY Press.

———. 2011. "The Impact of Political Consultants." In Stephen C. Craig and David B. Hills, Editors, *Electoral Challenge: Theory Meets Practice*. Second Edition. Washington, DC: CQ Press. 243–270.

Edsall, Thomas B., and Mary D. Edsall. 1991. *Chain Reaction: The Impact of Race, Rights, and Taxes on American Politics*. New York: W. W. Norton.

Edwards, George T. 1979. "The Impact of Presidential Coattails on Outcomes of Congressional Elections." *American Politics Quarterly*. Vol. 7, No. 1 (January). 94–108.

Eldersveld, Samuel J. 1949. "The Influence of Metropolitan Party Pluralities in Presidential Elections since 1920: A Study of Twelve Key Cities." *American Political Science Review*. Vol. 43, No. 6 (December). 1189–1206.

Engstrom, Erik. 2005. "The Partisan Impact of Malapportionment on the 19th Century and Early 20th Century House of Representatives." Presented at the 2005 Midwestern Political Science Association Meetings, Chicago, Illinois, April.

———. 2006. "Stacking the States, Stacking the House: The Partisan Consequences of Congressional Redistricting in the 19th Century." *American Political Science Review*. Vol. 100, No. 3 (August). 419–427.

Engstrom, Erik J., and Samuel Kernell. 2005. "Manufactured Responsiveness: The Impact of State Electoral Laws on Unified Party Control of the Presidency and

House of Representatives, 1840–1940." *Journal of Politics.* Vol. 49, No. 3 (July). 531–549.

Erikson, Robert S. 1971. "The Advantage of Incumbency in Congressional Elections." *Polity.* Vol. 3, No. 3 (Spring). 395–405.

———. 1972. "Malapportionment, Gerrymandering and Party Fortunes in Congressional Elections." *American Political Science Review.* Vol. 66, No. 4 (March). 1234–1245.

———. 1976. "Is There Anything Such as a Safe Seat?" *Polity.* Vol. 8, No. 4 (Summer). 623–632.

———. 1988. "The Puzzle of Midterm Loss." *Journal of Politics.* Vol. 50, No. 4 (November). 1011–1029.

Erikson, Robert S., and Kent L. Tedin. 1981. "The 1928–1932 Partisan Realignment: The Case for the Conversion Hypothesis." *American Political Science Review.* Vol. 75, No. 4 (December). 951–962.

Erikson, Robert S., and Thomas R. Palfrey. 1998. "Campaign Spending and Incumbency: An Alternative Simultaneous Equations Approach." *Journal of Politics.* Vol. 60, No. 2 (May). 355–373.

Erikson, Robert S., Michael B. MacKuen, and James A. Stimson. 1998. "What Moves Macropartisanship? A Response to Green, Palmquist, and Shickler." *American Political Science Review.* Vol. 92, No. 4 (December). 901–912.

Erikson, Robert S., and Gerald C. Wright. 2009. "Voters, Candidates, and Issues in Congressional Elections." In Lawrence C. Dodd and Bruce I. Oppenheimer, Editors, *Congress Reconsidered.* Ninth Edition. Washington, DC: CQ Press. 71–95.

Eubank, Robert B. 1985. "Incumbent Effects on Individual-Level Voting Behavior in Congressional Elections: A Decade of Exaggeration." *Journal of Politics.* Vol. 47, No. 3 (August). 958–967.

Ewing, Cortez A. 1947. *Congressional Elections 1896–1944: The Sectional Basis of Political Democracy in the House of Representatives.* Norman: University of Oklahoma Press.

Feinstein, Brian D., and Eric Schickler. 2008. "Platforms and Partners: The Civil Rights Realignment Reconsidered." *Studies in American Political Development.* Vol. 22 (Spring). 115–116.

Fenno, Richard F., Jr. 1977. "U.S. House Members in Their Constituencies: An Exploration." *American Political Science Review.* Vol. 71, No. 3 (September). 883–917.

———. 1978. *Home Style: House Members in Their Districts.* New York: HarperCollins.

Ferejohn, John A. 1977. "On the Decline of Competition in Congressional Elections." *American Political Science Review.* Vol. 71, No. 1 (March). 166–176.

Ferejohn, John A., and Randall L. Calvert. 1984. "Presidential Coattails in Historical Perspective." *American Political Science Review.* Vol. 28, No. 1 (February). 127–146.

Ferejohn, John A., and Morris P. Fiorina. 1985. "Incumbency and Realignment in Congressional Elections." In John E. Chubb and Paul E. Peterson, Editors, *New Directions in American Politics.* Washington, DC: Brookings Institution. 91–115.

Fiorina, Morris. 1973. "Electoral Margins, Constituency Influence, and Policy Moderation: A Critical Assessment." *American Politics Quarterly.* Vol. 1, No. 4 (October). 479–98.

————. 1977a. *Congress: Keystone to the Washington Establishment*. New Haven, CT: Yale University Press.

————. 1977b. "The Case of the Vanishing Marginals: The Bureaucracy Did It." *American Political Science Review*. Vol. 71, No. 1 (March). 177–181.

————. 1980. "The Decline of Collective Responsibility in American Politics." *Daedalus*. Summer. 109. 25–45.

————. 1981a. "Some Problems in Studying the Effects of Resource Allocation in Congressional Elections." *American Journal of Political Science*. Vol. 25, No. 3 (August). 543–567.

————. 1981b. *Retrospective Voting in American National Elections*. New Haven, CT: Yale University Press.

————. 1996. *Divided Government*. Second Edition. Boston: Allyn and Bacon.

————, with Samuel J. Abrams. 2009. *Disconnect: The Breakdown of Representation in American Politics*. Norman: University of Oklahoma Press.

————, with Samuel J. Abrams and Jeremy C. Pope. 2010. *Cultural War: The Myth of a Polarized America?* Third Edition. New York: Pearson Longman.

Fiorina, Morris P., David W. Rhode, and Peter Wissell. 1975. "Historical Change in House Turnover." In Norman J. Ornstein, Editor, *Congress in Change*. New York: Praeger. 24–46.

Fleisher, Richard, and Jon R. Bond. 2004. "The Shrinking Middle in the US Congress." *British Journal of Political Science*. Vol. 34, No. 3 (July). 429–451.

Fleming, Gregory N. 1995. "Presidential Coattails in Open-Seat Elections." *Legislative Studies Quarterly*. Vol. 20, No. 2 (May). 197–211.

Froman, Lewis A., Jr. 1963a. "Inter-Party Constituency Differences and Congressional Voting Behavior." *American Political Science Review*. Vol. 57, No. 1 (March). 57–61.

————. 1963b. *Congressmen and Their Constituencies*. Chicago: McNally.

Frymer, Paul, Thomas P. Kim, and Terri L. Bimes. 1997. "Party Elites, Ideological Voters and Divided Party Government." *Legislative Studies Quarterly*. Vol. 22, No. 2 (May). 195–216.

Gaddie, Ronald Keith, and Charles S. Bullock. 2000. *Elections to Open Seats in the U.S. House: Where the Action Is*. Lanham, MD: Rowman & Littlefield.

Galvin, Daniel J. 2010. *Presidential Party Building: Dwight D. Eisenhower to George W. Bush*. Princeton, NJ: Princeton University Press.

————. 2012. "Presidential Partisanship Reconsidered: Eisenhower, Nixon, Ford, and the Rise of Polarized Politics." *Political Research Quarterly*. Vol. 65, No. 1 (January). 1–15.

Garand, James C., and Donald A. Gross. 1984. "Changes in the Vote Margins for Congressional Candidates: A Specification of Historical Trends." *American Political Science Review*. Vol. 78, No. 1 (March). 17–30.

Garand, James C., Kenneth Wink, and Bryan Vincent. 1993. "Changing Meanings of Electoral Marginality in U.S. House Elections, 1824–1978." *Political Research Quarterly*. Vol. 46, No. 1 (March). 27–48.

Gardner, Michael. 2003. *Harry Truman and Civil Rights: Moral Courage and Political Risks*. Carbondale: Southern Illinois University Press.

Geer, John G. 1991. "Critical Realignments and the Public Opinion Poll." *Journal of Politics*. Vol. 53, No. 2 (May). 434–453.

Gelman, Andrew, and Gary King. 1990. "Estimating Incumbency Effect without Bias." *American Journal of Political Science.* Vol. 34, No. 4 (November). 1142–1164.

Gelman, Andrew, and Zaiying Huang. 2008. "Estimating Incumbency Advantage and Its Variation as an Example of a Before–After Study." *Journal of the American Statistical Association.* Vol. 103, No. 482 (June). 437–446.

Gilmour, John B., and Paul Rothstein. 1993. "Early Republican Retirement: A Cause of Democratic Dominance in the House of Representatives." *Legislative Studies Quarterly.* Vol. 18, No. 3 (August). 345–365.

Glantz, Oscar. 1960. "The Negro Voter in Northern Industrial Cities." *Western Political Quarterly.* Vol. 13, No. 4 (December). 999–1010.

Glazer, Amihai, Bernard Grofman, and Marc Robbins. 1987. "Partisan and Incumbency Effects of 1970s Congressional Districting." *American Journal of Political Science.* Vol. 31, No. 3 (August). 680–707

Green, Donald P., and Bradley Palmquist. 1990. "Of Artifacts and Partisan Instability." *American Journal of Political Science.* Vol. 34, No. 3 (August). 872–902.

______. 1994. "How Stable Is Party Identification?" *Political Behavior.* Vol. 16, No. 4 (December). 437–66.

Green, Donald P., Bradley Palmquist, and Eric Shickler. 1998. "Macropartisanship: A Replication and Critique." *American Political Science Review.* Vol. 90, No. 4 (December). 883–899.

______. 2002. *Partisan Hearts and Minds: Political Parties and the Social Identities of Voters.* New Haven, CT: Yale University Press.

Griffin, John D. 2006. "Electoral Competition and Democratic Responsiveness: A Defense of the Marginality Hypothesis." *Journal of Politics.* Vol. 68, No. 4 (November). 911–921.

Grofman, Bernard, William Koetzle, Michael McDonald, and Thomas L. Brunell. 2000. "A New Look at Split-Ticket Outcomes for House and President: The Comparative Midpoints Model." *Journal of Politics.* Vol. 62, No. 1 (February). 34–50.

Gronke, Paul, Jeffrey Koch, and J. Matthew Wilson. 2003. "Follow the Leader? Presidential Approval, Presidential Support, and Representatives' Electoral Fortunes." *Journal of Politics.* Vol. 65, No. 3 (August). 785–808.

Gross, Donald A., and James C. Garand. 1984. "The Vanishing Marginals, 1824–1980." *Journal of Politics.* Vol. 46, No. 1 (February). 224–237.

Grossman, Matt, and Casey B. K. Dominguez. 2009. "Party Coalitions and Interest Group Networks." *American Politics* Research. Vol. 37, No. 5 (September). 767–800

Hacker, Jacob S., and Paul Pierson. 2010. *Winner-Take-All Politics: How Washington Made the Rich Richer – and Turned Its Back on the Middle Class.* New York: Simon and Schuster.

Hale, Jon F. 1995. "The Making of the New Democrats." *Political Science Quarterly.* Vol. 110, No. 2 (Summer). 207–232.

Han, Hahrie, and David W. Brady. 2007. "A Delayed Return to Historical Norms: Congressional Party Polarization after the Second World War." *British Journal of Political Science.* Vol. 37, No. 3 (July). 505–531.

Harmon, Kathryn H., and Marsha L. Brauen. 1979. "Joint Electoral Outcomes as Cues for Congressional Support of U.S. Presidents." *Legislative Studies Quarterly.* Vol. 4, No. 2 (May). 281–299.

Harris, Louis. 1962. "Memorandum to the President from Louis Harris, Subject: Analysis of the 1962 Elections, November 19, 1962." Kennedy Papers, Part I, Reel 3.

———. 1963. "Memorandum to the President from Louis Harris, Subject: The South in 1964." September 3, 1963. Kennedy Papers, Part I, Reel 3.

Haynie, Kerry L., and Candis S. Watts. 2010. "Blacks and the Democratic Party: A Resilient Coalition." In Jeffrey M. Stonecash, Editor, *New Directions in American Political Parties*. New York: Routledge. 110–125.

Heberlig, Eric S., and Bruce A. Larson. 2005. "Redistributing Campaign Funds by U.S. House Members: The Spiraling Costs of the Permanent Campaign." *Legislative Studies Quarterly*. Vol. 30, No. 4 (November). 597–624.

Herrera, Richard, and Michael Yawn. 1999. "The Emergence of the Personal Vote." *Journal of Politics*. Vol. 61, No. 1 (February). 136–150.

Herrnson, Paul S. 1989. "National Party Decision-Making, Strategies, and Resource Distribution in Congressional Elections." *Western Political Quarterly*. Vol. 42, No. 3 (September). 301–323.

———. 2002. "National Party Organizations at the Dawn of the Twenty-First Century." In L. Sandy Maisel, Editor, *The Parties Respond: Changes in American Parties and Campaigns*. Boulder, CO: Westview Press. 47–78.

———. 2008. *Congressional Elections: Campaigning at Home and in Washington*. Fifth Edition. Washington, DC: CQ Press.

———. 2009. "The Roles of Party Organization, Party-Connected Committees, and Party Allies in Elections." *Journal of Politics*. Vol. 71, No. 4 (October). 1207–1224.

Hetherington, Marc J. 2001. "Resurgent Mass Partisanship: The Role of Elite Polarization." *American Political Science Review*. Vol. 95, No. 3 (September). 619–632.

Hetherington, Marc J., and Jonathan D. Weiler. 2009. *Authoritarianism and Polarization in American Politics*. Cambridge: Cambridge University Press.

Hibbing, John R. 1991. "Contours of the Modern Congressional Career." *American Political Science Review*. Vol. 85, No. 2 (June). 405–428.

———. 1991. *Congressional Careers: Contours of Life in the U.S. House of Representatives*. Chapel Hill: University of North Carolina Press.

Hillygus, D. Sunshine, and Todd G. Shields. 2008. *The Persuadable Voter: Wedge Issues in Presidential Campaigns*. Princeton, NJ: Princeton University Press.

Hinckley, Barbara. 1967. "Interpreting House Midterm Elections: Toward a Measurement of the In-Party's 'Expected' Loss of Seats." *American Political Science Review*. Vol. 61, No. 3 (September). 694–700.

———. 1970. "Incumbency and the Presidential Vote in Senate Elections: Defining Parameters of Subpresidential Voting." *American Political Science Review*. Vol. 64, No. 3 (September). 836–842

———. 1980. "The American Voter in Congressional Elections." *American Political Science Review*. Vol. 74, No. 3 (September). 641–650.

Hopkins, David A. 2009. "The 2008 Election and the Political Geography of the New Democratic Majority." *Polity*. Vol. 41, No. 3 (July). 368–387.

Humes, Karen R., Nicholas A. Jones, and Roberto R. Ramirez, *Overview of Race and Hispanic Origin: 2010*. U.S. Census Bureau, March 2011: http://www.census.gov/prod/cen2010/briefs/c2010br-02.pdf.

Hunter, James Davison. 1991. *Culture Wars: The Struggle to Define America*. New York: Basic Books.

Hurley, Patricia A. 1989. "Partisan Representation and the Failure of Realignment in the 1980s." *American Journal of Political Science.* Vol. 33, No. 1 (February). 240–261.

———. 1991. "Partisan Representation, Realignment, and the Senate in the 1980s." *Journal of Politics.* Vol. 53, No. 1 (February). 3–33.

Isserman, Maurice, and Michael Kazin. 2004. *America Divided: The Civil War of the 1960s.* New York: Oxford University Press.

Jacobson, Gary C. 1976. "Presidential Coattails in 1972." *Public Opinion Quarterly.* Vol. 40, No. 2 (Summer). 194–200.

———. 1978. "The Effects of Campaign Spending in Congressional Elections." *American Political Science Review.* Vol. 72, No. 2 (June). 469–491.

———. 1981. "Incumbents' Advantages in the 1978 U.S. Congressional Elections." *Legislative Studies Quarterly.* Vol. 6, No. 2 (May). 183–200.

———. 1983. *The Politics of Congressional Elections.* Boston: Little, Brown.

———. 1985. "Money and Votes Reconsidered: Congressional Elections, 1972–1982." *Public Choice.* Vol. 47 (1985). 7–62.

———. 1987. "The Marginals Never Vanished: Incumbency and Competition in Elections to the U.S. House of Representatives, 1952–1982." *American Journal of Political Science.* Vol. 31, No. 1 (February). 126–141.

———. 1989. "Strategic Politicians and the Dynamics of U.S. House Elections, 1946–86." *American Political Science Review.* Vol. 83, No. 3 (September). 773–793.

———. 1990. "The Effects of Campaign Spending in House Elections: New Evidence for an Old Argument." *American Journal of Political Science.* Vol. 34, No. 2 (May). 334–362.

———. 1990. *The Electoral Origins of Divided Government: Competition in U.S. House Elections, 1946–1988.* Boulder, CO: Westview Press.

———. 1993. "Getting the Details Right: A Comment on 'Changing Meanings of Electoral Marginality in U.S. House Elections, 1824–1978.'" *Political Research Quarterly.* Vol. 46, No. 1 (March). 49–65.

———. 1996. "The 1994 House Election in Perspective." *Political Science Quarterly.* Vol. 111, No. 2 (Summer). 203–223.

———. 2000. "Party Polarization in National Politics: The Electoral Connection." In Jon R. Bond and Richard Fleisher, Editors, *Polarized Politics.* Washington, DC: CQ Press. 9–30.

———. 2000. "Reversal of Fortune: The Transformation of U.S. House Elections in the 1990s." In David W. Brady, John F. Cogan, and Morris Fiorina, Editors, *Continuity and Change in House Elections.* Palo Alto, CA: Stanford University Press.

———. 2003a. "Party Polarization in Presidential Support: The Electoral Connection." *Congress and the Presidency.* Vol. 30, No. 1 (Spring). 1–36.

———. 2003b. "Reconsidering 'Reconsidering the Trend in Incumbent Vote Percentages in House Elections': A Comment." *American Review of Politics.* Vol. 24. 241–244.

———. 2007. "Explaining the Ideological Polarization of the Congressional Parties since the 1970s." In David W. Brady and Mathews D. McCubbins, Editors, *Party, Process, and Political Change in Congress,* Volume 2. Palo Alto, CA: Stanford University Press. 91–101.

———. 2009. *The Politics of Congressional Elections.* Seventh Edition. New York: Pearson-Longman.

Jacobson, Gary C., and Samuel Kernell. 1981. *Strategy and Choice in Congressional Elections.* New Haven, CT: Yale University Press.

James, Scott C. 2000. *Presidents, Parties, and the State: A Party System Perspective on Democratic Regulatory Choice.* New York: Cambridge University Press.

Jensen, Richard. 1971. *The Winning of the Midwest.* Chicago: University of Chicago Press,

Johannes, John R., and John C. McAdams. 1981. "The Congressional Incumbency Effect: Is It Casework, Policy Compatibility, or Something Else?" *American Journal of Political Science.* Vol. 25, No. 3 (August). 512–542.

Johnston, Richard, and Byron Shafer. 2010. "Structural Foundations of Divided Government, 1952–2008: A Reconsideration." Presented at the 2010 Annual American Political Science Association Meetings, Washington, DC, September.

Jones, Charles O. 1964. "Inter-Party Competition in Congressional Seats." *Western Political Quarterly.* Vol. 17, No. 3 (September). 461–476.

Jones, David R. 2010. "Partisan Polarization and Congressional Accountability in House Elections." *American Journal of Political Science.* Vol. 54, No. 2 (April). 323–337.

Kabaservice, Geoffrey. 2012. *Rule and Ruin: The Downfall of Moderation and the Destruction of the Republican Party from Eisenhower to the Tea Party.* New York: Oxford University Press, 2012.

Karol, David. 2009. *Party Position Change in American Politics: Coalition Management.* New York: Cambridge University Press.

Kawat, Sadafumi. 1987. "Nationalization and Partisan Realignment in Congressional Elections." *American Political Science Review.* Vol. 81, No. 4 (December). 1235–1250.

Kazee, Thomas A. 1983. "The Deterrent Effect of Incumbency on Recruiting Challengers in U.S. House Elections." *Legislative Studies Quarterly.* Vol. 8, No. 3 (August). 469–480.

Kazee, Thomas A., and Mary C. Thornberry. 1990. "Where's the Party: Congressional Candidate Recruitment and American Party Organizations." *Western Political Quarterly.* Vol. 43, No. 1 (March). 61–80.

Kernell, Georgia. 2009. "Giving Order to Districts: Estimating Voter Distributions with National Election Returns." *Political Analysis.* Vol. 17, No. 3 (Summer). 215–235.

Kernell, Samuel. 1977. "Presidential Popularity and Negative Voting: An Alternative Explanation of the Midterm Congressional Decline of the President's Party." *American Political Science Review.* Vol. 71, No. 1 (March). 44–66.

———. 1977. "Toward Understanding 19th Century Congressional Careers: Ambition, Competition, and Rotation." *American Journal of Political Science.* Vol. 21, No. 4 (November). 669–693.

Key, V. O., Jr. 1955. "A Theory of Critical Elections." *Journal of Politics.* Vol. 17, No. 1 (February). 3–18.

———. 1959. "Secular Realignment and the Party System." *Journal of Politics.* Vol. 21, No. 2 (May). 198–210.

Kinder, Donald R., and D. Roderick Kiewiet. 1979. "Economic Discontent and Political Behavior: The Role of Personal Grievances and Collective Economic Judgments in Congressional Voting." *American Journal of Political Science.* Vol. 23, No. 3 (August). 495–527.

King, Gary. 1991. "Constituency Service and Incumbency Advantage." *British Journal of Political Science.* Vol. 21, No. 1 (June). 119–128.

King, Gary, and Andrew Gelman. 1991. "Systematic Consequences of Incumbency in U.S. House Elections." *American Journal of Political Science.* Vol. 35, No. 1 (February). 110–138.

Kirkpatrick, Evron M. 1971. "'Toward a More Responsible Two-Party System': Political Science, Policy Science, or Pseudo-Science?" *American Political Science Review.* Vol. 65, No. 4 (December). 965–990.

Kleppner, Paul. 1970. *The Cross of Culture: A Social Analysis of Midwestern Politics, 1850–1900.* New York: Free Press.

Klinkner, Philip A. 1993. *The Losing Parties: Out-Party National Committees, 1956–1993.* New Haven, CT: Yale University Press.

——, Editor. 1996. *Midterm: The Elections in 1994 in Context.* Boulder, CO: Westview Press.

Koger, Gregory. 2010. *Filibustering: A Political History of Obstruction in the House and Senate.* Chicago: University of Chicago Press.

Koger, Gregory, Seth Masket, and Hans Noel. 2009. "Partisan Webs: Information Exchange and Party Networks." *British Journal of Political Science.* Vol. 39, No. 3 (July). 633–653.

——. 2010. "Cooperative Party Factions in American Politics." *American Politics Research.* Vol. 38, No. 1 (January). 33–53.

Kolodny, Robin. 1998. *Pursuing Majorities: Congressional Campaign Committees in American Politics.* Norman: University of Oklahoma Press.

Kolodny, Robin, and Diana Dwyre. 1998. "Party-Orchestrated Activities for Legislative Party Goals." *Party Politics.* Vol. 4, No. 3 (July). 275–295.

Kostrowski, Warren Lee. 1973. "Party and Incumbency in Postwar Senate Elections: Trends, Patterns, and Models." *American Political Science Review.* Vol. 67, No. 4 (December), 1213–1234.

Kousser, J. Morgan. 1974. *The Shaping of Southern Politics: Suffrage Restriction and the Establishment of the One-Party South, 1880–1910.* New Haven, CT: Yale University Press.

Kramer, Gerald H. 1971. "Short-Term Fluctuations in U.S. Voting Behavior, 1896–1964." *American Political Science Review.* Vol. 63, No. 1 (March). 131–143.

Krashinsky, Michael, and William J. Milne. 1993. "The Effects of Incumbency in U.S. Congressional Elections, 1950–1988." *Legislative Studies Quarterly.* Vol. 18, No. 3 (August). 321–344.

Krasno, Jonathon S., and Donald P. Green. 1988. "Preempting Quality Challengers in House Elections." *Journal of Politics.* Vol. 50, No. 4 (November). 920–936.

Krehbiel, Keith. 1993. "Where's the Party?" *British Journal of Political Science.* Vol. 23, No. 2 (April). 235–266.

——. 1999. "Paradoxes of Parties in Congress." *Legislative Studies Quarterly.* Vol. 24, No. 1 (February). 31–64.

Krehbiel, Keith, and John R. Wright. 1983. "The Incumbency Effect in Congressional Elections: A Test of Two Explanations." *American Journal of Political Science.* Vol. 27, No. 1 (February). 140–157.

Kritzer, Herbert M., and Robert Eubank. 1979. "Presidential Coattails Revisited: Partisanship and Incumbency Effects." *Midwest Journal of Political Science*. Vol. 23, No. 3 (August). 615–626.

Kuhn, David Paul. 2007. *The Neglected Voter: White Men and the Democratic Dilemma*. New York: Palgrave Macmillan.

Ladd, Everett Carll, Jr. 1970. *American Political Parties: Social Change and Political Response*. New York: W. W. Norton.

———. 1995. "The 1994 Congressional Elections: The Postindustrial Realignment Continues." *Political Science Quarterly*. Vol. 110, No. 1 (Spring). 1–23

Ladd, Everett Carll, Jr., and Charles Hadley. 1975. *Transformations of the American Party System*. New York: W. W. Norton.

Layman, Geoffrey C. 1999. "'Cultural Wars' in the American Party System." *American Politics Quarterly*. Vol. 27 (January). 89–121.

———. 2001. *The Great Divide: Religious and Cultural Conflict in American Party Politics*. New York: Columbia University Press.

Layman, Geoffrey C., and Thomas M. Carsey. 2002. "Party Polarization and 'Conflict Extension' in the American Electorate." *American Journal of Political Science*. Vol. 46, No. 4 (October 2002). 786–802.

Layman, Geoffrey C., Thomas M. Carsey, John C. Green, Richard Herrera, and Rosalyn Cooperman. 2010. "Party Polarization, Party Commitment, and Conflict Extension among American Party Activists." *American Political Science Review*. Vol. 104, No. 2 (May). 324–346.

Lee, Frances E. 2009. *Beyond Ideology: Politics, Principles, and Partisanship in the U.S. Senate*. Chicago: University of Chicago Press.

Lemann, Nicholas. 1992. *The Promised Land: The Great Black Migration and How It Changed America*. New York: Vintage.

Leogrande, William M., and Alana S. Jeydel. 1997. "Using Presidential Election Returns to Measure Constituency Ideology: A Research Note." *American Politics Quarterly*. Vol. 25, No. 1 (January). 3–18.

Levendusky, Matthew. 2009. *The Partisan Sort: How Liberals Became Democrats and Conservatives Became Republicans*. Chicago: University of Chicago Press.

Levendusky, Matthew S., Jeremy C. Pope, and Simon Jackman. 2008. "Measuring District-Level Partisanship with Implications for the Analysis of U.S. Elections." *Journal of Politics*. Vol. 70. No. 3 (July). 736–753.

Levitt, Steven D., and Catherine D. Wolfram. 1997. "Decomposing the Sources of Incumbency Advantage." *Legislative Studies Quarterly*. Vol. 22, No. 1 (February). 45–60.

Lewis-Beck, Michael S., and Richard Nadeau. 2004. "Split-Ticket Voting: The Effects of Cognitive Madisonianism." *Journal of Politics*. Vol. 66, No. 1 (February). 97–112.

Lichtman, Allan J. 1976. "Critical Election Theory and the Reality of American Presidential Politics, 1916–1940." *The American Historical Review*. Vol. 81, No. 2 (April). 317–351.

Liscio, Rebekah, Jeffrey M. Stonecash, and Mark D. Brewer. 2010. "Unintended Consequences: Republican Strategy and Winning and Losing Voters." In John C. Green and Daniel J. Coffey, Editors, *The State of the Parties*. Sixth Edition. New York: Rowman & Littlefield. 255–270.

Lowi, Theodore. 1963. "Toward Functionalism in Political Science: The Case of Innovation in Party Systems." *American Political Science Review*. Vol. 57, No. 3 (September). 570–583.

Lyons, Michael, and Peter F. Galderisi. 1995. "Incumbency, Reapportionment, and U.S. House Redistricting." *Legislative Studies Quarterly*. Vol. 48, No. 4 (December). 857–871.

Macdonald, Stuart E., and George Rabinowitz. 1987. "The Dynamics of Structural Realignment." *American Political Science Review*. Vol. 81, No. 3 (September). 775–796.

MacInnes, Gordon. 1996. *Wrong, for All the Right Reasons: How White Liberals Have Been Undone by Race*. New York: New York University Press.

Mackenzie, G. Calvin, and Robert Weisbrot. 2008. *The Liberal Hour: Washington and the Politics of Change in the 1960s*. New York: Penguin Press.

MacKuen, Michael, Robert S. Erikson, and James A. Stimson. 1989. "Macropartisanship." *American Political Science Review*. Vol. 83, No. 4 (December). 1125–1142.

———. 1992. "Question Wording and Macropartisanship." *American Political Science Review*. Vol. 86, No. 2 (June). 475–481.

Maestas, Cherie D., L. Sandy Maisel, and Walter J. Stone. 2005. "National Party Efforts to Recruit State Legislators to Run for the U.S. House." *Legislative Studies Quarterly*. Vol. 30, No. 2 (May). 277–300.

Mann, Thomas E. 1978. *Unsafe at Any Margin*. Washington, DC: American Enterprise Institute.

Mann, Thomas E., and Raymond E. Wolfinger. 1980. "Candidates and Parties in Congressional Elections." *American Political Science Review*. Vol. 74, No. 3 (September). 617–632.

Masket, Seth E. 2009. *No Middle Ground: How Informal Party Organizations Control Nominations and Polarize Legislatures*. Ann Arbor: University of Michigan Press.

Mason, Robert. 2004. *Richard Nixon and the Quest for a New Majority*. Chapel Hill: University of North Carolina Press.

Mattei, Franco, and Joshua Glasgow. 2005. "Presidential Coattails, Incumbency Advantage, and Open Seats: A District-Level Analysis of the 1976–2000 Elections." *Electoral Studies*. Vol. 24, No. 1 (March). 619–641.

Mayhew, David R. 1974a. 'Congressional Elections: The Case of the Vanishing Marginals." *Polity*. Vol. 6, No. 3 (Spring). 295–317.

———. 1974b. *The Electoral Connection*. New Haven, CT: Yale University Press.

———. 2002. *Electoral Realignments: A Critique of an American Genre*. New Haven, CT: Yale University Press.

———. 2005. *Divided We Govern: Party Control, Lawmaking, and Investigations, 1946–2002*. Second Edition. New Haven, CT: Yale University Press.

McAdams, John C., and John R. Johannes. 1981. "Does Casework Matter? A Reply to Professor Fiorina." *American Journal of Political Science*. Vol. 25, No. 3 (August). 581–604.

———. 1985. "Constituency Attentiveness in the House: 1977–1982." *Journal of Politics*. Vol. 47, No. 4 (November). 1108–1139.

———. 1988. "Congressmen, Perquisites, and Elections." *Journal of Politics*. Vol. 50, No. 2 (May). 412–439.

McCarty, Nolan, Keith T. Poole, and Howard Rosenthal. 2006. *Polarized America: The Dance of Ideology and Unequal Riches*. Cambridge, MA: M.I.T. Press.

McGhee, Eric. 2008. "National Tides and Local Results in US House Elections." *British Journal of Political Science*. Vol. 38, No. 4 (October). 719–783.

McGirr, Lisa. 2001. *Suburban Warriors: The Origins of the New American Right*. Princeton, NJ: Princeton University Press.

McMahon, Kevin J. 2003. *Reconsidering Roosevelt on Race: How the Presidency Paved the Road to Brown*. Chicago: University of Chicago Press, 2003.

Meffert, Michael F., Helmut Norpoth, and Anirudh V. S. Ruhl. 2001. "Realignment and Partisanship." *American Political Science Review*. Vol. 95, No. 4 (December). 953–962.

Mellow, Nicole. 2008. *The State of Disunion: Regional Sources of Modern American Partisanship*. Baltimore, MD: Johns Hopkins University Press.

Menefee-Libey, David. 2000. *The Triumph of Candidate-Centered Politics*. New York: Chatham House.

Merelman, Richard M. 1970. "Electoral Instability and the American Party System." *Journal of Politics*. Vol. 32, No. 1 (February). 115–139.

Merriam, Charles E. 1930. "Research Problems in the Field of Parties, Elections, and Leadership." *American Political Science Review*. Vol. 24, No. 1 (February). 33–38.

Merrill, Samuel, III, Bernard Grofman, and Thomas L. Brunell. 2008. "Cycles in American National Electoral Politics: Statistical Evidence and an Explanatory Model." *American Political Science Review*. Vol. 102, No. 1 (February). 1–17.

Mettler, Suzanne. 1998. *Dividing Citizens: Gender and Federalism in New Deal Public Policy*. Ithaca, NY: Cornell University Press.

Milkis, Sidney M. 1993. *The President and the Parties: The Transformation of the American Party System since the New Deal*. New York: Oxford University Press.

Milkis, Sidney M., and Jesse H. Rhodes. 2007. "George W. Bush, the Republican Party, and the 'New' American Party System." *Perspectives on Politics*. Vol. 5, No. 3 (September). 461–488.

Miller, Arthur H. 1979. "Normal Vote Analysis: Sensitivity to Change over Time." *American Journal of Political Science*. Vol. 23, No. 2 (May). 406–425.

Miller, Gary, and Norman Schofield. 2003. "Activists and Partisan Realignment in the United States." *American Political Science Review*. Vol. 97, No. 2 (May). 245–260.

Miller, Warren E. 1955. "Presidential Coattails: A Study in Political Myth and Methodology." *Public Opinion Quarterly*. Vol. 19, No. 4 (Winter). 353–368.

———. 1991. "Party Identification, Realignment, and Party Voting: Back to the Basics." *American Political Science Review*. Vol. 85, No. 2 (June). 557–568.

———. 1992. "Generational Changes and Party Identification." *Political Behavior*. Vol. 14, No. 3 (September). 333–352.

Mondak, Jeffrey J. 1993. "Presidential Coattails and Open Seats." *American Politics Research*. Vol. 21, No. 3 (July). 307–319.

Monroe, J. P. 2001. *The Political Party Matrix: The Persistence of Organization*. Albany: State University of New York Press.

Moos, Malcolm. 1952. *Politics, Presidents, and Coattails*. Baltimore, MD: Johns Hopkins University Press.

Nardulli, Peter F. 1994. "A Normal Vote Approach to the Study of Electoral Change: Presidential Elections, 1828–1984." *Political Behavior*. Vol. 16, No. 4 (December). 467–503.

______. 1995. "The Concept of Critical Realignment, Electoral Behavior, and Political Change." *American Political Science Review*. Vol. 89, No. 1 (March). 10–22.

______. 2007. *Popular Efficacy in the Democratic Era: A Reexamination of Electoral Accountability in the United States, 1828–2000*. Princeton, NJ: Princeton University Press.

Nelson, Candice J. 1978–79. "The Effect of Incumbency on Voting in Congressional Elections." *Political Science Quarterly*. Vol. 93, No. 4 (Winter). 665–678.

Newman, Brian, and Charles Ostrom, Jr. 2002. "Explaining Seat Changes in the U.S. House of Representatives, 1950–1998." *Legislative Studies Quarterly*. Vol. 27, No. 3 (August). 383–405.

Nie, Norman, Sidney Verba and John Petrocik. 1976. *The Changing American Voter* Cambridge, MA: Harvard University Press.

Niemi, Richard G., and John Deegan, Jr. 1978. "A Theory of Political Districting." *The American Political Science Review*. Vol. 72, No. 4 (December). 1304–1323.

Niemi, Richard G., and Patrick Fett. 1986. "The Swing Ratio: An Explanation and an Assessment." *Legislative Studies Quarterly*. Vol. 11, No. 1 (February). 75–90.

Nivola, Pietro S., and David W. Brady, Editors. 2006. *Red and Blue Nation: Characteristics and Causes of America's Polarized Politics*. Washington, DC: Brookings Institution.

Norpoth, Helmut, and Jerrold G. Rusk. 2007. "Electoral Myth and Reality: Realignments in American Politics." *Electoral Studies*. Vol. 26 (June). 392–403.

Okrent, Daniel. 2010. *Last Call: The Rise and Fall of Prohibition*. New York: Scribner.

Olson, Laura R. 2010. "Religion, Moralism, and the Cultural Wars: Competing Moral Visions." In Jeffrey M. Stonecash, Editor, *New Directions in American Political Parties*. New York: Routledge. 148–165.

Oppenheimer, Bruce I., James A. Stimson, and Richard W. Waterman. 1986. "Interpreting U.S. Congressional Elections: The Exposure Thesis." *Legislative Studies Quarterly*. Vol. 11, No. 2 (May). 227–247.

Parker, Glenn R. 1980. "The Advantage of Incumbency in House Elections." *American Politics Quarterly*. Vol. 8, No. 4 (October). 375–398.

______. 1986. "Is There a Political Life Cycle in the House of Representatives?" *Legislative Studies Quarterly*. Vol. 11, No. 3 (August). 375–392.

Parker, Glenn R., and Roger H. Davidson. 1979. "Why Do Americans Love Their Congressmen So Much More Than Their Congress?" *Legislative Studies Quarterly*. Vol. 4, No. 1 (February). 53–61.

Parker, Glenn R., and Suzanne L. Parker. 1985. "Correlates and Effects of Attention to District by U.S. House Members." *Legislative Studies Quarterly*. Vol. 10, No. 2 (May). 223–242.

Patterson, James T. 1965. "The Failure of Party Realignment in the South, 1937–1939." *Journal of Politics*. Vol. 27, No. 3 (August). 602–617.

______. 1967. *Congressional Conservatism and the New Deal: The Growth of the Conservative Coalition in Congress, 1933–1939*. Lexington: University of Kentucky Press.

Paulson, Arthur C. 2000. *Realignment and Party Revival: Understanding American Electoral Politics at the Turn of the Twenty-First Century.* Westport, CT: Praeger.

Payne, James L. 1980. "The Personal Electoral Advantage of House Incumbents." *American Politics Quarterly.* Vol. 8, No. 4 (October). 375–398.

Pearson, Kathryn. 2008. "Party Loyalty and Discipline in the Individualistic Senate." In Nathan W. Monroe, Jason M. Roberts, and David W. Rohde, Editors, *Why Not Parties? Party Effects in the United States Senate.* Chicago: University of Chicago Press, 100–120.

Perlstein, Rick. 2001. *Before the Storm.* New York: Hill and Wang.

———. 2008. *Nixonland: The Rise of a President and the Fracturing of America.* New York: Scribner.

Petigny, Alan. 2009. *The Permissive Society: America, 1941–1965.* New York: Cambridge University Press.

Petrocik, John R. 1987. "Realignment: New Party Coalitions and the Nationalization of the South." *Journal of Politics.* Vol. 42, No. 2 (May). 347–375.

———. 1989. "An Expected Party Vote: New Data for an Old Concept." *American Journal of Political Science.* Vol. 33, No. 1 (February). 44–66.

Petrocik, John R., and Scott W. Desposato. 2004. "Incumbency and Short-Term Influences on Voters." *Political Research Quarterly.* Vol. 57, No. 3 (September). 363–373.

Phillips, Kevin. 1969. *The Emerging Republican Majority.* New York: Anchor.

Pierson, Paul. 2004. *Politics in Time: History, Institutions, and Social Analysis.* Princeton, NJ: Princeton University Press.

Plotke, David. 1996. *Building a Democratic Political Order: Reshaping American Liberalism in the 1930s and 1940s.* New York: Cambridge University Press.

Polsby, Nelson W. 1968. "The Institutionalization of the U.S. House of Representatives." *American Political Science Review.* Vol. 62, No. 1 (March). 144–168.

———. 2004. *How Congress Evolves: Social Bases of Institutional Change.* New York: Oxford University Press.

Polsby, Nelson W., and Aaron Wildavsky, with David A. Hopkins. 2008. *Presidential Elections: Strategies and Structures of American Politics.* Twelfth Edition. New York: Rowman & Littlefield.

Polsky, Andrew J. 1997. "The 1996 Elections and the Logic of Regime Politics." *Polity.* Vol. 30, No. 1 (Autumn). 153–166.

Pomper, Gerald M. 1967. "Classification of Presidential Elections." *Journal of Politics.* Vol. 29, No. 3 (August). 535–566.

———. 1972. "From Confusion to Clarity: Issues and American Voters, 1956–1968." *American Political Science Review.* Vol. 66, No. 2 (June). 415–428.

———. 1978–1979. "The Impact of *The American Voter* on Political Science." *Political Science Quarterly.* Vol. 93, No. 4 (Winter). 617–628.

Poole, Keith T., and Howard Rosenthal. 1984. "The Polarization of American Politics." *Journal of Politics.* Vol. 46, No. 4 (November). 1061–1079.

———. 1985. "A Spatial Model for Legislative Roll Call Analysis." *American Journal of Political Science.* Vol. 29, No. 2 (May). 357–384.

Popkin, Samuel. 1994. *The Reasoning Voter.* Chicago: University of Chicago Press.

Press, Charles. 1958. "Voting Statistics and Presidential Coattails." *American Political Science Review.* Vol. 52, No. 4 (December). 1041–1050.

______. 1963. "Presidential Coattails and Party Cohesion." *Midwest Journal of Political Science*. Vol. 7, No. 4 (November). 320–335.

Prior, Markus. 2007. *Post-Broadcast Democracy*. New York: Cambridge University Press, 2007.

Ragsdale, Lyn. 1980. "The Fiction of Congressional Elections as Presidential Events." *American Politics Quarterly*. Vol. 8, No. 4 (October). 375–398.

Rapoport, Ronald B. 1997. "Partisan Change in a Candidate-Centered Era." *Journal of Politics*. Vol. 59, No. 1 (February). 185–199.

Ray, David. 1974. "Membership Stability in Three State Legislatures: 1869–1969." *American Political Science Review*. Vol. 68, No. 1 (March). 106–112.

Reichard, Gary W. 1986. "Democrats, Civil Rights, and Electoral Strategies in the 1950s." *Congress and the Presidency*. Vol. 13, No. 1 (Spring). 59–81.

Reiter, Howard L., and Jeffrey M. Stonecash. 2011. *Counter Realignment: Political Change in the Northeast*. New York: Cambridge University Press.

Reese, Matt. 1963. "Memorandum." LBJ Library, DNC Collection, Box 83.

Rieselbach, Leroy N. 1973. *Congressional Politics*. New York: McGraw-Hill.

Roberts, Gene, and Hank Klibanoff. 2006. *The Race Beat: The Press, the Civil Rights Struggle, and the Awakening of a Nation*. New York: Vintage.

Robinson, Edgar Eugene. 1934. *They Voted for Roosevelt*. Palo Alto, CA: Stanford University Press.

______. 1947. *The Presidential Vote, 1896–1932*. Palo Alto, CA: Stanford University Press.

Rohde, David W. 1991. *Parties and Leaders in the Postreform House*. Chicago: University of Chicago Press.

Rohde, David, and John Aldrich. 2010. "Consequences of Electoral and Institutional Change: The Evolution of Conditional Party Government in the U.S. House of Representatives." In Jeffrey M. Stonecash, Editor, *New Directions in American Political Parties*. New York: Routledge. 234–250.

Sanders, Elizabeth. 1999. *Roots of Reform: Farmers, Workers, and the American State*. Chicago: University of Chicago Press.

Savage, Sean J. 1991. *Roosevelt: The Party Leader, 1932–1945*. Lexington: The University of Kentucky Press.

______. 2004. *JFK, LBJ, and the Democratic Party*. Albany: SUNY Press.

Scammon, Richard and Ben Wattenberg. 1970. *The Real Majority*. New York: Coward-McCann.

Schaller, Thomas F. 2006. *Whistling Past Dixie: How Democrats Can Win without the South*. New York: Simon and Schuster.

Schattschneider, E. E. 1960. *The Semisovereign People: A Realist's View of Democracy in America*. New York: Holt, Rinehart and Winston.

Schickler, Eric. 2010. "New Deal Liberalism and Racial Liberalism in the Mass Public, 1937–1952." Presented at the 2010 American Political Science Association Meetings, Washington, DC, September.

Schickler, Eric, Kathryn Pearson, and Brian Feinstein. 2010. "Congressional Parties and Civil Rights Politics from 1933 to 1972." *Journal of Politics*. Vol. 72, No. 3 (July), 672–689.

Schlesinger, Joseph A. 1985. "The New American Political Party." *American Political Science Review*. Vol. 79, No. 4 (December), 1152–1169.

Segura, Gary M., and Stephen P. Nicholson. 1995. "Sequential Choices and Partisan Transitions in U.S. Senate Delegations: 1972–1988." *Journal of Politics*. Vol. 57, No. 1 (February). 86–100.

Sellers, Charles. 1965. "The Equilibrium Cycle in Two-Party Politics." *Public Opinion Quarterly*. Vol. 29, No. 1 (Spring). 16–38.

Serra, George. 1994. "What's in It for Me: The Impact of Congressional Casework on Incumbent Evaluation." *American Politics Quarterly*. Vol. 22, No. 4 (October). 403–420.

Serra, George, and Albert D. Cover. 1992. "The Electoral Consequences of Perquisite Use: The Casework Case." *Legislative Studies Quarterly*. Vol. 17, No. 2 (May). 233–246.

Shafer, Byron E., Editor. 1991. *The End of Realignment*. Madison: University of Wisconsin Press.

Shafer, Byron E., and Richard Johnston. 2001. "The Transformation of Southern Politics Revisited: The House of Representatives as a Window." *British Journal of Political Science*. Vol. 31. No. 4 (September). 601–625.

———. 2006. *The End of Southern Exceptionalism: Class, Race, and Partisan Change in the Postwar South*. Cambridge, MA: Harvard University Press.

Shannon, W. Wayne. 1968. *Party, Constituency and Congressional Voting*. Baton Rouge: Louisiana University Press.

Shelley, Mack C. II. 1983. *The Permanent Majority: The Conservative Coalition in the United States Congress*. Tuscaloosa: University of Alabama Press.

Silbey, Joel H. 2002. "From 'Essential to the Existence of Our Institutions' to 'Rapacious Enemies of Honest and Responsible Government': The Rise and Fall of American Political Parties, 1790–2000." In L. Sandy Maisel, Editor, *The Parties Respond: Changes in American Parties and Campaigns*. Boulder, CO: Westview Press, 2002. 1–18.

Simon, Dennis M., Charles W. Ostrom, Jr., and Robin S. Marra. 1991. "The President, Referendum Voting and Subnational Elections in the United States." *American Political Science Review*. Vol. 85, No. 4 (December). 1177–1192.

Sinclair, Barbara Deckard. 1977. "Party Realignment and the Transformation of the Political Agenda: The House of Representatives, 1925–1938." *American Political Science Review*. Vol. 71, No. 3 (September). 940–953.

———. 1982. *Congressional Realignment 1925–1978*. Austin: University of Texas Press.

Sitkoff, Harvard. 1971. "Harry Truman and the Election of 1948: The Coming of Age of Civil Rights in American Politics." *Journal of Southern History*. Vol. 37, No. 4 (November). 597–616.

Skinner, Richard M., Seth E. Masket, and David A. Dulio. 2012. "527 Committees and the Political Party Network." *American Politics Research*. Vol. 40, No. 1 (January). 60–84.

Smith, Rogers M., and Desmond S. King. 2005. "Racial Orders in American Political Development." *American Political Science Review*. Vol. 99, No. 1 (February). 75–92.

Sorauf, Frank J. 1968. *Party Politics in America*. Boston: Little, Brown.

Squire, Peverill. 1989. "Competition and Uncontested Seats in U.S. House Elections." *Legislative Studies Quarterly*. Vol. 14, No. 2 (May). 281–295.

Stern, Mark. 1992. *Calculating Visions: Kennedy, Johnson, and Civil Rights*. New Brunswick, NJ: Rutgers University Press.

Stevens, Arthur G., Arthur H. Miller, and Thomas E. Mann. 1974. "Mobilization of Liberal Strength in the House, 1955–1970." *American Political Science Review*. Vol. 68, No. 2 (June). 667–681.

Stimson, James A. 2005. *Tides of Consent: How Public Opinion Shapes American Politics*. New York: Cambridge University Press.

Stimson, James A., Michael B. MacKuen, and Robert S. Erikson. 1995. "Dynamic Representation." *American Political Science Review*. Vol. 89, No. 3 (September). 543–565.

Stonecash, Jeffrey M. 2000. *Class and Party in American Politics*. Boulder, CO: Westview Press.

———. 2003. "Reconsidering the Trend in Incumbent Vote Percentages in House Elections." *American Review of Politics*. Vol. 24, No. 3 (Fall). 225–239.

———. 2006. *Parties Matter: Realignment and the Return of Partisanship*. Boulder, CO: Lynne Rienner.

———. 2008. *Reassessing the Incumbency Effect*. New York: Cambridge University Press.

———. 2010a. "The Electoral College and Democratic Responsiveness." In Gary Baugh, Editor, *Electoral College Reform: Challenges and Possibilities*. Burlington, VT: Ashgate. 65–76.

———. 2010b. "Class in American Politics." In Jeffrey M. Stonecash, Editor, *New Directions in American Political Parties*. New York: Routledge. 110–125.

———. 2010c. "The Declining Swing Ratio: Incumbent Insulation or Realignment?" Presented at the 2010 American Political Science Association Meetings, Washington, DC: September

———. 2011a. "The 1966 Incumbency Effect Increase and the Study of Elections." Presented at the 2011 Southern Political Science Association Meetings, New Orleans, Louisiana, January.

———. 2011a. "Political Change and Party Identification: Stability versus Change and the Exclusion of Parties." Presented at the 2011 Midwest Political Science Association Meetings, Chicago, Illinois, March 30–April 3.

———. 2012. "Political Science and the Study of Parties: Sorting out Interpretations of Party Response." In Mark D. Brewer and L. Sandy Maisel, Editors, *The Parties Respond*. Fifth Edition. Boulder, CO: Westview Press.

———. Forthcoming. *Understanding American Political Parties: Democratic Ideals, Political Uncertainty, and Strategic Positioning*. New York: Routledge.

Stonecash, Jeffrey M., and Mack D. Mariani. 2000. "Republican Gains in the House in the 1994 Elections: Class Polarization in American Politics." *Political Science Quarterly*. Vol. 115, No. 1 (Spring). 93–114.

Stonecash, Jeffrey M., Mark D. Brewer, and Mack D. Mariani. 2003. *Diverging Parties: Social Change, Realignment, and Party Polarization*. Boulder, CO: Westview.

Stonecash, Jeffrey M., and Everita Silina. 2005. "Reassessing the 1896 Realignment." *American Politics Research*. Vol. 33, No. 1 (January 2005). 3–32.

Stratmann, Thomas. 2000. "Congressional Voting over Legislative Careers: Shifting Positions and Changing Constraints." *American Political Science Review*. Vol. 94, No. 3 (September). 665–676.

Struble, Robert, Jr. 1979–1980. "House Turnover and the Principle of Rotation." *Political Science Quarterly*. Vol. 94, No. 4 (Winter). 649–667.

Sundquist, James L. 1983. *Dynamics of the Party System: Alignment and Realignment of Political Parties in the United States*. Revised Edition. Washington, DC: Brookings Institution.

Swisher, Idella G. 1933. "Election Statistics in the United States." *American Political Science Review*. Vol. 27, No. 3 (June). 422–432.

Szymanski, Ann-Marie E. 2003. *Pathways to Prohibition: Radicals, Moderates, and Social Movement Outcomes*. Durham, NC: Duke University Press.

Theriault, Sean M. 2008. *Party Polarization in Congress*. New York: Cambridge University Press.

————. 2012. "Congressional Parties and the Policy Process." In Mark D. Brewer and L. Sandy Maisel, Editors, *The Parties Respond*. Fifth Edition. Boulder, CO: Westview Press.

Tichenor, D. J. 2002. *Dividing Lines: The Politics of Immigration Control in America*. Princeton, NJ: Princeton University Press.

Tidmarch, Charles M., and Douglas Carpenter. 1978. "Congressmen and the Electorate, 1968 and 1972." *Journal of Politics*. Vol. 40, No. 2 (May). 479–487.

Tufte, Edward R. 1973. "The Relationship between Seats and Votes in Two-Party Systems." *American Political Science Review*. Vol. 67, No. 2 (June). 540–554.

————. 1975. "Determinants of the Outcomes of Midterm Congressional Elections." *American Political Science Review*. Vol. 69, No. 3 (September). 812–826.

Turner, Julius. 1951a. "Responsible Parties: A Dissent from the Floor." *American Political Science Review*. Vol. 45, No. 1 (March). 143–152.

Turner, Julius. 1951b. *Party and Constituency: Pressures on Congress*. Baltimore, MD: Johns Hopkins University Press.

Turner, Julius, and Edward V. Schneier. 1970. *Party and Constituency: Pressures on Congress*. Revised Edition. Baltimore, MD: Johns Hopkins Press.

Valelly, Richard M. 2004. *The Two Reconstructions: The Struggle for Black Enfranchisement*. Chicago: University of Chicago Press.

Vertz, Laura L., John P. Frendreis, and James L. Gibson. 1987. "Nationalization of the Electorate in the United States." *American Political Science Review*. Vol. 81, No. 3 (September). 961–966.

Viguerie, Richard. 1981. *The New Right: We're Ready to Lead*. Revised Edition. Falls Church, VA: Viguerie Co.

Von Bothhmer, Bernard. 2010. *Framing the 1960s: The Use and Abuse of a Decade from Ronald Reagan to George W. Bush*. Amherst: University of Massachusetts Press.

Ware, Alan. 2006. *The Democratic Party Heads North*. New York: Cambridge University Press.

Waterman, Richard A. 1990. "Comparing Senate and House Electoral Outcomes: The Exposure Thesis." *Legislative Studies Quarterly*. Vol. 15, No. 1 (February). 99–114.

————. 1990. "Institutional Realignment: The Composition of the U.S. Congress." *Western Political Quarterly*. Vol. 43, No. 1 (March). 81–92.

Waterman, Richard W., Bruce I. Oppenheimer, and James A. Stimson. 1991. "Sequence and Equilibrium in Congressional Elections: An Integrated Approach." *Journal of Politics*. Vol. 53, No. 2 (May). 372–393.

Wattenberg, Martin P. 1981. "The Decline of Political Partisanship in the United States: Negativity or Neutrality?" *American Political Science Review*. Vol. 75, No. 4 (December). 941–950.

———. 1990. *The Decline of American Political Parties 1952–1988*. Cambridge, MA: Harvard University Press.

———. 1991. *The Rise of Candidate-Centered Politics: Presidential Elections of the 1980s*. Cambridge, MA: Harvard University Press.

Weed, Clyde P. 1989. "What Happened to the Republicans in the 1930s: Minority Party Dynamics during Political Realignment." *Polity*. Vol. 22, No. 1 (Autumn). 5–23.

———. 1994. *The Nemesis of Reform: The Republican Party during the New Deal*. New York: Columbia University Press.

Whitby, Kenny G., and Frank D. Gilliam, Jr. 1991. "A Longitudinal Analysis of Competing Explanations for the Transformation of Southern Congressional Politics." *Journal of Politics*. Vol. 53, No. 2 (May). 504–518.

Wiebe, Robert H. 1967. *The Search for Order, 1877–1920*. New York: Hill and Wang.

Wildgen, John K., and Richard L. Engstrom. 1980. "Spatial Distribution of Partisan Support and the Seats/Votes Relationship." *Legislative Studies Quarterly*. Vol. 5, No. 3 (1980). 423–435.

Wilkins, Arjun. 2011. "Electoral Security of Members of the U.S. House." Presented at the 2011 Midwest Political Science Association Meetings, Chicago Illinois, April.

Wolbrecht, Christina. 2000. *The Politics of Women's Rights: Parties, Positions, and Change*. Princeton, NJ: Princeton University Press.

Wolbrecht, Christina, and Michael Hartney. 2012. "Race and Resources versus Excellence and Exams: Explaining Changing Party Positions on Education Policy." Presented at the 2012 Southern Political Science Association Meetings, New Orleans, January.

Wood, B. Dan. 2009. *The Myth of Presidential Representation*. New York: Cambridge University Press.

Wright, Gerald C., and Michael B. Berkman. 1986. "Candidates and Policy in United States Senate Elections." *American Political Science Review*. Vol. 80, No. 2 (June). 567–588.

Wrighton, J. Mark, and Peverill Squire. 1997. "Uncontested Seats and Electoral Competition for the U.S. House of Representatives over Time." *Journal of Politics*. Vol. 59, No. 2 (May). 452–468.

Yiannakis, Diana Evans. 1981. "The Grateful Electorate: Casework and Congressional Elections." *American Journal of Political Science*. Vol. 25, No. 3 (August). 568–580.

Zaller, John. 1992. *The Nature and Origin of Mass Opinion*. New York: Cambridge University Press.